CLUETOPIA

For Captain James Barry Astle,
a loving father of few words

DAVID ASTLE

CLUETOPIA

The story of 100 years of the crossword

Published by Allen & Unwin in 2013

Allen & Unwin
Sydney, Melbourne, Auckland, London

83 Alexander Street
Crows Nest NSW 2065
Australia
Phone: (61 2) 8425 0100
Fax: (61 2) 9906 2218
Email: info@allenandunwin.com
Web: www.allenandunwin.com

Cataloguing-in-Publication details are available
from the National Library of Australia
www.trove.nla.gov.au

ISBN 978 1 74331 453 1

Set in 12/16 pt Adobe Caslon Pro by Bookhouse, Sydney
Printed and bound in Australia by Griffin Press

10 9 8 7 6 5 4 3 2

MIX
Paper from
responsible sources
FSC® C009448

The paper in this book is FSC® certified.
FSC® promotes environmentally responsible,
socially beneficial and economically viable
management of the world's forests.

CONTENTS

INTRODUCTION

Warning: this book is a folly. Nobody can hope to travel a century and look at every crossword along the way. But hey—if you're feeling game and I can keep my nerve then what say we do the next best thing?

Let's hit the road. Let's hunt down the most curious crosswords out there, the most dubious, the ground-breakers and the head-spinners, the slurs and secret messages. Let's riffle (and rifle) the papers of the world to single out clues that can't be believed—or solved.

After all, a centenary in anybody's language deserves a grand gesture. Happy 100th birthday, Crossword! Time to wheel out the cake. Light up the candles. The brain-tickler that began life as a quick fix in the *New York World* has since spread like thistle fluff upon the four winds. Czechs call it the *křížovky*, and Swedes the *korsord*; Arabic speakers know the diversion as the الكلمات المتقاطعة, while the Chinese go for the 填字游戏 (words-in-the-blanks game). Seems the one-time gimmick has gone global. Viral. Pathological. The fad is no longer a fad.

Cluetopia aims to prove how the pastime embraces all cultures and every appetite, no matter how fancy or uncooperative a country's alphabet might be. And, just to give our folly shape, let's find a landmark crossword for every year, from that panicky day near

Christmas 1913 until its very own black-and-white gala in 2013. Crazy I know, impossible even, but it seems the ideal way to celebrate the grid that Arthur Wynne first created.

Standing here at square one, peering into the distance, we have a prison in our sights, a French rocket ship, an Irish golf club. We shall visit a skyscraper in Lvov, which locals call Lviv. With any luck we'll encounter a piece of Hungarian revenge, a romantic plea in Brisbane, a Māori funeral, a sex scandal in Scotland and a Russian murder mystery. These are just a few of the stopovers across an itinerary devoted to serendipity. As we straighten our seats and stow our trays, I can promise you Superman and Winnie-the-Pooh, Nabokov and Sondheim. Within these pages you will meet Mahatma Gandhi and Lady Di, grapple with Japanese guitarists and Yiddish bedbugs. We'll brush against wartime and politics, crime and philosophy, romance and faith, sport and furniture.

Then there's the history side of things—not just the crossword timeline, but the human misadventures that blaze in the background. Crosswords are windows on an evolving world. As we travel, you will find each puzzle a porthole, a peephole, allowing us to glance at places where people do things differently.

By way of bearings, I have planted a milestone in each chapter, a shortlist of key events that occurred in that year, along with a clutch of words coined roughly in the same era. This way you can see the century flex as we go, the changing world and what words we needed to identify those changes.

The other inspiration behind this chase is the Greek hero Theseus. He's the man who entered the Minotaur's maze, sword in one hand, a ball of string in the other. At each blind turn, primed to slay the beast, he walked in dread of being lost, or lunch. His string was the ancient version of the satnav really, a trick to help him trace his steps from A to B. Should you read the Minotaur myth in a quaint translation you'll find the string bundle identified as the hero's *clue*, or possibly *clew*—the two words are close cousins. English sustains the legend with this same simple word. *Clues* are threads we follow to creep nearer to the truth, the monster lying at the heart of things. Check most dictionaries and you'll see how *clew* (spelt the older way) still means a bundle of yarn. In plural form the word applies to the ropes that keep a hammock suspended. Both ideas link back to the brainwave that saved Theseus's neck.

As we enter *Cluetopia*, try to keep that idea in mind. No matter where we go, what weirdness we encounter, we will always have the clues as our continuum, one small mystery solved as we move onward to face another, the solace of one yarn linking to the next.

Zigging and zagging through the century, we'll navigate the maze using crosswords as our stepping stones and clues as our comfort. I don't anticipate we'll meet a monster on our path, but then again I can't promise anything in black and white.

1913

The fibre of a gomuti palm (3)

Arthur Wynne caught a packet steamer from Liverpool to America around 1891. To earn some cash he planted onions in Texas. Later he moved to Liverpool, Ohio, where he took up duties as the local paper's society editor. Ink ran in the family veins; his father back home was a newspaperman. Versatility was Wynne's other asset. The migrant moved to Pennsylvania to run the sports desk in McKeesport, on the Youghiogheny River. Before too long he was playing violin for the Pittsburgh Symphony Orchestra, as well as reviewing stage shows and concerts for the *Pittsburgh Dispatch*. And some years down the track, when Arthur was 42, working as a section editor for the *New York World*, he started a revolution.

Not that he realised that at the time. It was a Sunday, four sleeps from Christmas. His brainwave was a last-minute filler before the

+ Henry Ford's assembly line begins to roll.
+ Stainless steel is invented in Sheffield.
+ Australia's capital, Canberra, is named—and eventually built.

New words: movie, vitamin, jazz, conscious

paper went to press, a small kite-shaped diagram to occupy a nagging space on the page. He called the invention a word-cross puzzle, adding the instructions: 'Fill in the small squares with words which agree with the following definitions.'

FUN was already part of the grid, giving the solver half a chance. The first Down answer was RULE (*To govern*), running through the U of FUN. Not that Down was part of the dialect back then. Instead, the clue was labelled as 1–32. If that sounds bewildering, see if you can solve this clue:

The fibre of the gomuti palm (3).

The answer hangs in the western corner of Wynne's diamond, listed as 10–18. What say I give you some thinking time before revealing the answer?

The reason behind the strange numbering lay in the grid's coordinates. Rather than modern crosswords, where every clue's opening square is numbered, this diagram hosted numbers in the first and last squares of each entry. The principle resembles the street address for the *New York World*, a skyscraper standing at 53–63 Park Row. The numbers tell you the building's extent, occupying five slots along the block. This basic navigation key was a big part of Arthur's revolution. Before 1913, word squares relied on all entries filling the grid's length or height. Here's what I mean:

C	A	P	E	R
A	L	I	V	E
P	I	N	E	S
E	V	E	N	T
R	E	S	T	S

As you can see, every answer needed to go the distance of the diagram. There was no scope for interior design. Further to that, as in our example, words were often charged with double duty, appearing in both directions, meaning only horizontal clues were needed. But then Arthur tweaked the formula. In the man's own words, 'All I did was to take an idea as old as language and modernise it by the introduction of black squares.' And with black squares came embedded coordinates. Two small wangles and a mania began.

Both changes seem obvious, as do most innovations in hindsight. If Hollywood ever tried to capture Wynne's finest hour on film, I'd bet the FARM (*To cultivate*) that screenwriters would succumb to anachronism. Picture the scene:

WYNNE. *Stares at the blank space. Chews his lip. Rubs the back of his neck. [A shot of the clock creeping closer to deadline. A wide angle of the empty office.] Then suddenly an idea strikes him.* **Doh!**

Two major problems wreck that flashback. One, Homer was exclusively a Greek poet at that stage of human history, as opposed to a Duff drinker of Springfield. And two, if you consult a dictionary of antiquity, you'll discover that DOH had only two meanings in 1913, namely a musical note, and the fibre of a gomuti palm.

1914–21

A heavy blow (4)

Before you could say 'Chapter 2', the word-cross of Arthur Wynne became the cross-word of the people. The switch in label was seen as a casual bungle—or maybe cross-word had a sweeter sound to a staffer's ear. However the flip-flop occurred, the word morphed early in 1914, making this book, this celebration, this whole hullabaloo, all about crosswords, not wordcrosses.

Bizarre, don't you think? Here we are toasting this verbal achievement, when the toastee's name was close to being arsy-versy. 1913 in fact was a big year for the English language. As Wynne enjoyed his eureka on Park Row, other words were being coined across the industrial world, like hubcap and bellhop, postcard and anti-freeze. Yet none of these newborns was transposed in infancy. You won't find books celebrating a century of hopbells and cardposts. A million bucks if your local library has a copy of *Spangle and Swirl: The Golden Jubilee of the Trotfox*.

Returning to the clue quest, our second puzzle mirrored the shape of Wynne's prototype—a hollow diamond of 40 answers. But there were several key differences. The gomuti palm had been lopped for more common words: the obscurest in this next puzzle was the *Sea eagle* nesting at 29–30. Mind you, if you've done your share of crosswords, you'll recognise ERNE as a serial offender. The bird sits high in the list of crossword words, up there with ETUI (needle case), ECRU (pale brown) and ERATO (the Muse of love poetry). And that's just the ES.

Another distinction was the lack of instructions. Solving crosswords is like riding a bike—a gentle exercise to get the cogs turning. After ten months of exposure, from start-up puzzle to this latest, 'Cross-Word 41', the diversion had become second nature to Gothamites, making directions redundant.

A far greater shock was a young woman named Della Sherry.

Arthur Wynne was pushed for time. Making the New Jersey commute every day was hard enough on his hours. The expat was stretched with sundry tasks for the paper that now included puzzle-making. Odds are, when he'd built his FUN diamond last December, he'd had no inkling of the passion he'd be planting. How could he? The diversion was some mental tinsel to decorate a Christmas page. Maybe if he had foreseen the fervour he'd never have invented the bloody thing in the first place, since one person's craze is another's albatross. As it was, Wynne was viewed as the city's sole compiler, his fingertips alone the holders of the alchemy.

Arthur, however, saw matters otherwise. He knew the challenge of drafting a grid was just as catchy as entering the answers. Or, as he phrased it that February, 'It is more difficult to make up a cross-word puzzle than it is to solve one. If you doubt this, try to make one yourself.' The statement was designed to be a red rag—and it worked. Dozens of DIY puzzles started landing on his desk. That number soon increased to bagloads, until Mrs MB Wood became the first citizen to craft a crossword for *World* readers. Indeed, the outsourced stream of newspaper puzzles, begun by Wynne's taunt, still flows through American culture today.

Della Sherry was part of the initial deluge, though her debut puzzle came with a tad more fanfare. Not only did the newbie get a byline for her crossword, Della also found her cover letter being published beside the grid. 'Instead of giving us a spelling lesson,' she'd written to Wynne, 'the teacher told us to compose a cross-word.' That's right: Della Sherry was a schoolgirl. We don't know her age for sure, but something-teen going by the puzzle's superior polish. More the point, her arrival was a portent. For a school to be challenging kids to make their own puzzles was a bright sign for the genre. I should know. That's how my own fever rose.

In my case, the teacher's name was Max. His portfolio was geography, but the class he was babysitting was Year 7 English. To pass the time he told the class to make a crossword. This was 1974—I was twelve, a closet compiler just spoiling for the invitation. Somehow I made a puzzle with symmetry and clues just before the bell rang. Max was obliged to make copies that soon passed around the playground. From that week forward I could imagine myself as a crossword-maker.

But high school is small beer compared to The Big Apple. God knows how Sherry felt, a century ago, the young woman a published setter on top of being a trailblazer. What a kick, while still in school, to know strangers in Manhattan were chewing on your *Prescribed food* to get DIET, to think commuters in Queens were contemplating *Black and white mixed* to make GREY.

You may think I'm overplaying this aspect of our second puzzle—some whiz-kid girl from New York makes a diamond 100 years ago—but there's a reason for it. A great reason, in fact, as 1914 was also the year when America began to pay full attention to Europe.

In August that year the Austrian army invaded Serbia. Germany soon pushed into France and Belgium. Month by month a remote crisis increased in ferocity, and proximity. Before long, Britain was enmeshed. The odds of American forces getting involved shortened by the week. Battles erupted along the Western Front, ramping up the death toll. Newspapers were filled with maps and bulletins of the conflict, pushing the glibness of puzzles to the margins, no matter how much fun they promised.

Crosswords, in fact, had every chance of being one more casualty of the Somme. If not for a few vital influences, Wynne's invention might have fallen in league with the pianola and zeppelin. Indeed, this chapter is the only one that will sweep across several years. You may think I'm fudging the calendar so early in the time-trip, but this period marks a holding pattern in the black-and-white game. For a good stretch the *New York World* was a lonesome source, continuing to publish the puzzles as Europe tottered on the brink of chaos. The crossword was yet to bite on a grand scale. Its time would come, but, until then, our search is obliged to march on the spot—and salute those vital influences.

For a clue to the deeper history, consider the clues embedded in our first two puzzles. The moment you notice the spelling of *fibre* in 1913, or the choice of GREY over GRAY in Della Sherry's grid, you will appreciate the ties that still bound America to Britain. Shared spelling is a glimpse of heritage, a symptom of continued closeness. Flimsy evidence, but it's there on display, the time-honoured loyalty of lettering. The two nations were bound in history. If the old mother was under threat, then the breakaway offspring felt compelled to assist. Before too long, in 1917, Woodrow Wilson committed forces to the front, helping to repel the Germans. Uncle Sam, in fact, remained entrenched in Europe until the job was done.

Curiously, on the puzzle front, *The Boston Globe* launched its own crossword in 1917, though this initiative was a rarity. Where puzzles might be comforts in anxious times, not to mention money-spinners, the war was providing its own circulation boost. Rival papers were in no hurry for these new-fangled cross-words, not when campaign updates held readers in lucrative thrall. Though the *Globe* puzzle, in tandem with the *World*'s influx of amateurs, some of them just teens, did no harm to the genre's future.

Another hero we must salute through this fallow stretch is Margaret Petherbridge, the spy who came in from the cold. The copy-spy, if you like: Margaret was recruited from Smith College, Massachusetts, in 1921, to oversee the *World* crossword. The young woman longed to be a journalist, but Arthur Wynne had a more pressing assignment for her. The puzzle department, such as it was, needed taming. He asked around, discovering his stepdaughter's roommate at Smith was looking for a job. She could spell, knew shorthand and was well organised. With a simple handshake, eight years from its fluky birth, the crossword puzzle gained its first full-time editor.

Margaret learnt quickly. It's fair to say the rookie saw the cross-word as bagatelle, a trivial corner of an important paper, but a few weeks in the chair taught her how dearly the diversion was held. And how closely it was surveyed, especially by a man named FPA.

Franklin Pierce Adams was a columnist at the *World*, hired for his outspoken character. Alas for Margaret, one target of Adams's blunt-ness was the paper's crossword. The man deplored its sloppy errors, its missing clues, its bungled numbering. He derided Margaret on a regular basis, using his column, The Conning Tower, as a soapbox.

The ridicule hit home, and the rookie editor took a pledge. 'Then and there,' she later wrote, 'with my left hand reposing on a dictionary and my right raised in the air, I took an oath to edit the cross-words to the essence of perfection.'

Margaret was the genre's saviour. She studied every submission. Chased out repetition. Culled typos. Fine-tuned definitions. If Wynne's acorn sprang a great oak, a metaphor she later used, then Margaret Petherbridge ensured the sapling flourished.

The woman was an innovator, too. Her mark on the crossword went far beyond quality control. For the first time in crossword history, a set of rules was drafted. The editor insisted that all grid patterns observe symmetry, as well as avoid isolated clusters in their makeup.

Nor was she finished there. On the suggestion of a reader named Radical, the world's first crossword editor ditched the dual-numbering system around this period, opting for the single-digit markers we know today. Consequently, clue 35–36 in Della Sherry's puzzle (*A heavy blow*) was labelled 27-Across in future editions to tell the solver where to enter BANG.

Speaking of bang, the crossword made its own deep impact soon after 1921. Following the heavy blow of World War I, the world was poised to ❤ the crossword. The flurry of Arthur Wynne's in-tray was nothing compared to the frenzy waiting in the wings.

1922

Non-professional (5)

We don't know his name, this chap in jacket and tie, but he dominates the comic strip. He crouches over the crossword, mulling on clue 127–128, *Non-professional*. A thought bubble rises over his head. He suspects the answer is AMATEUR. 'But it begins with L and is five letters,' he despairs.

The cartoonist was Clare Briggs, a Wisconsin draftsman who began his professional life in New York City sketching European battlefields to supplement the photo shortage. But after the Great War the artist tried his hand at being funny. This one-off gag for the *Tribune* was called 'Movie of a Man Doing the Cross-Word Puzzle'. As you can see, the hyphen in cross-word prevailed. Likewise, the Petherbridge system of modern clue-numbering had yet to influence every grid. Yet these were minor issues: the crossword bug was biting

---

+ The BBC is formed.
+ *Ulysses* is published.
+ Vegemite is invented.

New words: fascism, face-lifting, insulin

deep. How else to explain this graphic tribute, occupying a quarter of the sports page?

Stumped by *Non-professional*, our hero turns to the dictionary. He opens the book on his lap, the smoke from his cigar shaping a question mark above his head. 'Well it's L-A something, something Y.' The answer, he decides, is LAITY, which irks me a bit. Does it irk you? Put it this way: a layperson is a non-professional, not the laity. A quibble you may think, but a clue needs to reflect its answer's case. Laity is the mass noun, while the adjective is lay or laic. Though let's skip this debate for now. There's a time and place for disagreement. For a new trend to get the eight-panel treatment in a big-time broadsheet shows five-star approval.

The climax of this black-and-white 'movie' is the solver speaking in tongues ('mus— musi— mur— murd— mur—') until settling on MURRE, a northern sea bird. This inside joke, toying with arcane lingo, contemplating words that only seem to nest in crosswords, is more evidence of Arthur Wynne's fledgling taking off.

1923

An additional clause (5)

Years ago at uni I did a course called technical writing. Looking
back, I can't tell you why. Either I was conned by the course's label,
seeing writing in the title, or the subject suited my two-day timetable.

The final assignment was based on the game three-handed
euchre. To pass the course we had to explain the game's rules to a
visitor from another planet. Thankfully, the visitor spoke English,
but that was the only presumption we could make. Everything else
was ground zero. Hence, the task resembled a spoon-feeding exercise,
the whole shebang broken into tiny steps, every step a sentence, the
rigmarole arranged into a lucid sequence:

1 Cards are oblong slips of cardboard.

+ Louis Armstrong makes his first recording, 'Chimes Blues'.
+ The Mexican rebel Pancho Villa is shot.
+ Turkey becomes a republic.
+ Sydney and Brisbane are linked by trunk telephone.

New words: robot, runway, debunk

2 Each card has its own value.

3 A set of cards is called a deck.

4 Or a pack.

5 Did I mention that one side of each card is the same?

I didn't do very well. To this day I haven't met a euchre-loving Venusian, suggesting the message failed to reach its audience. Mind you, if I did learn anything from the course, it was that I'm not a technical person.

For years, in fact, I buried the trauma of this discovery in the backyard of my brain. Only to chance on a February 1923 edition of *The Queenslander*, a Saturday news summary with literary airs issued by *The Courier-Mail*, or *The Brisbane Courier* as it was then known. Going by the layout, it seems paragraphs were unfashionable between the wars. The occasional ads, most of which imply Queenslanders suffered bleeding gums and halitosis, constitute the lone relief in the five-column format. Tucked inside this edition is an American-style crossword, 15 by 15 squares, part of the first wave to reach Australian shores. The crossword has no named author, nor do the neighbouring instructions. In disbelief I grabbed a ruler to measure the 25 centimetres of column space devoted to the how-to passage. Seven words per line, three lines per centimetre: that's like taking half an hour to explain musical chairs to a ten-year-old, or 2000 steps to demystify three-handed euchre for Ewoks.

The column is headed 'The Latest "Craze"'. Quite rightly, this suggests the crossword was alien to most Brisbanites. But still, the level of detail implies your average banana-bender to be dumber than a bucketful of hammers. Sample this technical writing if you don't believe me:

'The "general idea"—to resort to military parlance—is to fill in the squares in a diagram with letters which make words, these words interlocking with each other according to a definite plan.

Each of the words is deduced from the clue given. It is often, but not necessarily, a synonym of the clue word, and some composers of puzzles take rather alarming liberties with definitions, and even with languages in the effort to tax the ingenuity of solvers. The clues are numbered to correspond with the numbers in the squares in the diagram, and letters in the adjacent squares themselves form words reading not only horizontally, but vertically. To find these words correctly—guess may be the more correct term—is the object of the puzzle. The number of squares in the diagram is not limited. In some puzzles there are as many as 400—20 rows of 20 each. Black squares—arranged according to a symmetrical plan, which may be varied in the case of each puzzle—and the border of the diagram limit the beginning and end of every word. That is, each word begins either at the border or after a black square and ends at the border or before a black square. In the example given here, for example, the first word begins in the square numbered 1, following a black square, and runs horizontally along to end in the open square before the next black square; that is, it contains five letters. These five letters form a word which is a synonym of or is described by the clue—in this case it must be a word which means "an additional clause"'.

PS, the aim of doing a crossword is to have fun (borrowing from the first entry ever coined), not to smother a simple diversion in one RIDER (*An additional clause*) after another. Seems I wasn't the only scribe to struggle with lucid instructions—the prime difference being I knew when to quit.

1924

Move (2)

The modest blue book was a world first. Cloth-bound, with its own bonus pencil, *The Cross Word Puzzle Book* was poised to launch a booming genre. Inside were 50 puzzles from a dozen first-time setters. The collection was the debut project of the Plaza Publishing Company, a New York start-up owned by two fresh Columbia grads, testing Wynne's baby in a new guise. And, just to keep the solvers guessing, the book opened with a murder confession.

The crime's trigger was a crossword. Newman Levy, a minor poet of the day, was sharing the fireside with his wife, or so went the verse he'd submitted to the *New York World*. He was happily lost in *Lord Jim* by Joseph Conrad when his focus was diverted. Let's hear the killer's story in his own words:

+ Lenin dies—and Stalin takes over Soviet Russia.
+ IBM is founded.
+ The first fax is sent by Swedish inventor Ernst Alexanderson.

New words: Band-Aid, beautician, Geiger counter

When suddenly I hear my wife's voice say,
'What word for "female child" begins with G?'
'The word is "Girl",' I growl. Again I try
To catch the shattered magic of my tale.
I find my place. Again with Jim I sail
Upon the tropic sea. My wife says, 'My,
What pronoun in three letters starts with Y?'

Before we get to the gore, let's take a breather and look at the puzzles inside the book. The 50 chosen had been sifted from thousands sent to the *World* after a public appeal for new material. One sifter was Margaret Petherbridge, a lady we've met before. By this time she waded in crosswords, ensuring the flood was properly managed and the 'water' quality high. To help her curate the puzzles for the collection, Petherbridge was joined by editors Prosper Buranelli and F Gregory Hartswick.

The trouble was, the team was limited by the puzzles the *World* had received over the time. As a prime example, the book's opener is called 'A Soft Beginning' by Gregorian. The pattern is plagued by two-letter words—sixteen, altogether—a truckload, when you consider the modern American grid holds none. In ho-hum fashion the first Horizontal clue is *Pronoun*, where the answer is HE, linking with the first Vertical, *Exclamation* (HO). But let's not judge the genre with too much hindsight: Gregorian was playing with the toys of the day.

Yet even the editors rued the two-letter tedium. To quote Hartswick in the prologue, 'Parts of the verb 'to be'; prepositions; the Egyptian Sun God, Ra; pi, em, me, pe, i.e., e.g., so, to, go, do, are to be found in almost every cross-word puzzle, and the solver gets heartily tired of them.'

So it was that Petherbridge turned this debut volume into a platform for reform. Before long, every occupied square in the grid would be crossed twice, while the hodgepodge of itsy-bitsy words had to *Move* (GO)—the final entry in 'A Soft Beginning'.

Other puzzles in the book had grander ambitions with ritzier titles to match, including 'A Quadripuntal Asteroid' and 'A Lingual Labyrinth'. Stretching belief, a setter named Helen V Christ made 'At the Crossroads', just as Frank A Ford did 'Crank Her Up'. There was 'Honeymoon Hokum', composed by Mr and Mrs William Stern II, as well as the troubling byline of Kross Korner Knut, or KKK. Posterity should know, however, that 'A Central Swastika' was *not* the handiwork of Joseph E Austrian, who actually crafted 'Small but Neat'.

Whatever the medley, *The Cross Word Puzzle Book* was a smash, selling close to 200 000 copies by its twelfth reprint. The bonanza boosted the coffers of business newbies Richard Simon and Max Schuster, those two Columbia grads, providing seed capital for an empire set to flourish. Like no other venture, this humble book convinced the world of the crossword's appeal. Mind you, the world was already included in many abstruse clues, like *Australian catfish*, *Chinese weight* and *East Indian climber*. And if you think cryptics are hard, try your luck with these head-scratchers:

The solan goose (6)
Facing toward the direction from which a glacier impinges (5)

To confirm the answers, just follow the instructions on the flyleaf: 'If you wish a copy of *The Book of the Correct Answers* for *The Cross Word Puzzle Book—First Series*, sent with our compliments, use the enclosed postal.' Yes, the first ever crossword book couldn't trust citizens to avoid peeking, asking them instead to lick a stamp for GANNET and STOSS.

Speaking of licking, I promised you a murder. But be warned, unless Punch and Judy tickle your fancy, the crime is brutal. Next time you're stalled on a crossword clue, think twice before consulting your nearest and dearest.

Calmly I rise and search about the place
To find a weapon of sufficient weight.
Aha! Upon our wall an ancient mace,
Studded with knobs of steel. The very thing.
I seize it, and with easy, graceful swing
Wallop my darling wife upon the pate,
The sconce or bean, or dome, or what you will.
Silent she tumbles headlong in the grate.
I take my book and leisurely resume
My tale, and peace and quiet fill the room.

1925

What is it that is good for everyone and is good at any time? (6,3,5)

Kaboom! If any year marks the crossword explosion, it's 1925. This moment like no other marks the mania's big bang. Not just on the page, but in all levels of society.

Groovy women hastened to Greenwich Village, or Bussell's Emporium on Elizabeth Street in Melbourne, to buy crossword frocks and scarves. According to *The Argus*, the chequered garments were 'available in navy, fawn, cinnamon and cocoa'. Crossword handbags were cropping up in swank boutiques on Bond Street. Songs arose, perhaps the most notable being penned by Sidney Clare

---

+ The Great Sphinx is unearthed in Egypt.
+ Double-decker buses run in London.
+ Mussolini seizes power in Italy.
+ The Melbourne Cup is broadcast on radio for the first time.
(The winner is Windbag.)

New words: lesbian, bitchy, blind date

and William Raskin. The catchy tune, crooned by Frank Crumit, was called 'Cross-Word Mamma, You Puzzle Me (But Papa's Gonna Figure You Out)'.

On the legal front, Mary Zaba described herself as a 'crossword widow'. Standing in a Chicago court, she claimed her man devoted more time to synonyms than matrimony. The judge restricted the addict to three puzzles a day, a compromise to avoid divorce.

Librarians across the Western world limited the use of reference books. In Dulwich Library, south London, staff members blacked in the white squares in newspaper crosswords, a ruse to stop the papers being savaged or stolen. London's *Daily Express* lamented the death of the novel. Editorials deplored the plunge in fiction sales versus the focus newly placed on almanacs and glossaries. If society wasn't solving, it was frothing at the mouth. Look around you now and you'll see how the debate surrounding social media taps into similar alarm for declining standards of reading and writing.

Big-S Society was stricken by the fever too, claimed the *Hull Daily Mail*. 'You see fashionable women sitting in their limousines as they drive about town, not deep in the pages of a novel, but in the far more intriguing problems of solving a cross-word puzzle.'

The same article went on to add, 'Half-pay Colonels, and retired Admirals who used to sleep the hours away in their Club in the afternoon are now sitting up in their chairs surrounded by dictionaries searching for solutions.'

American commuters had the same luxury on the Baltimore and Ohio trains. Every morning and evening the service kept the *Webster's Dictionary* handy in each carriage, a bonus boost to help undo that last stubborn corner. What better way to ride, watching the East Coast slide past as you double-checked STOA, your *Greek portico*, in transit? And if a traveller couldn't wait for his fellow-passenger to finish checking, then he might consult his special nerdy bracelet, a sturdy chain that carried a miniature dictionary like a lucky charm.

Not that such a talisman worked wonders for a Californian named WE Carruthers. A snippet in the *New York American* claimed Carruthers incurred the first grievous injury from the addiction. 'Fatigued by hours of futile study, [the man] stretched his mouth in such a yawn that he dislocated his jaw.'

Of course, for every red-hot trend, there's always a rival in freefall. In this case, the casualty was mahjong. Before Arthur Wynne interrupted, the Chinese tile game had dominated the family parlour. Parks and kitchens once rang with the clatter of ivory, but the racket had subsided to a desultory peck by 1925. Capitulation came on Valentine's Day, when mahjong-makers sent a doggerel to *The New Yorker*. The poem was addressed to all crossword editors.

Roses are red
Violets are blue
We'd like to cut
Your throats for you.

Back in London, the East Ham Palais de Danse warmed to the gimmick of crossword dances. A kind of elimination waltz, participants solved random clues in order to last until the prize rounds.

Further north, the *Evening Post* of Nottingham identified the modern ailment as *cluemonia*, a bug as potent as any epidemic. The scourge was liable to ransack an evening at the theatre, the paper reported. Matheson Lang, by all accounts a diligent thespian, missed his entrance at the city's New Theatre while musing clues in the wings. Even the era's rising playwright, Noël Coward, indulged in the curse, admitting his day was complete if he could make 1-Across fit with 1-Down.

Naturally, the clergy was concerned with such misplaced devotion. In a story posted by the *Western Daily Press*, Reverend EC Atherton of St James in Keyham, Leicestershire, urged parishioners to exercise restraint over Lent by rationing their crossword-solving. 'There are many who seem to be at the mercy of any new craze which comes along . . . This is very bad for us physically, mentally and spiritually.' Worshippers in Tamworth, northeast of Birmingham, according to the same piece, were found to be hiding puzzles inside their hymn books, the better to mull on 'a six-letter word meaning idler' while mouthing with the choir.

As for affairs in Australia, the first crossword to appear in *The Sydney Morning Herald* was essentially a booby-trap. A browser probably took the grid to be a genuine arrival at first glance, with some answers already entered, much like Wynne's template. Yet a closer look revealed the words to be advertising copy, reading, 'What is it that is good for everyone and is good at any time?'. The answer was the agency's client, PETERS ICE CREAM.

Over in Adelaide, a correspondent in *The Register* went cuckoo with the letter c. The japery opened like so: 'Curse cross words! Cacophonous collections of the colloquial and cabalistic, catches and connotations, carefully culled converses and cognate complements, causing cerebral callisthenics.' Wynne's invention had even reached Tasmania, where Hobart's *Mercury* published a poem by Anon. The fix was bittersweet:

> I have no comfort now or ease
> My temper's like a bear's.
> All day I peg away at these
> Confounded little squares.

Regardless of the hemisphere, old world or new, nowhere seemed exempt from the crossword tide. Twelve years had seen the trickle swell to torrent. The big bang of 1925 had shattered the universe into infinitesimal squares with hypnotic patterns. Even the innocence of childhood was corrupted by cluemonia. The *Sunday Times* ran a cluster of semi-familiar verses. These so-called 'Cross-Word Nursery Rhymes' captured just how deeply the devotion gnawed:

> Old Mother Hubbard went to the receptacle for nourishment
> To get her poor dog an osseous titbit.
> When she got there the cupboard was entirely denuded of its
>   contents,
> And so the poor doggie got the opposite of any.

1926

Point was (6)

Squinting in the half-light, I can see how the grey squares might resemble insect antennae, a weevil built out of blocks. That was the hope of Edward Powys Mathers, crafter of the first crossword in London's *Observer*, a puzzle he called 'Feelers'. So why the weevil in the first place? The motive lies in the accompanying preamble, which describes the feature as 'a putting out of feelers from setter to solver, and from solver to setter. A beginning has been made with an unusual number of varied lights [answers].'

No question, this virtual bug was a crossword milestone. Many pundits consider 'Feelers' as the first cryptic offshoot, despite most of its clues playing straight. Different from the American fare, the setter's style dances with mischief.

+ Francisco Franco rises to become General of Spain.
+ Scotsman John Logie Baird demonstrates TV.
+ Escapologist Harry Houdini dies of a ruptured appendix.

New words: cozzie, kitsch, recycle, totalitarian

Take MET, for example. In America such a word would have been matched with the clue *Encountered*, or *Converged*, or *Satisfied*. But 'Feelers' took another tack: *Livingstone and Stanley did*. More than simply playful, though, the clue implies a story, which befits a man like Mathers, who was a literary critic and poet. He also drew a wage translating Middle Eastern literature, including *1001 Arabian Nights*. Indeed, among the literati Mathers was something of a name (not that he latched his byline on to this creepy-crawly, going for a pseudonym instead).

So what alias did he choose? If you know your Spanish Inquisition, then you'll be familiar with Torquemada, the chief convertor of non-Christians during the 1400s. The priest's main tools of persuasion were life imprisonment and the stake. Half a millennium later, the new Torquemada was swapping torch and woodpile for oblique clues and deletion recipes: *Dose without circle* (DSE).

To be pedantic, this was not the poet's first crossword. Before 'Feelers' crept into the light, on 14 March 1926, Mathers had composed similar puzzles for friends, with rhyming couplets as clues. Evidently, one friend blew the whistle, showing the handiwork to the editor of the *Saturday Westminster*, who agreed to run a dozen samples as the first feeling-out. Called Puzzles for Supermen, the novelties acted as candlelight to moths, and soon Mathers was balancing writerly duties with an *Observer* commission.

His opening clue, in fact, exudes literature. It also acts as a terrifying sign of the mayhem we have coming. Brief but brutal, the clue reads: *Point was*. To spare you pain, I shall tell you the answer is JESTER, a reference to Jack Point, a jester in Gilbert and Sullivan's operetta *The Yeomen of the Guard*. And if you think that's tough, bear in mind this was Torquemada playing nice, trying to seduce the moths before he tore off their wings.

The plan worked—both plans. The giant bug infected the British bloodstream, obliging the setter to follow up his critter with more radical diagrams. Pattern-wise, it's hard to believe one man, in a single calendar year, could generate a doll's house, a peacock, two sparring boxers, a spider, a chess knight, a devil mask, Romeo and Juliet, a cat, an ugly duckling, a zodiac scorpion and Oojah the Elephant.

To shadow this sequence is to see the birth of cryptic crosswords in time lapse, as orthodox clues lose out to baby-step anagrams—*Money made out of a rail accident* (LIRA)—and tentative double-meanings—*You get this measure from a bill* (PECK). In time we'll chart these twists in closer detail, nasty traps invented by other torturers in other papers. For now the focal point is a new subgenre, with Mathers the jester at the centre. His bug would mutate into 670 more marvels across a 14-year career. In a way this cryptic series would see the Brits win back a little of the intellectual property that America had pegged out. Or, as Mathers himself jeered in a later collection, 'It soon happened, therefore, that the crossword split into two crosswords, one taking the highbrow and one the lowbrow.'

1927

A young hostess of recent times (6)

The routine evokes a border crossing, my library card as visa. To pass beyond the front desk and enter the Rare Books Room properly, I need to state my name and the nature of my business. The registry requires my phone number, address and time of visit. Everything but allergies and next of kin.

'That's a pen,' says the supervisor.

It is, yes. A blue ballpoint. I show him.

'Pencils only,' he reminds me.

My reason for worshipping in this chapel-like chamber, the inner sanctum of Victoria's State Library, awaits me on one of the tables: a Domesday ledger of deckle board. Etched on the cover are the magic words '*Yorkshire Evening News*, 1927'.

<hr>

+ The People's Liberation Army forms in China.
+ The first talkie—*The Jazz Singer*—is released in America.
+ Gangster Squizzy Taylor is shot in Melbourne.

New words: modernist, televise, Rorschach test

By necessity, there was always going to be a pot-shot randomness to this clue safari, a blind belief in fate doing the uncovering. Pick a year; pick a paper. I open the ledger and start with January. The pages are thin and yellow, redolent of dust. By February I'm sneezing as I skim the tobacco ads, the lamb sales, the constipation fixes.

The puzzles are daily and anonymous. I make a list of clues that could be keepers, seeking a touchstone of 1927. I jot down the vernacular, *Silly fool—vulgar* (MUG); the parochial, *Wycliffe's river* (TEES); the erudite, *Stevenson's blind villain* (PEW); and the accidentally smutty, *Ejaculation, most used with another* (OH). Aside from quotes and the occasional wordplay—*Character in the mail?* (LETTER)—there seem to be no firm steps in a cryptic direction. (Not yet, though the mutation was radiating.) Exclamation marks grab the attention, such as *Most girls!*. The answer is FLIRTY, which would struggle to pass modern muster.

Then a clue catches my eye: *A young hostess of modern times (6)*. My first response is GEISHA—perhaps the word had migrated to Sheffield by that stage—yet no letter agrees as I mentally solve the surrounding clues. The answer, I check in the next day's edition, is ISHBEL.

Ishbel who? Ishbel what? That's the joy of any crossword: a single clue can prise apart the curtains, show a new landscape, a lost time, another continent. No doubt, ISHBEL is going to be the year's souvenir, so long as I can solve the solution.

Notes away, pencils away, I leave the holy room and head back down the marble stairs into the library's main atrium. The room is packed with people Facebooking on laptops. I find a spare nook to join the wifi stream, checking the status update of a girl called Ishbel.

The name is Gaelic for Isabel, I learn, but which Ishbel was in the setter's mind? My first suspect is Ishbel Maria Hamilton-Gordon, otherwise known as the Marchioness of Aberdeen and Temair. A good egg, her ladyship was based in Canada for most of her life, presiding over the International Council of Women. She campaigned for females to enter the clergy, as well as lobbying for legal brothels. She introduced the golden retriever to Ontario and wrote a comical memoir called *The Musings of a Scottish Granny*. But her timing is out of whack. At the time the crossword appeared, this 'young hostess' was 70 in the shade.

Methuselah compared to the next spring chicken, Ishbel MacDonald, who was 24 when the clue appeared. The lass was the oldest of five children, her mother dying of blood poisoning when Ishbel was only eight. Her father, Ramsay MacDonald, never remarried. By and large this obliged his oldest daughter to fulfil a mothering role, as Ramsay embraced his career with the Parliamentary Labour Party. A talented statesman, Ramsay soon rose to be party leader, going as far as 10 Downing Street when Ishbel was 21.

Apologies if you know the story already, but I'm staggered to think a Scottish girl accompanied her widower father into the nation's head office, a gaggle of four younger bairn in their care. There, she adopted the ceremonial duties of a quasi-wife, minding her siblings and receiving the world's high and mighty—and I for one have never heard of her. And I'd wager no Tweeter in this atrium has heard of her either. Yet she never left her father's side, being the fresh face of duty for three whole terms in office, from 1924 to 1935, spending half her life as the PM's other half. And as a measure of her fame the girl was a crossword clue in her early twenties. More than that she was an epithet—*young hostess*—answered by a first name only. Ishbel was Britney minus the viral video, Beyoncé without a booty being licious.

Later in life Ishbel had a crack at politics but soon lost the drive, preferring to run a country pub than the country. She saw out her days at the Old Plow, in High Wycombe, eventually dying childless in 1982, aged 79.

I power down the laptop and study the crowd around me, a sea of twenty-somethings enrapt in cyberspace. Knowledge is lurking at our fingertips, yet so few surfers know of Ishbel. Where is the Channel 4 costume drama? The postage stamp? The Ishbel MacDonald Foundation for Single Parents? Unless that revival occurs, this random Yorkshire crossword will remain a rare reminder of a former household name that has dwindled into obscurity.

1928

Big bird (3)

Owl sat down in his favourite chair. He wore an old shawl around his shoulders and a pair of pince-nez lodged on his beak. Across his lap was a copy of the *Ornithological Times*, folded to the crossword page.

Big bird (3), said the first clue, causing Owl to hesitate. His quill froze above the paper. He scratched behind his ear and read the clue a second time.

Best thing to do was fetch a scrap of paper. He wrote down EGL, but that looked odd. Maybe the letters would improve in the mirror—but no, even odder. He took a sip of tea and had a new idea. But try as he might he could not fit OSTRIDGE or HORK into the boxes.

+ The Royal Australian Flying Doctor service begins operating.
+ After 70 years, the *Oxford English Dictionary* completes its final volume.
+ Mickey Mouse appears in *Steamboat Willie*.

New words: fat cat, commentator, racketeering

The doorbell rang. Of course, being a bird of superior wisdom, Owl could easily have finished the puzzle if left alone, but the doorbell was more important in the Scheme of Things. He went downstairs to find Pooh and Piglet standing outside. They wished to talk about Christopher Robin. Their friend had only just returned to Hundred Acre Wood, riding a blue bicycle. Where had he been all this time, and was there any risk he was going back?

Truth be told, Christopher Robin had been away for 81 years. The boy was last spotted in 1928, sharing cakes and jellies in AA Milne's final book of Winnie-the-Pooh stories, *The House at Pooh Corner*. Back then, every animal in the wood had made their peace with him. They'd given him presents and waved him good luck for his next big adventure—off the page.

Yet here he was in 2009, back in full colour, with longer legs and shorter hair but essentially the lad who'd left. For that matter, neither Owl nor Rabbit nor any other animal had gained a freckle. Better still, Hundred Acre Wood had not been subdivided into medium-density housing.

I grew up with Winnie-the-Pooh. I loved his talent for daydreaming, a vital hobby in any crossword-making career. Sometimes your best clues will surface during a stroll, or while you are staring into the distance. But that was the Pooh of 1928, the bear with little brain depicted through EH Shepard's drawings and the gentle magic of Milne's language. The book made a modest splash between the wars. (*Winnie* the name honoured a black bear called Winnipeg that a Canadian soldier gave to London Zoo.) Since those days, the characters have flourished, appearing as soft toys and puppets, in cartoons and pantomimes, the Milne title never falling out of print.

But a sequel? With a bicycle? And an otter called Lottie? And a crossword puzzle? Heresy to some. Needless to many. Even the author, David Benedictus, was terrified when his story collection reached the book shops. 'At worst everyone will hate me,' he confessed to *The Guardian*, 'and I'll just crawl under a bush and hide.'

The jury however was mainly impressed. From gramophones to billycarts, these ten new chapters in the Pooh canon almost justified the 81-year wait. Benedictus himself had waited ten years between submitting his first speculative stories to the Pooh Properties Trust and receiving the board's wary yes.

Without knowing the contract's small print, I can only surmise that part of the sequel's aim was to emphasise a certain Britishness to life in the woods, not just through the marmalade and daisy chains, but also in the ritualism. How else to explain a game of cricket (where Eeyore plays the 'wicked-keeper') or hoopla at the harvest festival or a crossword?

Owl eventually works out OWL, the answer, but not without the aid of Christopher Robin's thesaurus, which Piglet thinks sounds ten times scarier than a Heffalump. As for the spelling bee to end the crossword chapter, Pooh agrees to go along only because of one True Thing he knows: where there are bees, there is always hunny.

1929

ИМЯ ДЕВУШКИ (3)

Or, said another way, *Girl's name*. It's the kind of clue I despise as a rule. The solver is faced with a mountain of choices. Worse than that, despite this being a so-called quick clue, there's no way of pinpointing the mystery girl quickly. Even if you have the last letter, which here is an A, you still flounder. The long list may well diminish, yet more than a dozen options remain: Ava, Eva, Mia, Pia . . . Muddying the waters further, this same *krestoslovitsu* already has two girls in the grid, and Ingrid ain't one of them! Instead, they are IRMA and OKSANA, two Russian lasses.

All three girls appeared in the first puzzle to run in the newspaper *Rul'* (The Rudder), in 1929. The time-passer was intended for Russian exiles in Berlin, fugitives from the 1917 revolution. Among their number was the Nabokov family, including Vladimir

+ Wall Street crashes.
+ Conscription ends in Australia.
+ Popeye and Tintin both make their comic debuts.

New words: zucchini, sasquatch, greenhouse effect

Dmitrievich, the paper's founding editor, and his wordy son Vladimir Vladimirovich, the crossword's creator.

Berlin had heralded tough times for the Nabokovs. From the moment Lenin had derailed their comfy existence in St Petersburg, the aristocrats had been living in limbo, moving to Yalta in the Crimea and later to Britain before finally relocating to Berlin. Tragically, two years after creating *Rul'*, Nabokov Senior was murdered. The liberal politician was shot while trying to defend a colleague at a tsarist conference in 1922. His death only tightened the financial squeeze on his widow, Elena Ivanovna, and her five children.

As the eldest, in his late twenties, Vladimir juggled several jobs to keep the clan's lifestyle intact, turning his hand to translation work, language-teaching and tennis-coaching. At least these gigs raised funds, compared to his two real passions—literature and lepidoptery. As it happens, butterflies remained a lifelong passion for Vladimir, while his renown (and reward) as a fiction writer remained, ahem, in the wings.

Most budding novelists might have considered journalism at this point, earning a quid through his late father's *Rul'*. Not Vladimir. He zigged where others would zag. His writing was more a private obsession, a ritual that he often observed at night. By day, however, to grub some extra coin, he invented chess problems and *krestoslovitsu.*

Even native speakers might stall at that last word. Vladimir didn't just construct crosswords, he also contrived the very word—*krestoslovitsu*—to label them. With cruciverbal virus just edging into Europe, the Russian languages lacked a term for the pastime, so Nabokov made one up. His coinage didn't stick, however; in the end, the English term was adopted, or its calque, кроссворд, to be precise, an approximation of the foreign word, where кросс almost mimics the English word 'cross'. Over time the puzzle grew to a favourite pursuit for millions of Russians, with their émigré novelist recognised among the art form's pioneers, despite his label failing to catch on.

Unfazed, Nabokov persisted with his neologism, using *krestoslovitsu* in his best-known novel, *Lolita*, 20 years later. Translated, the passage captures the Nabokovian flair for imagery and wordplay. At one stage, Humbert Humbert, Lolita's lover, notices 'seven empty bottles in the wooden squares of the tray that look like an incomplete *krestoslovitsu*.'

Speaking of incomplete, many *Rul'* readers would have abandoned their crossword, thanks to such terse clues as *Girl's name*. Or, if the dilemma of names didn't thwart solvers, Nabokov's other clues might have obstructed them. *Obstruction*, in fact, is quirkily answered by ROOM SCREEN, keeping with the transliteration, while *Expression of aversion* is BRRR.

Perhaps the fairest clue on show is *Promise*. Neat and simple, all roads lead fairly to vow. Which makes me wonder, how many solvers sensed the real promise of this innovative compiler? Even Nabokov himself might have been surprised to learn that Ada, the missing girl in his maiden *krestoslovitsu*, would eventually serve as the title of his fifteenth novel and last great work, three decades down the track, the culmination of a glittering career.

Then again, maybe not. The name held a special place in the butterfly-lover's heart. From the cradle, Nabokov was affected by a condition known as synaesthesia, where letters and numbers were linked to specific colours in his mind's eye. With a name like Ada, not only did the palindrome evoke something of a butterfly's symmetry, but the three letters released gold-black-gold in the Russian's imagination, the colour scheme of the swallowtail, one of his favourite catches. In a sense the insect's beauty is trapped inside a puzzling rarity, a colourful imago pinned forever in a literary master's *krestoslovitsu*.

1930

Red loam (anag.) (7)

I should write this chapter as a boustrophedon, that eccentric Greek method of two-way writing. If you haven't seen the system, the first line will travel outwards from left to right, as per usual, only for the next line to pivot and reverse the direction, heading back to the left margin. The word *boustrophedon* comes from *bous* (ox) and *strophe* (turn). Combine both elements and you have the rhythm of the plough, furrowing a field with text.

The reason for such a gesture would be to celebrate Adrian Bell. Epitaphs describe the man as a journalist-farmer, but that's selling him short. Bell was an idyllist in the Virgil tradition, a poet of the harrow. In the early 1920s, barely out of his teens, he fled the bohemian turpitude of London to take up farmhand duties in

---

+ Mahatma Gandhi embarks on his Salt March.
+ Haile Selassie is crowned as Ethiopia's emperor.
+ Pluto is discovered by 23-year-old Kansan, Clyde Tombaugh.
+ Donald Bradman scores 334 against England.

New words: drive-in, heist, whodunit

Suffolk. During this time he wrote three books about rural life: *Corduroy*, *Silver Ley* and *Cherry Tree*. All three were destined to be classics, not just for their quality but also because they were pocket-sized, perfect for soldiers to smuggle to war, portable reminders of why they were fighting. At World War II's peak, postmen lugged whole sacks of appreciation to Bell's smallholding near Beccles. His books were valued talismans of an endangered Britain. Yet writing was not the only sideline the farmer pursued: there's another feather in the Bell cap, with feather being the operative word.

If this book came complete with pictures, like Bell's idylls, I'd have campaigned for the *Times*' photo of him in velvet jacket and cravat, a quill jutting from the hand that rests against his chin. He's looking to the window, if the balance of light is any guide, patiently awaiting the phrasing of his next clue. Scattered on the desk are three careworn dictionaries and as many crossword grids. Fresh feathers stand in two inkwells. The wall at his back is a private library of solemn tomes. It's an endearing vision of a pioneer, as Bell was the instigator of the world's best-known cryptic, from *The Times*.

His father actually worked for the paper. The editor was eager to begin a puzzle series, since *The Daily Telegraph* was stealing a march on them—that paper had been running the gimmick for five years already. Call it nepotism, but Bell Senior knew young Adrian was up to the task. After all, the boy was lost in furrows all day dreaming up pretty sentences, so crosswords should hardly present a leap.

The hunch was well founded. His son was born to the art. Adrian Bell (a near-jumble of BALLERINA) twisted and turned London minds for almost 50 years. His output tallied a staggering 4520 puzzles. The chap had style and humour, intellect with a sense of joy, not to mention a velvet jacket and quill.

His initial clues, on 1 February, carried every sign of that potential, as well as the rural glimpses that were soon his other mainstay. As was the flavour back then, the inaugural *Times* crossword was a mix of quick and cryptic, the rules of engagement still on the drawing board. Things got down to an earthy start with 1-Across: *Spread unevenly* (SMEAR) and turned muckier only at 18-Across: *Denizen of the ultimate ditch* (DIEHARD). But the ploughman's fingerprints were seen most clearly in a purebred anagram. What's more, *Red loam (anag.)* also leads to EARLDOM, a buried reference to the new domain *The Times* came to distinguish. Though let's not forget the seed-sower, Adrian Bell, the journalist-farmer who turned the first sod.

1931

A Siamese functionary (6)

DH Lawrence was playing silly buggers, I swear. One of his novellas is called *The Virgin and the Gypsy*, a title guaranteed to get any schoolboy sniggering. Ditto can be said for some of his other novels, notably *Aaron's Rod* and *The Escaped Cock* (seriously). Sex was always foremost on the writer's mind—on every human mind, should you subscribe to his tales of suppressed libido. His true heroes were thatchers with a small t, miners and gamekeepers, men in their naked prime, unguarded hedonists. His ideal women were awake to their id, given to Dionysus and rolls in the hay.

Not that Yvette and Lucille get too many chances to hit the straw in *The Virgin and the Gypsy*. The young sisters are trapped in their father's vicarage, the household ruled by a blind grandmother.

+ Japan occupies Manchuria.
+ The Empire State Building is completed.
+ Dame Nellie Melba dies.

New words: Filofax, kibbutz, underpants

The elephant in the room is the missing mother, a fugitive of sexual passion whose name and crimes are seldom broached.

This was Lawrence's last work, written in 1929 and published after the author had succumbed to tuberculosis, aged 45. A good portion of the story is spent in the dark dining room at the rectory. Here the clock ticks, the fire crackles, and the girls yearn for elsewhere. One evening, father and Uncle Fred 'played crossword puzzles with Granny'. This phrase alone suggests the contempt in which DH held such bourgeois diversions. You don't *play* crosswords; you *solve* them. But the semantics were lost on Lawrence, who despised primness and order: qualities embodied by a symmetrical box.

The author's scorn is confirmed in the only clue the rector reads aloud, for the benefit of his blind mother. 'Now, Mater, are you ready?' he asks. 'N blank blank blank blank w: a Siamese functionary.'

Granny is hard of hearing. She mistakes the N for an M, then *Siamese* for *Chinese*. Once the muddles are cleared, the room falls into contemplation. Or oppression, as far as Yvette is concerned. The title's virgin wishes she could open a window, if not to escape her destiny, then to alleviate the Granny smell.

The clue is never solved, and there's a reason for that. My first response, had I been sitting by the vicarage fire, would have been to suspect NEPHEW, a match for the pattern but not the clue. Likewise for NARROW, a word evoked more actively by the room than the puzzle. Beyond that, I strike a wall. This obliges me, like Lawrence's coalmining father, to go digging. I delve the dictionary to unearth such obscurities as NAPHEW (a small turnip), NANDOW (a Brazilian ostrich) and NIPKOW (a German inventor). Reading further, I learn that Paul Nipkow played a seminal role in creating television, a gadget poised to usurp crosswords in a matter of years. All very interesting, but light years from Siam.

That's when the brainwave comes. Lawrence *was* playing silly buggers. Dying in New Mexico, depleted by his stricken lungs, the man had more pressing issues to consider, like oxygen and sex, rather than the niceties of a word puzzle. What we get then in this claustrophobic scene is a fusion of truth and recollection, a pastiche of a real clue and an approximate array of letters. I can't say this for certain, but I do recall meeting this very subterfuge in older crosswords, usually with a question mark attached. *Siamese functionary* is something of a crossword cliché, in fact, suiting Lawrence's purposes to the bone. The formula is a pun, a misdirection to make solvers think of Siam, the kingdom, rather than a cat. A synonym of *functionary* is *cat's paw*, which may seem a liberty given the details supplied in the pattern the rector reads, but who's to say the invalid's own letters were correct, let alone his mathematics?

If I were there, a wild-mopped gypsy sandwiched between two sisters, I'd offer that solution in a heartbeat. Tell the rector the word derives from a fable in which a monkey cons a cat to fetch his chestnuts from the fire, so making CAT'S PAW a metonym for minion. Granny may be impressed. Uncle Fred could harrumph with surprise. But, being a pagan love god, I remain silent, my gypsy brain entrenched in a different rut.

1932

'So Eustace dedicated his book on tubers to you! We English are no longer farmers, I am afraid; the sight of a decayed swede or fetid parsnip no longer thrills us.' (Hidden) (4)

Did you ever see *Dad's Army*? I can still see my own dad sitting in his favourite chair, turning purple with laughter as Captain Mainwaring tried to marshal his hapless troop through the latest episode. Part of the squad was the silver-haired Sergeant Wilson, a bank-teller in khaki played by John Le Mesurier. His catchphrase was uttered in every second show, gently spoken in the captain's earshot: 'Do you think that's wise, sir?'

+ Franklin D Roosevelt replaces Herbert Hoover as president.
+ Sydney Harbour Bridge is opened.
+ The ABC is established.

New words: skivvy, technocrat, iron lung

I'm not sure if there's a blood link, but the creator of our next crossword has the surname Le Mesurier also. This chap was in the real military: mounted infantry, if my research is sound. And being a genuine soldier, Lieutenant-Colonel HG Le Mesurier could have benefited from heeding the rhetoric of the make-believe version. I'm referring to the prologue of the Lieutenant-Colonel's book, *Pattern and Patchwork: A Book of Crossword Puzzles*. This is the same preamble where Le Mesurier deplores a certain formula of clue to be found in the popular press. He writes, 'Sentences in which words have been 'hidden' are, perhaps, slightly less idiotic than those usually associated with these puzzles.'

Either I'm missing the irony here, or the day-to-day clues of other puzzles must have been bloody ludicrous to eclipse the efforts of Le Mesurier. In all my trawlings I can't bring to mind longer-winded or loopier examples of the hidden formula than those that appear in his collection.

If you don't know the recipe, a hidden clue buries the answer in its body. A modern sample is *Taste balsam, pleasantly bottled (6)*. Examine the clue and you'll find your answer hiding among the letters: a word of encapsulation (*bottled*), adjoining a loaded phrase (*balsam pleasantly*) and a definition (*taste*) that together yield the answer (SAMPLE). But in 1932 the regulations were looser. Lax, almost. For starters, the formula didn't require a definition. Instead, if a compiler could string a sentence together—sometimes two—and manage to secrete the clue's solution along the way, then his mission was complete.

After such an immodest intro, Le Mesurier's technique was on show. And if I was playing drillmaster, I'd send him back to the barracks for a spit and polish. With few exceptions, his hidden work is a dog's breakfast. This chapter's heading is the Lieutenant-Colonel's bid to camouflage SNIP. That's 140 characters, better known as Tweet-max, to convey four. Even that's ignoring the fact that the same blather smuggles thirteen other four-letter words, including the military whiff of CEDE and RAID.

Yet perhaps I'm being unfair. Multiple options were doubtless part of the historic game, especially with no definition to serve as compass. Indeed, in some puzzles, clues drew further words from the one verbose source. But Le Mesurier was showing how doolally the formula had become. Indeed, greater restraint and more concision (plus an inbuilt meaning) awaited at decade's end. SNIP the answer soon doubled as 'Snip!' the command, something the army of modern solvers, with the aid of hindsight, would recommend as wise.

1933

Army unit (4)

There comes a point at which you can't keep selling pencil-sharpeners for a living. At the age of 35, on a cold day in Chicago, Edgar Rice Burroughs had reached that point. It was 1911, a cusp in the Age of Exploration. A treasure-hunter had just uncovered Machu Picchu in the Andean jungle. Norwegians were racing to the North Pole. Yet here was Edgar—with a wife and two kids to support—dragging his bones across town with a two-bit gimmick in his valise.

If anything, the job's big perk was spare time. Edgar filled his days by reading *Argosy All-Story Weekly*, a pulp anthology of high-sea stories, the Zorro stuff, cannibals in Africa. He came to think he could write better page-turners. Why not? He had the pencils for it, and the imagination—both sharp.

+ Adolf Hitler is appointed as German Chancellor.
+ A US physicist discovers radio waves emitting from the Milky Way.
+ Sydney gets its first traffic lights.

New words: escapism, supermarket, pesticide

So he invented a planet called Barsoom as the setting of his first escapade, *Under the Moons of Mars*. The recipe was romance with a dash of violence and a race of nasty Green Martians. The single earthling on Barsoom was an ex-soldier named John Carter. *Argosy* parcelled the tale into chapters throughout 1912. In case the experiment flopped, Edgar chose the alias of Normal Bean, though an editor took the name to be a typo, converting the creator into Norman Bean.

Regardless, the story made a splash, encouraging Edgar to treat John Carter as a template for his next he-man series. This one he called Zantar, which shrewd staffers rejigged into Tarzan, and Edgar was on his way. By 1933, in fact, with eight Barsoom books under his belt and twice as many Tarzan yarns, Burroughs could buy as many pencil-sharpeners as he damn well pleased.

But let's return to outer space. Barsoom was steeped in flora and fauna, culture and history, plus an ingredient missing in most fiction of the day: an invented language. Direct and guttural, Barsoomian was devoid of any ornate phrases. It seems the aliens of Thark and Ptarth were seldom in the mood for small talk. All up, Burroughs coined 400 words in his eleven-book series, with most barely a syllable long. Barsoomian animals include the *banth*, the *apt* and the equine *thoat*. Measurements were equally punchy, with *ads*, *sofads*, *haads* and *karads*.

I know such oddities thanks to a Swedish IT journalist named Fredrik Ekman, who, at 42, doesn't do things by halves. He role-plays in Middle Earth with other Tolkien fans, has a black belt in jujitsu, and edits the newsletter of an all-male choir named Orphei Drängar. (Curiously, the same group is dubbed the 'crossword choir' in Sweden, since its initials occur frequently in that nation's diagrams.) Anyhow, Ekman also speaks a dozen programming languages—on top of English and Barsoomian. His obsession began in 2000, when revisiting the Martian series with an eye to harvest the artificial words. 'I grew fascinated by the language,' he told me. 'I wanted to have a dictionary of the words but found no compilation of the sort. So I started creating one of my own.'

After each book Fredrik noted the latest acquisitions. Soon his dictionary overflowed, causing him to wonder what to do with it. 'Don't ask me how I got the idea exactly . . . I'd already made a few small crosswords in Swedish, so I knew I could do it.' But there was a hitch. The potential fill for a Barsoomian crossword was severely limited. The Swede's first compromise was asymmetry. His next was running words and names in any direction, before hitting a dead-end and starting again.

After a mountain of pencil shavings, Fredrik did the impossible. Not that he took the credit. Instead, he placed the Barsoomian puzzle with *ERBzine* (a Burroughs fanzine), claiming the creation had appeared in *The Helium Times*, the planet's chief gazette. The ruse echoed Burroughs's technique, as he claimed his Martian series arose from John Carter himself, alleging his hero to be an uncle and the novels so many chunks of a bequeathed memoir.

As for solving the crossword, Ekman described the challenge as 'ridiculously difficult. Even a diehard Burroughs fan would only get ten words.' *Sak*, say, is Barsoomian for jump, the first word Carter learnt when arriving on the planet via astral projection. But the real fan-tester among them is the clue *Army unit (4)*. If this was plain English and not Barsoomian via Swedish, half-a-dozen options would exist: RANK? FILE? Or maybe BASE, FORT or CAMP? None applies here, I'm afraid. To crack the code you need military intelligence of the cosmic kind. The book to target is *Swords of Mars*, number eight in the saga that *Argosy* ran in 1933. The plot is pure pulp, in which a lowly soldier (Hadron of Hastor) falls for a hot princess (Sanoma Tora) who's kidnapped by a depraved baddie (Tul Axtar of Jahar). Before you can say *sak* a *karad*, the army intervenes.

For the record, a *padwar* is an extraterrestrial lieutenant, the brass in charge of a *utan*, or 100 soldiers, better known as *thans*. Yet UTAN is not our prize, since the answer ends in K, owing to A-KOR, the son of O-Tan the Jeddak, running along the base. Confused? You need to keep reading the novel's skirmish to encounter the *umak*, or a force of 10 000 Barsoomian grunts.

Bingo. One unique puzzle solved, an opus conceived in Östergötland by a black-belted fantasist, via speakeasy Chicago and the inner solar system. And you thought crosswords were vanilla distractions? Or the only word Edgar Rice Burroughs invented was Tarzan's yodel, AAAARRGHH-AAAR-AAAH?

1934

Ren makes the plural of this (5)

Sydney Elliott Napier, creator of the first crossword for *The Sydney Morning Herald*, was an enigma in his own right. Better known by his middle name, the ex-solicitor was also an ex-soldier, serving as a sergeant in World War I. After the war, he took up journalism with the *Herald*. Some of the stories he covered for the paper eventuated into books, touching on such topics as great lovers of history, great British walks, or the Great Barrier Reef—yet it was the Great War that pervaded his more personal pieces. Track down any of his poetry and you'll find it embodies the trauma of the battlefield. Even his debut crossword carried a wartime echo:

Telling beer (anagr.) = BELLIGERENT
A poison gas = PHOSGENE

+ Persia becomes Iran.
+ Qantas is formed.
+ The first Loch Ness Monster photo appears in the UK press.

New words: ESP, evacuee, spiv

The puzzle itself was hidden in *The Women's Supplement*, between tea-making tips and a bridge column. Despite most clues being quick, several refuse to yield to the modern gaze. Test yourself on this one:

Long-haired rider (8)

Only by the mercy of cross-letters (giving a _ A _ A _ I _ R pattern) might you twig to the possibility of CAVALIER. Yes, that's the answer—but why? The solution sent me digging for its logic. I chanced across a popular chocolate box of the period, a line of soft-centred treats known as Cavalier Chocolates. The logo on the lid showed a debonair horseman with a full-blooded mullet, the logo evidently a Georgian meme.

Another stumper in the so-called quick category was this:

Nasty if not gilded (5)

The letter breakdown was P_L_S. To my shame, I peeked at the next week's solution to confirm the answer was PILLS, versus POLES. A gilded pill? That made no sense. In desperation I floated the mystery in my Wordplay column, a weekly feature of the very same *Herald*, and a reader named John Moyse came to the rescue. He told me the clue trifles with a line from *Yeomen of the Guard* in which a piece of advice is handed down: 'For he who'd make his fellow-creatures wise should always gild the philosophic pill!' Believe it or not, the advisor in question is the jester, Jack Point, a name you may recall from 1926. No question, Gilbert and Sullivan were the Lennon and McCartney of their day.

As a sergeant, Napier no doubt knew the value of order—and of following orders. Rules and respect are crucial in the face of conflict. Yet peacetime was a different hill of beans, going by the renegade treatment the compiler paid to cryptic etiquette. True, a lot of these rules had yet to be promulgated, and griping about hairy cavaliers is more about distance than disdain, but the demobbed sarge showed a real talent for insubordination. Exhibit A would be the indirect anagram:

Instruct a twisted swindler = TEACH, an anagram of *cheat*

Or if that's being harsh, then try the next taboo, pretty much apologising for an obscure entry by citing the answer in the clue:

A small ode = ODELET

Yet EN (as Elliott Napier would be known to modern *Herald* solvers) soothes all umbrage with a dose of old-world charm. A large sample of his clues displays that whimsy that Torquemada—another setter-poet—was peddling five years before. Such clues spritz the usual sobriety found in the dictionary, looking at words with a cheeky smile:

As a whistle proverbially = CLEAN
Privately is in this = CAMERA, as in camera, means in private,
or in the room as the Latin translates.

But the cheekiest in this vein ignores the definition altogether. Instead, Napier just has fun with the answer's unique quality:

Ren makes the plural of this (5)

The answer is a fitting term for this ancestral puzzle, as 1934 marked the birth of cryptics in Australia. Down under, in the cryptic game, we all share a few genes with this opener. In some small way, the diverse family of Australian compilers, from yours truly to the newest kid on the block, are all the CHILD-REN of EN.

1935

Unua verso de tre konata poemo
(3,5,7,8,2,4)

'So what's the thing about crosswords?' That's a question I cop a lot. 'Surely they're just boxes with words inside them?' Uh-huh, in the same way JS Bach's *Mass in B Minor* is a string of notes along a stave, or Jackson Pollock's *Blue Poles* is a bunch of daubs. My point being, each box holds a ticket to somewhere new. Look no further than this clue from 1935: *Unua verso de tre konata poemo*. What language is that? Some words will seem half-familiar, like *verso* and *poemo*, while *de* and *tre* have an Italian vibe, or maybe French. They're actually both in a way. Translated, the clue reads, *First verse of a famous poem*, granting us two mysteries to solve now: What language? And which poem?

+ Amelia Earhart is the first to fly solo from Hawaii to California.
+ The German Luftwaffe is created.
+ Monopoly hits the market.
+ Cane toads are introduced to Queensland.

New words: ecosystem, autopilot, pizza

The clue belongs to a *krucvortenigmo*—literally, a cross-vortex puzzle. The feature appeared in a monthly review entitled *Literatura Mondo*. The magazine was assembled in Hungary, though the language is not Hungarian. Indeed, to answer the first question we need to travel to Białystock. Despite being in northeast Poland nowadays, the city was part of Prussia 200 years ago, and an annex of Russia after that. During the Russian phase, in the 1880s, a young Jew called Ludwig Lazarus Zamenhof lived in the city's centre. No linguist by training, he was nevertheless fluent in many languages. His mother tongue was Russian, but his home also flowed with Polish and Yiddish, while his father taught German. Talk on the street wove in strands of Lithuanian and Belorussian, making Białystock a European Babel. Blessed and cursed by the same fate, the city was divided by ethnic schisms, persecution and prejudice. Ludwig started to wonder how life would be if every fishmonger, every bureaucrat, every duchess, every gangster shared a single language, not just in Białystock, but around the world.

So at the age of 28 the optician invented a language. Like a car mechanic ransacking parts to make an engine, Zamenhof borrowed words from English and German, Latin and Greek, French and Russian. He dubbed his creation a *lingvo internacia* and published its vocabulary and sixteen rules of grammar in 1887, relying on the alias of Doktoro Esperanto (one who hopes).

Esperanto became the system's name, a social experiment tinged with utopia. Soon the language found an audience, for obvious reasons. The spelling was logical. The grammar was clear. Here was a language in which all nouns ended in o, all adjectives in a, all adverbs in e and all plurals in oj. Esperanto was a gift from Dr Hope encouraging humans to go forth and unify.

A movement began as the century turned. A pre-web flash mob met in 1905, at the first Universala Kongreso de Esperanto. Almost 700 speakers walked the boulevards of Boulogne-sur-Mer.

Zamenhof, a dapper man in self-prescribed specs, led the throng in 'La Espero', his customised anthem.

Schools blossomed. Seminars and associations were organised, including an Esperanto bicycle club. Stories and poems prolifer-ated—enough to justify the Budapest magazine *Literatura Mondo*, in 1922.

Yet these were fraught times in Europe, the Great War inflicting a wound on the psyche and a severe mauling of idealism. Millions of innocents had been slaughtered along multiple fronts, making hope of a universal language seem bereft. *Literatura Mondo* reflected that volatility. From 1922 until its demise in 1949, the periodical was periodical at best, releasing just sixteen issues in three separate incarnations.

Despite Zamnhof's invention attracting over two million students, the difficulties hampered the language's inbuilt promise. After so much bloodshed, could one language be the panacea?

But hope sits at the heart of Esperanto. The magazine persevered even as one war fermented a second. Every issue, in a stateless language, held a fresh raft of essays, poems and stories, articles and reviews, plus a *krucvortenigmo*. And in 1935, one cross-vortex puzzle opened on our chapter's clue. The poem is not 'Le Espero', as sung at the first *kongreso*, but another Zamenhof composition called 'Le Vojo' (The Road), a stirring war-cry for peace. For many Esperanto speakers, the poem's first line was a household mantra to get them through Europe's bleakest days: *Tra densa mallumo briletas la celo* (Through a thick darkness the objective glows). Humanist scripture, the line was vital, as perhaps the nameless setter feared: a solace to recite in the face of great horrors lurking around the corner.

Keep in mind this was 1935. A year later Stalin launched his Great Purge, a murderous campaign against saboteurs and dissidents, with Esperantists high on his list. He viewed these non-Russian-speakers as a threat to statehood and killed thousands while sending still more to die in Siberian labour camps. Before too long Hitler followed suit, casting Esperanto as a piece of Jewish cleverness, a furtive bid for world dominion, *der Führer* impounding any speakers he could find.

So runs the anguish of world history, but what about Dr Hope? How did destiny treat the inventor of Esperanto? None too kindly, I'm afraid. The idealist passed away in 1917, quietly in Warsaw, yet Zamenhof would not be immune from the horrors of World War II. All three of his children would die in the Holocaust, yet his brainchild did not perish. Eighty years later, Esperanto perseveres with a million-plus speaker across *la mundo*, the numbers soaring in Africa and Brazil. The dream perseveres. Despite the punctuation of conflict and terror, the optometrist's vision has held its gaze—the optimist's vision.

1936

Il dit la même chose autrement (10)

If a particular Parisian author born in 1936 had thrown his individuality into this world-ranging book, you wouldn't find a scrap (not a jot, not a damn scintilla) of our most popular orthographic symbol, found in almost all forms of writing, including fiction and non-fiction, playscripts and philosophical discussions. And, odd as it may sound, crosswords.

That symbol is e. Shit, I just said it. The shackles are off. The secret is out. That first paragraph contains over 300 letters, with every vowel except e. But now that the parlour game is over, the boycott has been lifted, and we can restore the alphabet to its full size. Suddenly, I can say words like *suddenly*, or *alphabet*, or *secret* again. Phew.

━━━

+ Stalin's Great Purge begins.
+ The Spanish Civil War erupts.
+ Jesse Owens wins the 100-metre dash at the Berlin Olympics.
+ The last Tasmanian tiger dies in Hobart Zoo.

New words: magazine, Oscar, curvaceous, decrypt

But imagine writing a chapter minus that crucial vowel. How would you even say *vowel*, without e at your disposal? *Sound unit*? *Lingual building block*? *Polish lingo rarity*? It's lunacy, but that didn't deter Georges Perec from writing *La Disparition* (The Disappearance), a 300-page novel that eschews e. Sorry, avoids a particular sound unit throughout its wondrous duration.

A possible motive for the stunt lies in the writer's origins. Perec was the only child of Polish Jews, born in a blue-collar district of Paris. His father died of shrapnel wounds before he was four, while his mother vanished on the Auschwitz train a few years later, neither her body nor fate ever verified. Disappearance exerted a terrible presence on the orphan's life, just as a name like Georges Perec, should it lose its most frequent letter, might be sorely diminished.

Through a bookworm boyhood, Perec found comfort in words and wordplay. Yet for all his élan with languages, he ended up shuffling data for the Neurophysiological Research Laboratory. The low-paid gig lent him time and security to toy with words and story forms. He dabbled in radio plays, essays and reviews. He joined a group called OuLiPo, or *Ou*vroir de *Litt*érature *Po*tentielle (The Workshop of Potential Literature). The coterie was devoted to experimental writing, as the triple-humped CamelCase of its acronym might suggest. The OuLiPo crowd enjoyed doing lipograms, an erudite game in which 'players' had to write a narrative with one letter removed, an exercise to see how the restriction affected their work. Perversely what followed for many writers was a new sense of freedom. Raymond Queneau, a novelist and OuLiPo member, described this paradox in laboratory language: '[We are] rats who must rebuild the labyrinth from which we propose to escape.'

Small wonder, then, that crosswords appealed to the game-playing Perec. The French style of the puzzle, the *mots croisés*, was compact, a typical grid being 10 by 10 with a scarcity of black squares. Symmetry was seldom heeded. Georges began making them for a weekly called *Le Point* from 1976, until his untimely death six years on. His success in fiction—he won praise and prizes for his finest work, *La Vie Mode d'Emploi* (Life: A User's Manual)—was furthered as a clue-monger.

In the ultimate collection of Perec crosswords, you'll find untold fresh hints for familiar words. My favourite is a touchstone of this maverick creator: *Il dit la même chose autrement* (He says the same thing differently). The answer is INTERPRETE.

Old words, new skins—that was the Perec trademark. He reinterpreted language and storytelling. Clue-writing, too. For evidence, take the name Io. A Greek nymph seduced by Zeus, her name is as common as muck in French puzzles, for reasons of length and a generous vowel count. Perec labelled such a word *une cheville* (a peg), essentially the dowel pin a lengthy plank requires in order to bear a load. Other typical French pegs are EON, LAI (a poem), RU (a university restaurant) and UTE (a Native American people). In Perec's eyes, each one was a regrettable component slotted in to the carpentry to make the whole puzzle hold firm.

Yet an intellect like Perec resented the inherent need for pegs. (Try writing that sentence without an e, our alphabet's quintessential peg.) Whenever his interlocks required a *cheville*, Perec went to extremes to invent a novel clue. IO, for example, was usually denoted by the obvious *Greek nymph* or by her mythical fate: *Zeus turned her into a cow*. (Once the god had seduced Io, he turned the maiden into a heifer to allay the suspicion of Hera, his other half.) Passé stuff for Perec. He'd seen that yarn implied so often on the puzzle page that he felt compelled to say the same thing differently. Hence, his radical collection of *mots croisés* includes 28 variations for that single nymph, over two dozen kinky roads accessing the one destination. Some refer to the legend itself, like *Aurait pu faire meuh* (She could moo); others are crafty, such as *Coeur de lion* (Heart of a lion); while another handful celebrates the name's physical composition, as in

Voyelles (Vowels) and *2 sur 5* (2 over 5—that is, 10 is two-fifths of AEIOU). But let's finish in honour of Perec and the huge debt *I owe* to this linguistic explorer. After all, the French man of letters himself would insist this chapter *se termine avec brio*.

1937

Enterprising one makes more money at Xmas (4)

Do schoolchildren learn FABLES or TABLES? You can't be sure which one applies. Children hear about the dangers of crying wolf as readily as they recite, 'Three times four is twelve.' Maths may seem likelier than folklore, but, even if your hunch is right, that's just one dilemma solved out of the 36 you are facing.

Welcome to the prize puzzle, or pruzzle as Americans knew it in the late 1920s. The spin-off was a hit during the Depression, thanks to its apparent ease combined with the quick-cash lures for a correct solution. As the economy cooled and poverty deepened, the prize puzzle glittered like a leprechaun's pot of gold.

Unlike the standard crossword, this novel grid came with half the letters already filled in. One entry might offer T _ _ E, for

---

+ The Hindenburg airship bursts into flames in New Jersey.
+ Volkswagen is founded.
+ Mrs Wallis Simpson marries the Duke of Windsor, once Edward VIII.

New words: oomph, logo, existential, yeti

example. Dozens of words could match that pattern, so you try the clue: *Important in music*. TUNE, of course, is pretty significant, but then the doubts arrive. What about TONE? That's important too. Even TIME has its place, if you treat that as a synonym for *tempo*. TAPE is handy as well. Not that cassettes existed in 1937, but you get the predicament. Cleverly, the grid was designed to maximise the doubts. Do fishermen cherish a COD or a ROD? Does a light GLINT, GLEAM or GLARE? Every answer was prone to the flip of a coin. A gamble, in other words. A generation became hooked, betting pennies or nickels on whether a *Tree* was an ALDER or an ELDER. Or maybe even a CEDAR.

To boost the cash pool, magazines began to offer two and more grids, allowing solvers to enter numerous combinations for an added fee. Can you see where this is heading? Put it this way: did punters lose their dough to a SCAM or SCUM? On paper, the con was a cinch. All it took was one unscrupulous pruzzle operator to settle on a combination of answers that no other punter submitted, and so secure the jackpot as his. Without full scrutiny, the contests were liable to such corruption. Most states in America sought to ban the fishy business, while the Betting and Lotteries Act warned Brits against the less reputable contests.

Regardless of the flak, the crossword contests continued, including the grand Christmas edition of *Answers*, a stapled tabloid of puzzles, riddles, cartoons and stories issued by Fleetway Publications. While I make no suggestion that the winner for their back-page crossword was improperly judged, I can't ignore the successful solver's potential booty. Imagine this: if you can decide correctly whether an enterprising SHOW or SHOP makes more money at Xmas, then you may be eligible to win £100 and a giant hamper worth five guineas. Then again, if you guess wrong but somehow manage to fudge the other CAT and RAT pickles, you may glean cold comfort in one of 50 frozen turkeys.

1938

Vozidlo (5)

Karel Čapek was Bohemian by birth and inclination. The Czech writer loved theatre, nature, Persian carpets, photography, rhododendrons, laminated records and *ohavné šarády z ameriky* (heinous charades from America), the last of these better known as crosswords, or criss-cross puzzles, as he sometimes dubbed them in his letters to Věra Hrůzová, an old flame. He was a fan with licence to whine: that 'heinous charade' bleat was part of a warning he passed on to Věra about the addictive qualities of these new scourges:

'Madam,' he wrote, 'I advise you emphatically that you never allow your husband to solve criss-cross puzzles for the consequences are terrible. Imagine you just falling asleep when he asks you, "What fish contains three letters, or what goddess has an o in the middle?"'

+ Kristallnacht takes place across Germany.
+ Oil is discovered in Saudi Arabia.
+ Hungarian László Bíró patents the ballpoint.
+ Superman appears.

New words: nylon, fave, Muzak

Even in translation you can sense the mock-outrage. This gifted novelist revelled in the challenge of the jumbo grids found in the national paper *Lidové Noviny* (The People's Newspaper). The larger examples jammed in 200 clues below complex grids. One clue was *Vozidlo* (Vehicle), which gave the Bohemian a dull pain in his frontal lobe: 'Apparently KODRB is a vehicle, yet there is no 'traffic' [of other words] from these letters, which makes me think there is something wrong in my solution.'

According to my research, *kodrb* is not a word in any language. The closest thing I could find was *kord*, the Czech word for sword, and probably what Karel wished to run through the compiler's vital organs.

Nonetheless, the impasse had a beautiful irony. Eight years before Karel collided with *Vozidlo* in a criss-cross puzzle and invented a word out of cruciverbal desperation, he had coined another five-letter word out of artistic desperation. That word was *robot*, arising from the Czech *robota* (slave labour). The word's vehicle, so to speak, was Karel's play *R.U.R. (Rossum's Universal Robots)*, a jaundiced peek at a demeaning future in which humanity falls victim to smart machines—and quite possibly those god-awful charades out of America.

1939

Longed to have twelve months in front of the secret hiding place (7)

To write a crossword history without mentioning Lindsey Browne would be like compiling the *Who's Who of Chariot-Racing* devoid of Ben-Hur. Even today his initials conjure delight in Australian word-lovers of a certain age. Say 'LB' and wait for a favourite clue in return. You're bound to cop the man's comical anagrams or cheeky puns, his metier for more than 60 years of setting. *Laden pythons*, for example, could writhe to spell SHETLAND PONY. The Sydney suburb of WOOLOOMOOLOO reliably enlisted an owl and cow and two toilets. Yet perhaps his most famous clue insisted that *Toothless emaciated Menzies is a whatchamacallit (9,3)*, or in other words a THINGUMMY-BOB after the era's PM.

+ Nazi Germany invades Poland.
+ Robert Menzies gains office in Australia.
+ *The Wizard of Oz* premieres in Hollywood.

New words: jukebox, lip gloss, muesli

Lindsey started life in Melbourne, in 1915, shouldering the burden of Ernest as a first name, though his parents and five younger sisters preferred his middle name, shortened to Lin. So did Lin, who taught himself piano and won a string of essay contests, all the while aspiring to take up journalism.

His break came early in the war, earning a cadetship with *The Sydney Morning Herald*. The Melbourne lad was going places. Soon he was covering federal politics from the Canberra bureau. The cub was there to observe the cogs and levers of power first-hand, though Lin's deeper passions ran to sport and music—plus a fellow journalist named Nancy Moore. By this stage, in case he wasn't busy enough assessing senate hearings by day and philharmonic concerts by night, Lin was sole hand on the *Herald*'s crossword page—the perfect platform, he figured, for the wooing of Nancy.

His first overture of love came late in 1939, using 'Puzzle No. 304' in the *Women's Supplement* to make his feelings known—not to every Tom, Dick or Harry, but just to those who detected the code, including Nancy he hoped. As publication date drew near, Lin kept dropping hints about a special message for a special someone hiding in the puzzle.

INVERTEBRATE was the opening answer. The definition element referred to a spineless one, which Lindsey certainly wasn't. To bury a private message inside a public diversion was downright gallant, if not foolhardy. For most solvers, though, once they snared INVERTEBRATE (*Upset the vulgar young rascal with ease*), they progressed oblivious of either the romance or the acrostic based upon the first letter of all the Across answers.

To your average commuter, INVERTEBRATE was a handy start, a dozen letters helping to unlock the northwest corner. But to Lin and Nancy, the opening word was important for its opening letter, I, which was also the message's first letter. Then came the next Across answers. Scan their initials and you'll see how this December crossword was a premature valentine: LOOT, ORGAN, VOLE, EVENT, NEEDLES, ASTER, NETTLES, CURES, YEARNED, MISER, OPAL, OASES, RIPS, EXTRAVAGANCE. Note too that the code contained VOLE, the mammal's name creating the ideal anagram. As for YEARNED, this was attached to the clue *Longed to have twelve months in front of the secret hiding place (7)*.

Connoisseurs will grumble how the clue lacks a signpost, that inbuilt command telling the solver to reverse DEN, the secret hiding place. No matter: LB had that eccentric flair, not to mention a distracted focus. Often his appetite for mischief made him sidestep the rulebook. Take OPAL in the same puzzle, which earnt these clunky instructions: *Make circle first and an unusual circuit last for a stone*. Hardly poetry, compared to the alternative story of a friend (PAL) receiving a ring (o), but LB was merely timing his run.

On 12 March, a few months after the declaration puzzle, another message appeared. Once more the code was buried in 'the secret hiding place' of a statewide newspaper. Same formula, but this time a different message: WOODCUTTER, IRKS, LOOPHOLES, LOUSE, SATURNALIA, HOGMANAY, EREBUS, MIRAGE, ARBITERS, RANUNCULUS, ROARS, YESTERDAY, MAIM, EMBLAZONED.

The answer was yes. Nancy and Lindsey were deeply in love. A date was set, the ceremony squeezed in to their busy working lives. Families from Sydney and Melbourne filled St James's on King Street to witness the event—the crossworder's golden chance to bestow that ring on his pal for real.

1940

Ho! Let's go in (anag.) (10)

Gentlemen in the clubs of London licked their lips. How easy was today's 4-Down in *The Times*? See for yourself, dear boy: *Ho! Let's go in (anag.).* There you have it: everything on a plate. The formula identified, plus the ten letters holding the answer: HOLETSGOIN. Rearrange those ten and pop in your word.

ANTHOLOGIES? Too long. LONGISH TOE? Too ridiculous. Clearly, the letters could be reset into a single word . . . SHOOLETING? Nothing leapt out. Or not so far. It was only a matter of time.

From the opening clue, another painless anagram, the puzzle had felt benign. Any dolt could see DISRAELI hiding in *A Victorian statesman lurking in a side lair (8).* Next to fall had been *Pugilists' wear*: that had to be BOXERS, a double-meaning, the shorts and the sportsman. At this rate a personal best was in the offing. Or so the

---

+ The Blitz devastates London.
+ Lascaux cave paintings are found by French hikers.
+ The first McDonald's opens.

New words: commando, machismo, intercom

'half-pay Colonels and retired Admirals' must have hoped, but those plans were quickly squashed by the clues that followed.

A Manx beverage, for example. That reeked of deletion. *Manx* is the sure-fire cryptic indicator of tail-docking, turning the likes of RAISING into RAISIN, the device depending on the tailless breed of cat unique to the Isle of Man. So for this clue one merely had to snip a drink's final letter, such as BEER for BEE, or WINE for WIN, and create . . . what? There seemed to be no definition element, as if the clue itself had been docked.

Wordsworth's fan mail?

A nudist's aunt?

'Pray tell,' came the chorus. 'What the deuce is going on?' Every second clue felt too terse. *Four toes are broken.* A breeze at first reading—the solver needed to break FOURTOES—yet to render what? Was there a word at large in FOURTOES? Was there a definition, even if there was a word?

In desperation the members' eyes moved on to the other cocktail: *Ho! Let's go in (anag.).* ETHNOLOGIST? Again, one too many. GO THE LIONS? But go whither? The clue possessed a quaint sheen, allowing the letters to swirl like so many balls being juggled. This was how the game had begun, some fifteen years earlier, pioneered by the likes of Torquemada in *The Observer*. Before slyer subterfuges arose, a solver might juggle *Dry nab (anag.)* to create BRANDY, no definition required. But that didn't seem to work with this latest misery. Old-fashioned, newfangled: it made no difference. The puzzle was diabolical.

About this stage, the foiled solver would likely browse the paper as a whole: always a sound move when struggling in public. Next time you strike an impossible puzzle, I suggest you feign interest elsewhere. You need to persuade any onlooker that you weren't really solving anyway—or to persuade yourself. Who, me? Stumped by a puzzle? Never. Doubtless, club members let their eyes wander the law lists, the gold stocks, the weather forecast, the personal apology from Max Beerbohm. Hang on—Max Beerbohm? Why on earth was he running a letter beside the crossword?

Beerbohm was quite the name in literary London. The chap had enough charm to call Oscar Wilde a chum. He was the theatre critic for *The Saturday Review* and also a beloved author, mainly in the realm of parody, on top of being a feted caricaturist.

His other vocation was pranking. At this point in his late sixties, the gentleman of letters had a warranted notoriety. One of his more elaborate stunts involved George Bernard Shaw, his predecessor at the *Review*. Somehow Beerbohm had gained access to a dozen publicity shots of the playwright. Using pen and ink, he lengthened Shaw's nose, or deepened his furrows, or buckled a tooth, and then sent the tampered snaps to colluding friends. The lark saw each of these accomplices pursue Shaw for an autograph, whether it meant mailing the image to his agent or accosting the star in a foyer. By all accounts, the author of *Major Barbara* was majorly ticked off, wondering how his visage had been so deftly violated.

Another Beerbohm gotcha took place in a well-to-do garden. This time the saboteur removed every label from among the roses, replacing their horticultural names with those of psychopaths and murderers, shocking the garden's ladyship when she next led guests on a tour. And then there was the outrage entailing Herbert Trench, the Irish poet and celebrated romantic best known for the poem 'Apollo and the Seaman', a brooding meditation on matters of the soul. Beerbohm perverted that tone with the aid of a studio scalpel, seizing the British Library's copy and removing every initial H uttered by the sailor. Overnight, the god of music and knowledge began conversing with an 'andsome 'earty from the East End.

Yet the jewel in Beerbohm's crown was his *Times* crossword of 1940. The letter he had sent to the newspaper accompanying the crossword explained his motives:

'No doubt you, like most people, have sometimes thought of some utterly awful thing that you could do if you chose to, some disastrous and devastating thing the very thought of which has brought cold sweat to your brow? And you may have at some time thought: "Suppose I released into the columns of *The Times*, one of these fine days, a Crossword Puzzle with clues signifying nothing—nothing whatsoever."'

The editor had insisted that a public announcement adjoin the puzzle for him to agree to the hoax, and Beerbohm had accepted the compromise.

As to why he targeted the crossword, a clue lies in his prior pranks: roses, peers, West End theatres and high-end literature. There was something so English about his victims, almost TOO ENGLISH you could say. The crossword was part of an irreverent continuum. Ten thousand clever Charlies in London and Oxbridge stared bereft at the blank institution of Albion, trying to untangle HOLETSGOIN, and Max Beerbohm didn't give a SINGLE HOOT.

1941

Gargarisme (6)

A pilot crashes in the desert. He is lost, distraught, thirsty, delirious. A symptom of his stupor, he believes, is the sight of a young boy approaching. The boy has golden hair and a flowing scarf. And, in case that sounds vaguely credible, the boy undermines the impression, saying, as he arrives at the scene, that he is a prince and hails from an asteroid with three volcanoes and a beautiful rose.

Maybe the story is familiar to you, since *Le Petit Prince* has been translated into more than 250 languages. The author, Antoine de Saint-Exupéry, was a French pilot who crashed his own plane in the Sahara, in 1939, as Word War II was heating up. Somehow, he and his companion survived for four days on a single orange, a few grapes, crackers and coffee dregs until a Bedouin (with a scarf) lobbed on a camel.

―――――――――――――――――――――――――――――――――――――――

+ Japan bombs Pearl Harbor.
+ Germans mount the Siege of Leningrad.
+ Australian forces capture Tobruk.

New words: gremlin, radar, snafu, hipster

Returning to the novel, the pilot is busy repairing his plane as the little prince recounts his travels from asteroid to earth. He tells of the planets he visited en route, each one occupied by a narrow-minded human. There was the ancient geographer so engrossed in latitude and longitude that he never ventured anywhere. Then there was the drunkard so ashamed by his condition that he drank to eliminate his shame. And then the crossword-solver so absorbed in his puzzle that he neglected to observe the wonders surrounding him.

Smelling a rat? Sorry. That crossword chap never made the final draft, his role most likely usurped by the businessman determined to count all the stars he thought he owned. But papers brought to light in 2012 at the Morgan Library and Museum (formerly the Pierpont Morgan Library) in New York revealed that Saint-Exupéry dabbled with the crossword, the resulting story shaping as chapter 19 for a good while. The manuscript is dated 1941, the year after France had fallen to Nazi Germany, when the pilot and his Nicaraguan wife sought asylum in America. According to the author's scrawl, the crossword-solver was stuck on the one-word clue of *Gargarisme* (gargling), in dire need of a six-letter solution. No answer is announced in the text, the prince too keen to take his spaceship elsewhere, and the marooned solver too mesmerised to even realise the golden-haired boy has skedaddled.

1942

Un direttore pedante
Come capo ha inver ragione . . .
Ma che barba venir fa . . .
Allorquando lui ti espone
Le sue estreme volontà (10)

Annoyingly, for my bank balance at least, this book won't be available in any non-English markets. Why? I defer to the great American poet Robert Frost, who claimed, 'Poetry is what gets lost in translation.' Or, translating the quote into Italian, '*La poesia è ciò che si perde nella traduzione.*' Wordplay is just as resistant as verse to translation. Every clue is its own little haiku, defying easy conversion—or a quick buck in a Spanish *librería*.

+ Anne Frank hides in an Amsterdam annex.
+ Japanese midget subs infiltrate Sydney Harbour.
+ The OXFAM charity is founded.

New words: napalm, underbelly, strafe, plutonium

By the same token, hoping to find outstanding clues in other languages was always on the wishful side. Naïve, you could argue. Ten times easier if the clue were quick, I suppose, or if the focus fell on the story behind the clue. But to think I'd find true gold was optimism speaking. Cryptic clues especially are locked inside their culture of origin.

And then there was the other distant grail: a foreign clue in verse.

Did I quit? No. Did I whine? A little, but hey. You would too if you came upon an eye-catching clue only to realise the wording was Babelfish-proof. The fact this book has made daylight is testament to a small army of human translators I mobilised by favours, bribes and flattery. Yet for all their generous help, there was no guarantee of complete success, as this Italian clue will prove.

The morsel belongs to *La Settimana Enigmistica*, which means The Enigmatic Weekly, but even that translation is off-kilter. There's nothing enigmatic about what this weekly gazette offers its readers, not in terms of intention at least. The gist is puzzles, and puzzles are what you get. Loaded with riddles and rebuses, codes and crosswords, *Setti* has been around longer than Silvio Berlusconi and is twice as much fun to decipher.

When I lived in Rome—briefly, in the mid-1980s—I fell into the trap of using the magazine as a language tutorial, hoping to glean some handy Italian from the various puzzles. Boy, did I fail. Walking along the Via Catanzaro spouting clues, I must have struck the Romans as a Pentecostal fugitive with heatstroke. My basic etiquette was reduced to telling strangers that *piscina* (pool) was *un anagramma* of *spinica* (spinach), causing young mothers to come gather their *bambini* from the swing set.

La Settimana Enigmistica began life in Sardinia in 1932, funded by a nobleman called Giorgio Sisini. In its first decade, the magazine pioneered an A to Z of clue types, from the *aggiunta d'estremi* (addition of extremes, in which *Mahatma Gandhi*, for example, produces

MAGI with its four outer letters) to the *zeppa* (wedge, whereby *sto* (I am) in *melo* (apple) creates MESTOLO (ladle)). Another formula was the *doppio soggetto* (double-subject rhyme clue), in which the verse would often stand alone in a page's corner, or was occasionally aligned with the *parole cruciate*—the Italian term for *crossword*.

Being so vowel-rich, Italian is ideal for snipping into smaller pieces. Even MESTOLO, the ladle we just met, can subdivide differently, into *mesto* (sad) and *lo* (the). The double-subject rhymes explore these fault lines, alluding to the fragments in the opening lines, then unifying the segments into an overall clue in the coda. If you find that bemusing, then you haven't tried your hand at translating our chapter's ditty. *Mio Dio*, it's a can of worms. Here it is for easy reference:

> *Un direttore pedante*
> *Come capo ha inver ragione . . .*
> *Ma che barba venir fa . . .*
> *Allorquando lui ti espone*
> *Le sue estreme volontá*

This exercise feels like tightrope-walking. I'd delegated this doggerel to three different translators, and all three came back with variable approximations. Umberto Eco, the great Italian writer, likens translating to haggling. You see a rug you like in an Eastern bazaar. You ask how much, and the fun begins, where both parties adjust their stance on a sliding scale of compromise, eventually reaching a tolerable truth. So then, assembling the wisdom of all three versions, here is my bravest rendering:

> A fussy boss
> As the head with the most reason . . .
> But how boring . . .

Whence he exposes you
To his ultimate paperwork

The wordplay pivots on two ideas uniting to create a third. *Testa* (the head) is the first stage, a notion embodied by the opening two lines, where the operator at the top possesses superior reasoning. *Il capo* is not just Al Capone, or Tony Soprano, but the head on your shoulders too, the centre of reasoning and logic.

What follows next is idiom, the stumbling block for any translation. With Eco's analogy resonating, the so-called haggling begins now. Being literal for a tick, *ma che barba* converts into 'But that beard', yet actually means 'But how boring'. If that makes little sense, then consider the perversity we take for granted in English: raining cats and dogs, chip on your shoulder, brass tacks. All three must seem codswallop to a new speaker, not to mention codswallop. The key element, however, looking more closely at the Italian expression, is *barba*, or beard. Where does the beard grow? On the chin, or *mento* in Italian. This association is underlined by the idea of exposure—*espone*. Just as fussy bosses can expose others to your faults, or expose you and your colleagues to mindless work, so can a *barba*'s removal expose a *mento* (or chin).

Our last trick as solvers is the final click of the two fragments. As soon as we combine the acquired words, *testa* and *mento*, we create *testamento*, or will in the legal sense. This word is implied by the notion of 'ultimate paperwork', a phrase that doesn't just evoke workaday drudgery, but life's final document, and our ultimate solution.

As you can see, the pieces are all on show, distorted by the fractured stanza, and the handicap of translation. The head and chin, as it were, have been warped inside a carnival mirror that stands between two languages. Furthermore, the poem shows that other ineffable aspect of *La Settimana Enigmistica*. Um, I'm looking for the word. *Innovation?* Maybe. *Italianness?* Certainly. Or maybe the word is *timelessness*. Wander back through the magazine's archives and you'll find thousands of clever clues just like this *doppio soggetto*: experimental formulae that have been sating the national appetite for 91 years. The title is a national treasure, in many regards, a testament to the vision of Giorgio Sisini. As my principal translator, Barbara Amalberti, asserts, 'Every Italian has had *Setti* in their lives at some stage, in some way, somehow.'

The magazine halted production only once, late in World War II, when Italy was in peril. Otherwise, *La Settimana* hasn't skipped a week. Pick a year, any year, and you'll find a mix of puns and picture puzzles, crosswords and chess problems, with no ads and no editorial, and, of course, with the enduring banner on the cover: '*Prima per fondazione e per diffusione*' (First for foundation and for diffusion), which, as translations go, is way off-beam.

1943

German composer (4)

Ingvar Kamprad is the IK in IKEA. During the war, as a farm boy, he sold matches for pocket money. Then it was fish, and later tinsel. Soon one thing grew into another, and the young Swede set up shop in 1943, when just seventeen, selling furniture by mail order. As we know, the empire expanded to generate more money than most African republics, employing roughly the population of Pasadena: 140 000 designers, packers and meatball-makers.

More than tables and chairs, IKEA has given the world a new language. A popular theory insists that such labels as Floro and Trondheim, two beds found in the catalogue, belong to Norwegian fishing ports for a reason. Not because kippers need a queen-size, but to combat Kamprad's mild dyslexia. Names like Benno and

---

+ Italy joins the Allies.
+ French Resistance leader Jean Moulin is killed by the Gestapo.
+ Zoot suits appear—despite austerity measures in the West.

New words: bazooka, disposable, squillion, permafrost

Galant (a DVD tower and desk, as well as Swedish boys' names) beat the confusable gibberish of CQ409TX.

Benno, in fact, was the template for an ingenious IKEA ad that appeared many years after the first stick of furniture was sold. The concept was hatched by Marketforce, an Australian advertising agency based in Perth. If you've not met Benno, then picture a clean, upstanding unit of square pigeonholes, just a tick over two metres in height, with nine apertures to hold your movies and CDs. Now juxtapose eight more Bennos beside the first tower, and suddenly you're facing a vertical waffle of 81 hollows in a nine-by-nine square. These spaces are adjustable, of course, though Andrew Tinning (the ad's creative director) and Julia Elton-Bott (the art director) were happy with things just the way they were, the nine adjacent Bennos being custom-made for a crossword reno.

Compact discs and music files filled up half the squares, acting as the blacks in the crossword grid. As for the blank squares, some now bore a tiny numeral, Photoshopped into their top left corners. To fulfil the crossword vibe, a set of clues was listed below the décor, every answer leading to a singer or a band that fitted the remaining pigeonholes. But given we're in 1943, the year Kamprad's idea morphed into IKEA, I've selected the copy-line that makes sense in this era: *German composer*. The man missing from the shelves is Johann Sebastian BACH, not to be confused with Sebastian, the low-backed barstool.

1944

Big-wig (8)

arly days, as I tried to plot a path for *Cluetopia*, the horizon was clear. Crosswords might well spring up from anywhere, I figured. A clue could grab my attention from any year, any backwater. So it was, in the Don Quixote tradition, I dropped the reins to let chance take its course. The only brief I carried in my pocket was the desire to find the oddest, the best, the unique. My timeline was open slather, and my map a void, save for two must-see landmarks along the road: the first crossword, in 1913, and then the most scandalous, in 1944—the D-Day crossword, in other words.

Perhaps you know the crux already, or think you do. Whenever I speak on radio, canvassing listeners to share their crossword stories, the D-Day yarn is sure to be mentioned. It's the crossword story

---

+ Adolf Hitler escapes an assassination attempt.
+ The Cowra breakout of Japanese prisoners-of-war occurs.
+ Australia's first aerogrammes are issued.

New words: angst, superpower, vegan

many people half-know. Even now, decades on, the freaky episode gleams in popular memory—but do you know the *real* story?

Folks with a rough idea will tell you how a bunch of words ran in the *Daily Telegraph* crossword, words that betrayed sensitive military operations. That's true. But how did those words come to be there? And why? That's where the intrigue really exists.

Espionage was suspected at the time. Or treason. Take your pick. But the story of compiler Leonard Dawe and his nine fateful answers was always scheduled to be part of our itinerary, even before a dotted line was signed.

As a young buck, Dawe played football for Southampton, gaining a cap with the English amateurs as well as a spot on the Olympic team in Stockholm, 1912. He might have gone further born in a later era, when contact lenses were more sophisticated. As it was, the spectacles he wore on the pitch augured an academic future.

Life after football was no less illustrious, however. Before finding his stride as a classics teacher, Dawe served as a second lieutenant with the Hampshire Regiment, helping to liberate Baghdad as part of the Mesopotamia campaign. Returning from Arabia, resuming his classroom duties, he made swift progress through the ranks, ending up as principal at Strand School in south London. A few years into his teaching life, in 1925, he began making crosswords for the *Telegraph*.

Then came 1944, the *annus horribilis* for Dawe. First up, his headmaster role was made more onerous by the government ordering his school to evacuate London. Staff and students were forced to pack up books, leaving their patch south of Brixton and relocating to Effingham, in Surrey. Amid the flux, Dawe also pumped out most of the *Telegraph* puzzles across the week.

I should note that an early blot in his copybook was DIEPPE. (Here's a game: see how long your belief in coincidence can last, the deeper this chapter goes.) The Dieppe scandal occurred in 1942, with the war at full kilter. The *Telegraph* had been pared to a skerrick of pages, enough for wartime news and the balm of crosswords. On 18 August one of Dawe's clues was *French port (6)*. Eerily, this came on the eve of a secret raid in which Allied forces were poised to strike Dieppe harbour, in northern France. The occupying Germans were quick to repel the raid, as if savvy to the strike, with 1400 Allies killed and nearly 2000 Canadian soldiers captured in one swoop. A disaster, in any language.

An investigator with the Potteresque name of Lord Tweedsmuir was delegated to delve into the crossword matter, and Leonard Dawe in particular. After months of stone-turning, his lordship admitted, 'In the end it was concluded that it was just a remarkable coincidence—a complete fluke.'

Nonetheless, a risky fluke can leave a black spot beside a setter's name. Two years later, eyebrows rose further when Dawe wheeled out a medley of alarming entries inside ten weeks, each one giving a classified reference to a different beach in the crosshairs of Operation Overlord, the secret Normandy invasion scheduled to begin on 6 June—D-Day.

Early that year, the first three in the spotlight were SWORD, GOLD and JUNO, codenames for beaches assigned to the British. Can you blame MI5 for getting jumpy? Dawe's DIEPPE was already a nagging doubt in their minds, and now suspicions began to fester. Intelligence officers must have spent their days with one eye on the *Telegraph* puzzle, just to see if the outrages persisted.

They did. In quick succession. On 2 May the crossword carried the clue *One of the U.S. (4)*. The answer, UTAH, was the codename for a beach assigned to the American 4th Assault Division. On 22 May the clue *Red Indian on the Missouri (5)* led to OMAHA, a beach assigned to the 1st Assault Division. And on 27 May *Big-wig (8)* was solved by OVERLORD.

The closer the calendar crept to D-Day, the more Dawe's clues seemed to murmur treachery. On 30 May *This bush is the centre of nursery revolutions (8)* yielded MULBERRY, the codename for the floating harbours to be used in the landings. And on 1 June the clue *Britannia and he hold the same thing (7)* was answered with NEPTUNE, code for the naval assault phase.

Enough was enough. Another visit to Mr Dawe was overdue. I can't confirm the exact day the interrogators went knocking in Effingham—for obvious reasons—but my money says OVERLORD was the tipping point. Odds are the agents paid a call in the dead of night. Whenever, the tone was far from social.

Consider the tension. Here was a British headmaster, the model of all things British—from sport star to armed services, from school figurehead to crossword darling—propagating hush-hush vocabulary. Could the man's Prussian haircut be deemed a sinister sign of his true allegiances? Was such a noble career assembled to serve as a cover story? The investigators' concerns were far from eased when they uncovered a further twist, in which Dawe was found to have a brother-in-law within the Admiralty.

'They turned me inside-out,' Dawe later recalled, in a more genial interview on BBC television. 'They went to Bury St Edmunds, where my senior [crossword] colleague Melville Jones was living, and put him through the works. But they eventually decided not to shoot us after all!' Granted, but the nerves continued to twitch at MI5.

Textbooks will tell you that the Normandy landings were a powerful blow against the Nazi occupation. In one resolute pounce, five new beachheads were established into mainland Europe. The Axis powers carried clout for barely a year longer. The result cast the crosswords of Leonard Dawe as one grand coincidence—until 40 years after his death, when a former student at the Strand School put up his hand. Ronald French had a secret to impart.

The Wolverhampton property manager had been under the tutelage of Mr Dawe during the war. As a mental exercise, the principal would challenge the brighter boys to fill out empty cross-word grids freestyle, without the aid of clues. This exercise had the dual advantage of keeping idle hands busy and giving Dawe new interlocks in need of clueing.

French was typical of many Strand lads, a fan of the heroic war effort raging around him. Thanks to the school's relocation to Surrey, the battle zones felt a few degrees closer, as an army camp was only a short walk from the new grounds. Most afternoons the students loitered among the young Canadians and Americans stationed in the town. Whether it was through soldierly bragging or general osmosis, the code words for the Normandy invasion were absorbed by the schoolboys. As careless as that sounds, the adult French was quick to add that gleaning the vocab was a far cry from knowing its deeper meanings. No doubt the upcoming mission shaped the soldiers' talk, which in turn migrated to the headmaster's blank patterns.

French also admitted that Dawe contacted him after the invasion, grilling him about from where he'd harvested the terms. The boy was matter-of-fact about it. He even fished a journal from his bag, a chronicle of his months spent skulking in the army camp. ('I became a sort of dogsbody about the place,' French confessed in a 2004 *Telegraph* article, 'running errands and even, once, driving a tank.') Dawe was horrified. He demanded the boy destroy the evidence immediately. In a burst of flames the incriminating language was reduced to ash, leaving an extraordinary series of crosswords as the only telltale residue.

1945

This storm has something to beat (9)

Kite, Breakaway, Marcoo: I know the names by heart, the classified names buried under the Maralinga sand, codenames for the bombs detonated on the Nullarbor Plain—the ground blasts, the tower tests and the nuclear airdrop, the black rainfall, the toxic dust cloaking the workers and the Yankunytjatjara people, the balloon explosions and the weeping sores. Every Australian should know these names—Antler and Buffalo, Totem and Vixen—the innocuous nouns of havoc. But no: speak them in the street and the words will fall on deaf ears.

Despite the time that has passed, the aftermath radiation, the scandal still lies below the surface, off the curriculum, invisible.

+ Germany surrenders.
+ Atom bombs are dropped on Hiroshima and Nagasaki.
+ The United Nations is founded.
+ Occupying 170 square metres, ENIAC is the world's first electronic computer.

New words: cold war, Teflon, snog

I know the names only thanks to a play I drafted in 2007, a story based on the misled bomb crews, working bare-chested amid the mushroom clouds. The actors who read the parts at the workshop were staggered. The details were new to them. The names and the fallout. Over ten years of atomic tests were conducted in the 1950s—all in the name of military intelligence. The outback and the Montebello Islands, off Western Australia, were pummelled by more than 100 kilotons of warhead. That's a private Hiroshima detonated in Australia's backyard, signed and sealed by Canberra, and largely lost to time.

But not to two crosswords, each with a psychic twist.

Spookily, *The Leisure Time Crossword Puzzle Book* was published ten years before a bomb was triggered in Maralinga, which makes this discovery feel a little like the D-Day uproar you've only just read about. A little. Let's call this Australia's Little Overlord.

The coincidence would have escaped a contemporary solver's notice, since the fallout lay in the future. There's a chance, of course, if *Leisure Time* stayed in circulation, that a later purchaser could have seen it, but the book seems to have been a diversion of the moment, published in the year of Nagasaki.

Even yours truly, leafing through the pages, nearly missed the omen. The hardback is coffee-brown, the image on the cover of a modern couple solving puzzles by lamplight. (Well, he's solving, dressed in a woollen three-piece. She, in a sashed frock, looks on, admiring her man's genius.)

I started with 'Puzzle 1', cracking the clues in my head. The first section was straightforward, followed by a detour in the cryptic arts. The clues were more clumsy than hard. The compiler, Hayden Dru, opted for naked anagrams, like *Creep (anag.)* to denote CREPE. Or half-arsed sandwiches like FOLIO being clued as *Foo is about 51—a book proves it.*

Then I struck the double whammy, shared across adjacent puzzles. At first, the warning bells were hushed. The first Down answer in 'Puzzle 31' is TOTEM, the second major test in Maralinga. The next is REIGN: *Seems to hold sway in the clouds?*. Then I found a trilogy of clues, harmless on the surface but sinister in combination:

Something put on? = STYLE
Latest in the explosion = BLAST
There's nothing in it = EMPTY

Fanciful, I decided. A mild resonance at best. To invoke explosions and clouds and emptiness is hardly the stuff of political intrigue.

In the weeks that followed I did my best to learn more about this Hayden Dru—whether he had ties to the military or a government department—but every avenue I tried was a cul-de-sac. In the end I deemed TOTEM to be an historical hiccup, only to turn the page and collide with 'Puzzle 32'. The first clue involves a play on the word cane: *This storm has something to beat*. The answer is HURRICANE, the other major test on Australian soil. Did I say test? Then try the next clue: *Trail (anag.)*. There's only one possible solution: TRIAL. If you ask me, Dru had his finger on Canberra's pulse, or possibly a little red button. Either that, or I needed to escape the National Library and grab some air.

Outside, everything became clearer. Random words and clues have a supernatural knack of foreshadowing history. I call this crossword voodoo, where selecting an answer out of ether can sometimes invite that word into your life. You choose AVALANCHE for no other reason but its sequence of letters, and two days later a Thredbo snowboarder is buried under three tonnes of snow.

Or the time Andrew Fisher—not the Australian PM, but Australia's best Scrabble player—won the first series of *Letters and Numbers* on SBS. The year was 2011. As dictionary umpire on the show, I knew full well that Andrew had shaded his Scrabble nemesis, Naween Fernando, in a white-knuckle final. But as the show was pre-recorded, I wasn't allowed to tell a soul. After six long weeks of obligated silence, the episode went to air. On the same day a setter called Brendan, alias Brian Greer, aired a double-definition clue in *The Guardian*:

Effort finally revealed name of top solver on TV (9)

Conspiracy? What conspiracy? The wording was a fluke and nothing more. As a resident of Portland, Oregon, Greer has no inkling of the lounge-room butterflies swarming in Australia. No doubt Hayden Dru—and his totem explosions—belonged in the same basket. Mashing up language every day, crosswords can generate this *déjà vu*. Indeed, the answer to Brendan's teaser is a double shot of voodoo. Not only did the clue pre-empt the quiz result, but the answer—ENDEAVOUR—is a name destined to emerge some 40 years (or 123 pages) from now. Peek ahead if you can't bear the suspense. Or let's rush onward and wait for history to do the repeating.

1946

Assyrian bubble and squeak . . . (?)

This was a time when gay meant happy, people played housie-housie, the gentry drank brandy, and a waiter on a ship could be described as Mongoloid and nobody would take offence—except the waiter, perhaps. The ship, like the waiter, has no name. They both serve the main action, involving two middle-aged couples, the Pughs and Pomfrets, on a seagoing holiday. The opening scene contains deckchairs, on one of which we meet Julian Pugh, the crossword-solver. Or the aspiring solver, as his chance for quality time is cramped by the others—his glamorous wife, Jane, who soon arrives for a smoke, and the Pomfret pair, a couple given to brandy and chitchat.

+ The Nuremberg Trials take place.
+ Bikinis arrive.
+ Juan Peron takes power in Argentina.
+ Sidney Nolan begins his Ned Kelly series.

New words: data, space age, cleavage

On the surface, that's the gist of *Clutterbuck: An Artificial Comedy*, written by Benn Wolfe Levy, a British Labour MP and writer who yoyoed between the House of Commons and the West End. He dabbled in film as well, scripting romantic dramas and schlock horrors for the early talkies. But his true passion was theatre, second only to Constance Cummings, his bombshell American wife, to whom he was married for 40 years.

Constance in fact played Jane Pugh when *Clutterbuck* was first produced, in 1946, at the New Theatre in Hull. Her claims to fame as a movie star included a Frank Capra crime romp, *American Madness*, and kicking up her heels beside Lucille Ball in *Broadway thru a Keyhole*. She was jaded by the glitz, however, and had decided that Hollywood was not her scene. Soon after marrying, she migrated to Britain, limiting her work to theatre, her hubby's stuff included: romcoms mainly, with a bent for envy. For proof, you need only glance at the titles: *Ever Green*, *Mrs Moonlight*, *The Jealous God* and a stage adaptation of *Madame Bovary*. It seems most of Levy's output relied on a love–hate triangle, and *Clutterbuck* is no exception, though geometrically this shipboard play is more a love–hate pretzel.

The ship's other passenger is Clutterbuck, no first name supplied. The man is a mystery figure in the past of the women, a Lothario who left a fond impression on Jane Pugh and Deborah Pomfret both. Melissa is the other character to mention, the current wife of Clutterbuck. A poppet with a diminutive bathing dress, the young lady possesses 'the appeal of a responsible kitten'.

So what's Clutterbuck's appeal? It's hard to gauge. The roué belongs to that great tribe of characters who influence the action without uttering a single word. Think of Maggie Simpson, Gromit, Snoopy, Boo Radley and Wilson the volleyball. Nonetheless, it's what Clutterbuck manages to achieve offstage, in his locked stateroom, that makes the biggest impact.

The audience had to join the dots, of course. This was 1946, and promiscuous bonking was not for the spotlight. Indeed, Levy was a prime mover, as both MP and playwright, in trying to abolish theatrical censorship, though without success. The writer was obliged to settle for the implicit, like so many of his peers. Thus Clutterbuck has his presumed way with both exes, unsussed by the husbands, who in turn become rivals in their bid to impress the kittenish Melissa.

Befuddled? That spirit is likewise captured in the play's half-clue. 'Let's see,' mumbles Julian in Act 1, pencil poised above a folded *Times*, '*Assyrian bubble and squeak . . .*'

The womenfolk don't understand, while Arthur Pomfret studies his snifter. Somehow, six pages later, Julian has finished his puzzle, merrily 'blacking out' the grid, which possibly means inking out the entire diagram to form a pleasing square. We never know. We're never allowed to see.

So what was the Assyrian answer? Or the full clue, at least? The letter count? Did he have any cross-letters to work with? Again we must clutch at straws. Though the moral of *Clutterbuck* is clear: don't give all your attention to a crossword. You may be wiser to allocate a portion of your wits to ensure your partner isn't straying amidships.

1947

It was one in the eye for Harold,
900 years ago (6,2,8)

There's a macabre joke doing the rounds of *The Sydney Morning Herald*. The gag entails a piece of grim advice to aspiring crossword-setters who apply to the paper for work: 'The only way a new compiler can get a start is to push an old compiler under a bus.'

As an 'old compiler', I need to emphasise the statement is a joke—despite its grain of truth. Crossword-making is a lifetime career, assuming you can ever get started. Most of my *Herald* colleagues are of an age to retire yet show no signs of doing just that. Nor should they, or any other stablemate, as long as their clues still crackle and solvers still relish the challenge. May we deceive you for a good while yet.

+ British coal mines are nationalised.
+ Libya wins independence from Italy.
+ The Dead Sea Scrolls are discovered.
+ Edwin Land demonstrates his Polaroid camera.

New words: flying saucer, baby-sit, methadone, unputdownable

On one condition. Such limpet-think shouldn't prevail at the expense of the new breed. How can crosswords grow if we don't widen the gene pool? I am grateful to Lindsey Browne for tolerating the juvenile clues I sent him as a schoolboy. My plan embraced the Chinese theory, in which a drip-feed of puzzles would eventually see the man admit a new torturer to the ranks. The plan worked; I found a niche. And that was 30 years ago. Since then I've been repaying the debt at leisure. Lately, I've mentored two promising setters, handpicking both from the deluge of newbies the paper receives every year. One is Liam Runnalls, the setter on Mondays. The other is poised to find her mark if and when a chair can be found at the table.

Be that as it may, the bus joke resonates. It ain't easy out there. My best advice to tyros is to make the most of new media: join crossword forums, compete in clue contests, upload your own puzzles to a greater audience. You need to get noticed to get hired.

The other secret lies in your ability to discover fresh takes on familiar words. Anyone can make droll jumbles out of the latest movie title, but can you jazz up BUS? Or USUAL? That's where the Zen lies. You also need to ensure your tenth crossword is as good as—or ten times better than—your pampered first.

In Birmingham in 1947 the limpet situation was suffocating. Rock stars blaze and fizzle in bursts, but clue-mongers tend to linger for decades, refining their craft as they age. So editors at the *Birmingham Mail* resolved to fix the problem and came up with a win–win. They launched a reader's puzzle offering a moderate two-guinea payment. Not a pittance, but likely less than the veterans were charging. Regardless, a drove of hopefuls stampeded the paper with hand-drawn grids and DIY clues.

What transpired was a testing ground. Brilliant compilers of the future were groomed in the public eye. Tom Johnson—a future *Spectator* maestro—achieved his breakthrough with the schools' crossword, a variation on the general reader's puzzle. Another upstart to seize his chance was Guy Haslam, still the youngest winner of the *Times* Crossword Championship, aged 29. Then there was Ken Guy, the manqué Mercury of *The Guardian*. Geoff Adams, the editor overseeing the influx, went on to craft clues for *The Glasgow Herald*. But the setter to take the biscuit, if only for his chutzpah, must be Eddie James, a British Telecom worker by day, and the future Brummie (*Guardian*) and Cyclops (*Private Eye*) by night. The inspiration was a peculiar grid size of 16 by 16 squares that the *Birmingham Mail* was kite-flying. The dimensions served as Eddie's inspiration.

BATTLE OF HASTINGS, knew Eddie, added up to 16 letters. Even better, this was 1966, and the anniversary was fast approaching. (To help you with your maths, the reader's puzzle platform lasted 35 years before a change of editor saw the institution vanish.) So Eddie made his crossword with 1066 and all that, and the puzzle won a place on the main stage. As Eddie confessed via email, he'll never forget the thrill of seeing his oversized baby on the 203 bus to Edgbaston, the weekday route he travelled to and from Telecom.

'A favourite trick of mine,' he confessed, 'was solving my own puzzle on the way home from work, inking in the answers at super speed with a nonchalant air that clearly impressed fellow travellers. (Though no-one ever made a comment, which sums up the British reserve I suppose.) The puzzle I remember best was in 1966. The clue went something like: *It was one in the eye for Harold, 900 years ago.*

Eddie entered his own answer. He smugly looked around. Nobody blinked. No-one spoke. And then the bus lurched to one side. Tyres squealed. A sickening thud was heard on the street. What Eddie didn't realise, since I've just invented this last bit, was that the 203 had just flattened an old compiler, and the Telecom employee was on his way to a crossword career.

1948

Dry (3)

Superman may be able to fly over buildings, see through walls and outmuscle a locomotive, but he doesn't know squat about crossword shortcuts. The situation is dire. His newspaper cohorts—Lois Lane and Jimmy Olsen—have vanished into thin air. The key to their whereabouts, our hero's been told, lies in last Saturday's *Daily Planet* crossword. Call me devious, but wouldn't the man of steel be wiser to grab the Monday edition and crib the solution than to attempt to solve the puzzle from scratch? That way he'd see more quickly that the answer to the crisis is MOUNDVILLE, a mining shanty just past Desert Town, and Jimmy and Lois are trapped there. But no, mild-mannered Clark Kent gets a pencil and rubber and wrestles with the clues to find MOUNDVILLE running slash-like from top left

---

+ Mahatma Gandhi is assassinated.
+ Israel is created.
+ Apartheid policy commences in South Africa.

New words: simulcast, ginormous, canasta

to bottom right. This suggests firstly that the *Planet* favours a 10 by 10 grid, and secondly that Superman is honest to a T.

Nor is the puzzle easy, and certainly not with a noisy boss at your elbow, barking out advice and insults. Perhaps with the aid of super-focus Clark handles the clues. *Dry* is SEC and *Arena* is RING, though *Ancient musical instrument (9)* stalls the reporter. Perry White, the editor, is getting apoplectic. 'Kent, what the hell are you doing? Working a crossword puzzle? Have you gone crazy?'

No, Mr White, he's gone audio, with sound FX and Wurlitzer organ. *The Crossword Puzzle Mystery* was a thirteen-episode radio play produced by the in-house writing team as part of the new Superman cult. The hidden location lying in the *Planet* puzzle is a coded signal for gold-smugglers, summoning gang members to Moundville for bloodshed and bullion. Lois, alas, has fallen victim to the brigands, followed by the gormless Jimmy, leaving Kent to assemble the clues in their wake. While resisting Monday's answers and nutting out FLAGEOLET take Kent more than a Metropolis minute, the business of making haste to Moundville is achieved by his alter ego in a sec.

1949

The kind of wine Johnnie's drinking— Sydney's on it, too (4,7)

If you ever want to see Australia grow up before your eyes, just pluck a few spools from the microfilm drawers of *The Bulletin*. What you will observe, from 1880 to the magazine's demise, in 2008, is a brash ragamuffin with a British grudge evolve into a pugnacious investor with a right-sided lean, while in between lurk a lot of deplorable 'teenage' phases.

The adolescent peak was the postwar cockiness of the Australian heyday. Mining boomed. The first fleet of Holdens rolled off the line. The Snowy River dam and the Gold Coast facelift were in full swing. Workers won the right to a 40-hour week, and the Lucky Country scooped the Lotto as £10 Poms and other Europeans joined the abundance. And there to distil the spirit was *The Bully*.

+ West Germany is established.
+ The Soviet Union secretly tests Joe 1—its first hydrogen bomb.
+ Australia reaches a population of 8 million.

New words: telethon, Newspeak, New Australian.

Columns teemed with xenophobia, spurning Asia in particular. Cartoons depicted pipe-smoking chaps outfoxing plump, exasperated women, while the small print dwelt on wheat tariffs, amoral barons and limericks. All in all, a soft landing for the country's second regular cryptic, fifteen years after *The Sydney Morning Herald* had first tested the water.

A casual glance may lead you to take the puzzle for a British import. Are you serious? Not with *The Bully*'s history. Through a turbulent century the magazine nurtured a legion of literary and artistic talents destined to become household names. Poets Henry Lawson and Banjo Paterson were just two of its contributors. Also in the ranks were CJ Dennis and Steele Rudd, Ethel Turner and Dorothea Mackellar, plus the artist Norman Lindsay. Then there was one of the founding journalists, JF Archibald, who bestowed his name upon the nation's biggest art prize.

Thus the crossword had to be Australian, a poke in the eye for John Bull, bold proof that this punk could find its own way in the world. Or possibly that's the alcohol talking. The maiden Down clue in *The Bulletin*'s debut puzzle did two things: underlined the parochial and grabbed for the bottle: *The kind of wine Johnnie's drinking—Sydney's on it too (4,7)*.

The formula is Charade 101: PORT (*wine*) plus JACKS (a more common shortening of *Johnnie's*) plus ON (Aussie vernacular linked to binging). You'd struggle to find a more quintessential clue, pulling in slang, mateship and grog, with the pay-off identifying the harbour where Sydney and the magazine's base were situated. A British compiler might have taken a more sophisticated tack—doubtless resisting the anagram option of NO JOCKSTRAP—but the rambunctious magazine didn't give a tinker's cuss. Nor did the anonymous creator behind 'Puzzle No. 1'. In signature style, the cashed-up, loud-talking tearaway was off and running.

1950

Wander (but not too far, please) (?)

The meaning of *farrago* is mishmash. It stems from Latin, in which the word applies to a mix of grain for cattle, a kind of pastoral muesli, if you like. *Farrago* with a big F, however, is the campus paper at Melbourne University. The Latin is retained by the paper's motto: *Quidquid agunt homines nostri farrago libelli est* (Whatever men do forms the motley subject of our page). Motley, medley—the rag is a miscellany combining varsity news, sports results and general silliness. Though silliness, I should note, was not part of the original formula. Browse *Farrago*'s first editions, from 1925, and you'll detect a socialist preoccupation, largely of the fond persuasion. Yet year by year this undergrad leaning has tilted more towards buffoonery. For evidence I present a ditty from 1950:

+ The Korean War begins.
+ Myxomatosis is introduced to cull Australia's rabbit plague.
+ Shirley Temple quits showbiz, aged 22.

New words: aqualung, big bang, hi-fi, ergonomics

In days of old when nighties were bold
And Foo Tanks sogged increasingly,
The Winged-Swapard drank-loved
And hydro-gooned unceasingly.

The poet was Anon, though I sense he/she owes a debt to Messrs Carroll and Milligan—or Norman Lindsay, which may explain the Anon bit. The zaniness operates in tandem with the file photo of a lingerie model captioned: 'Voted the girl with whom the staff would most like to be locked in the office.' How's that? Sexism with grammatical purity.

Sustaining this absurdity was the Annual *Farrago* Crossword, which appeared only once, in 1950, to the best of my knowledge. At first glance the puzzle seems legit. A symmetrical pattern adorning a box of 11 by 11 squares. Clues arrayed in sober blocks. But in the muesli mix of student life, this is one more morsel of *caveat lector.*

The first warning you get is in the mismatched numbering. *Gloss* is the clue for 20-Across, say. SHEEN would have half a chance, if 20-Across existed in the grid. There is a 20-Down, but that has three letters and lacks a clue. Meanwhile, 28-Across reads like vernacular: *It is very cold now (3).* At least this clue's number corresponds to the grid. Could the answer be YES? Maybe. Though this issue ran in October, mid-spring, when lingerie modelling was lodged in the editorial mind. Even if you take time to mull the answer, your eye might *Wander (but not too far please)* to other clues, in which the silliness plainly declares its hand. In fact, I've picked four clues to serve as a sequel to Anon's doggerel, minus the rhyme this time:

Don't bother, we're in paradise.
If it wasn't bald it would be beautiful.
The River Queen wore nylons.
Screw it or crack it—yes, I am mad.

1951

Meubelstuk dat te los kan worden (5)

Now and then, during a crossword talk at a school or library, a bright spark near the front (always the first or second row) will ask, 'Do other languages have cryptics?'

Six months ago, before I embarked on this book, my answer would have been, 'Yes, well, kinda.' Without much more to add, I'd sit on the fence and dodge any plea for tangible detail. But thanks to our centennial quest I can now paraphrase Mr Spock: 'Other languages have cryptics, but not as we know them.'

Take the Dutch. They've been making their own devices for decades. Their two leading lights are HA Scheltes and Jelmer Steenhuis. Scheltes was born eight years after Arthur Wynne made his first word-cross. He worked as a journalist on the *NRC Handelsblad* in Amsterdam and, in 1951, won a contest to be the

---

+ Greek women get the vote.
+ The School of the Air connects to the outback.
+ *Catcher in the Rye* is published.

New words: biopic, nerd, Day-Glo, fast food

paper's chief setter. By then the cryptic genre had already crossed the Dutch border. A weekly specimen appeared from 1949 onwards in *De Groene* (The Green—after the magazine's initial use of green ink), but that puzzle was tame compared to the places Scheltes took his *cryptogram*, as Netherlanders call the cryptic.

If you know your clue types—the deletion, the container, the homophone—then you'd recognise most of the Dutch counterparts, once translated. Here's an anagram clue from an early Scheltes: *Meubelstuk dat te los kan worden (5)*. In English this reads, 'Piece of furniture that may become too loose.' The answer is STOEL (chair). A dainty piece of carpentry, as not only do chairs succumb to wear-and-tear wobbles, but the letters of *stoel* can be rejigged to make *te los* (too loose).

That was the Scheltes difference. His clues told stories. In contrast, the 'green' cryptic clues had an inbuilt looseness, a clunky betrayal of procedure. They wobbled compared to the sleek carpentry of Scheltes. A cult following soon spread across the Netherlands, convincing the paper to launch a new feature—the Scrypto, or Scheltes Cryptogram. In the words of Henk Verkuyl, a scholar of Dutch puzzling and *Cluetopia*'s guide through these nether regions, 'The Scrypto was a radical change from the British style. A lot less anagrams, making room for more puns, sound affinity and semantics.'

This shift is best illustrated by the work of Jelmer Steenhuis, an Amsterdam lawyer and Schelte's successor. He filled the loose chair vacated by Schelte in 1987. Happily, with the S initial shared by both men, the Scrypto label could be retained—though not its style. Where a Schelte clue asked the solver to take a creative leap, a Steenhuis clue tested the bungee cord's stretchability.

I'll keep with the furniture motif to prove the point, so long as I can issue a warning before we begin. You may not fully fathom the clue you're about to read unless you speak Dutch. I can order a Heineken in Le Hague, or a gram of *magische paddestoel* (magic mushroom) in Amsterdam, but that's about my limit. If nothing else, this exercise will prove how cryptics are welded into their own language, designed to collapse the minute they cross the border. Be that as it may, let's be gallant, and enter the world of Steenhuis.

The clue reads: *Familie van trapkast en klaptafel?* (Family of stairway closet and folding table?). The answer is SCHOPSTOEL, which lacks a pure equivalent in English. The literal translation is kick-chair. This is the object upon which a condemned man stands, his neck in the noose, awaiting the executioner to kick the chair away. The sinister item is preserved in Dutch idiom, as any worker who's feeling at risk of losing his job, can be said to be sitting on the *schopstoel*, awaiting a grim inevitability at any moment. (In English we might say one's head is on the chopping block, the execution vibe in dire harmony.) But if kick-chair is the answer, how does it work?

Strip back each coupling and you will see the logic. Being literal, *trapkast* means kick-closet, since the storage space sits below the household's daily footfalls. A close cousin, the folding chair—or *klaptafel*—can be broken into hit-table, owing to the blow you need to administer to the hinged legs, if you wish to fold them away. *Schopstoel*, or kick-chair, sustains the theme of violent-verb-meeting-item-of-furniture, thus belonging in the broader family, at least in a semantic way.

Satisfied? Mystified? Perhaps you're both. The exercise demonstrates how exotic clues can mirror, and distort, our own wordplay, as well as defy any facile translation. And the next time I'm asked about cryptics in other languages, I promise to hop off the fence and discuss the joinery of Dutch furniture.

1952

Laundry fiddler (3)

Steal a boat and you could sail across the lake to New York State. And don't think the inmates of Kingston Penitentiary—KP for short—didn't dream that scenario. Any time the prisoners caught a glimpse of the outside world, the backdrop was the glassy blue of Lake Ontario.

Kingston sits midway between Toronto and Montreal, built around the remnants of an old French fort. The place once made the most of its waterways, trading fur with Europe and nearby America, though more recently the main exports have been soldiers (training at the Royal Military College) and ice-hockey legends.

KP, of course, is the other industry, a city within a city. The prison can house over 400 inmates, needing the same again in wardens,

---

+ Queen Elizabeth II assumes the British throne.
+ In Michigan's Harper University Hospital, a mechanical heart is used during surgery.
+ Agatha Christie's *Mousetrap* begins its marathon run on London's West End.

New words: credit card, wolf whistle, wok, Ms

cooks and admin staff. While clouds hang over its long-term future, it has claims of being the longest continuing jail in the world, running since 1833 until the time of writing.

Speaking of writing, Charles Dickens dropped by this bleak house in 1842, back when women were part of the manifest. One woman who spent time inside was Grace Marks, a maid hailing from Northern Ireland. She copped a life sentence in 1843 for her part in strangling a fellow domestic with a scarf. Canadian author Margaret Atwood based her novel *Alias Grace* on the story, but that's where the high-end literature ends. KP is a place better known for monsters than for novelists.

Your blood will chill to read about the worst residents—bank-robbers and child-killers with nicknames like Mad Dog and the Vampire Rapist. Over the years KP has also been called home by the depraved and deranged—or the maladjusted, as criminal psychologists prefer to say, a brand of thinking that mobilised the 'socialisation projects' of the late 1940s. The argument was that prisoners needed skills not only to cope with life inside the jail's limestone walls, but also to resume life outside. They needed job-training, pastimes, hope. And a newspaper, too, aka *The K.P. Telescope*.

The masthead said it all, carrying not just the logo, a spyglass aiming beyond the page, but also the mission statement: '*The K.P. Telescope* is published to provide the inmate with a medium of creative expression and communication, in order to cultivate a better understanding of the outside world.' The first edition circulated the corridors in September 1950, beginning life as a monthly for subscribers only. Runs were sporadic at best, stopping and starting depending on matters like copy supply, work ethic or the infamous baseball riot of 1954. But the paper was vital, lasting well into the 1960s, when it became a bimonthly, and later a quarterly. Eventually, though, the whole thing sputtered, in 1967.

Issues today are hen's teeth. For months I pestered the patient souls in Canada's correctional department, in particular the *conseillères en relations avec les médias* Lori and Sara, sensing there was gold in this elusive *Telescope*, for hearsay insisted there was once a crossword as part of the paper's mix. Better than that, it was a crossword crafted by an inmate's hand: such was the way socialisation worked. Prisoners needed to be enabled, to borrow the jargon. For the *Telescope* to honour its mission statement, every article had to be penned inside the pen, so to speak, every television column, sports piece and poem. Every crossword. And here our search was in luck.

During a major retrofit within the KP complex in 1990, a builder spotted a scrap of paper lying in an abandoned cell. Curious, he picked it up to discover it was a crossword, smudged with age and typewriter ink—a commonplace diversion to the casual eye, perhaps, until he read the clues more closely. Later that day the puzzle was sent to the warden's old residence, home now to Canada's Correctional Museum.

Knowing the puzzle to be the work of a hard-core prisoner tends to inform your view. It's like holding a telescope back to front: your field of vision fixes on every letter, every comma, searching for the biographical hints beyond the clues. The only bankable fact was that the puzzle's compiler was a man with a long sentence to his name, yet what was he telling us? What was his mindset at the time he created it?

MOOD, in fact, is among the answers, along with a strong expression of desire. In every quadrant you find it: ACHE, EROS, YEN, LOVE, LUST and AMOR. Some clues seem emphatically penal (*Ruffians, A mass of blood, To decay, Length of time*), while others murmur contraband (*One who deals in seeds, A very small quantity*).

Doubters who say the puzzle was a buy-in need only look at the typos within the text ('devergence', 'Assytrian'), the missing clues, or the bungled interlock (where ETE is a *Greek letter*, and VATO is

Forbid). Each flaw is proof of a pent amateur, yet the surest sign of an inside job is the strangest clue of the lot: *Laundry fiddler (3)*.

Surrounding answers confirm the last two letters to be ED. Who can this mysterious fiddler be? Possibly RED, since Norman 'Red' Ryan escaped KP in 1923. (Red set fire to a shed and clambered the wall during the chaos.)

But no. The letters don't play out. Maybe TED is the culprit? Or JED? Safe to say we can rule out NED, as he's already popped up as *Man's name*.

Or wait. The answer to run across the top, the entry to give us the missing letter, is TANGENT, that 'divergence' I was talking about. The fiddler, therefore, is NED—or was Ned. Once more the setter is unlocking the door, allowing us to glimpse his obsessions. For Ned is far more than an incidental name. The guy appears twice in the interlock, once as a meat-and-potatoes name, and the second time as our alleged perpetrator of a laundry incident. Who knows what happened? A scandal? A crime? Revenge? Or maybe the answer is a keepsake, some long-lost moment of steaminess held captive within a *Telescope* crossword.

1953

Ein europäischer Staatsmann (4)

Die Wahrheit means the truth in German. But whose truth? The question flared up late in April 1953 when the communist weekly called *Die Wahrheit* accidentally carried the wrong sort of propaganda. Slanting the news to the left was fine, but when a crossword clue attempted to present an alternative view? Well, that was unconscionable.

The puzzle was an import from sources unknown. The offending clue was *Ein europäischer Staatsmann* (A European statesman). Before I reveal the answer, let me sketch your typical *Wahrheit* reader.

War-torn Europe was still awash in refugees. Many were communists in limbo, staunch believers in Mother Russia and the East German state, who found themselves in places like Austria,

---

+ Everest is climbed by Edmund Hillary and Tenzing Norgay.
+ DNA is discovered.
+ *Casino Royale*, the first James Bond novel, is written by Ian Fleming.

New words: boutique, snorkel, rotisserie

Belgium and West Germany. A paper such as *Die Wahrheit* unified the scattered tribe, chiefly due to its hatred of fascism.

Can you guess the statesman yet?

Once upon a time, Josip Broz was a communist brother, a Croatian soldier enlisted in the Red Guard, serving in Siberia. Returning home during World War II, he joined the Communist Party, carrying its creed into power as the war drew to an end. The new Balkan leader took on the name Tito, a palatable crossword solution for your average communist solver, at least through most of the 1940s, but not when he decided to go rogue.

As the prime minister of the newly formed Democratic Federal Yugoslavia, Tito went from being an ally to a dedicated foe of Stalin, introducing economic reforms, a softer socialism, new relationships with the West. His actions amounted to betrayal in the eyes of any Red onlooker.

Of course, if the Jackson 5 had been making music in 1953, then TITO might have been clued as *Michael Jackson's brother*. Mind you, Tito Puente was the Mambo King by that period, cranking out some wicked Afro-Cuban beats from New York—but clearly the sounds hadn't reached Hanover, where *Die Wahrheit* was published. For better or worse, at least those two musos were not deemed to be turncoats.

The backlash against the Tito solution was seismic. I'd lucked upon this story due to the uproar that had registered in the archives. Headlines in the London press shouted, 'A Purge of Crosswords', the stories conveying the deep regrets of *Die Wahrheit*'s editor. Central authorities censured the paper, obliging the editor to explain his 'lack of watchfulness' in a public statement.

As you'd expect, part of the penance was a delicious bit of conspiracy-cooking, in true communist tradition. To give you a taste of the editor's apology: 'You can see how cleverly imperialist propagandists squeeze anti-communist propaganda even into such non-political things as crossword puzzles. From now on our puzzles will be devoted to the fight for peace and German unification.'

If only the clue had been *Ein gefährlicher Zehelappen von den Balkan* (A treacherous toe-rag from the Balkans). Then the puzzle would have been speaking the acceptable truth.

1954

It's a draw. 'Queen Anne's dead, chum!' (9)

No favouritism had been shown, swore the editors at *Country Life*. The crossword contest had been open to all comers, highborn or low, the sender of the first correct entry drawn from the pile crowned the winner. That lucky person in May 1954 went by the name of Margaret Rose Windsor, better known as Princess Margaret, making 'Crossword 1266' the closest the lass would come to a coronation.

Her big sister, Elizabeth, had been crowned queen the year before. Going by the law of blood, Elizabeth's two children (a stripling Charles and an infant Anne) leapfrogged their aunt in the British line of succession, behind their father, Prince Philip, the Duke of Edinburgh.

+ Vladimir and Evdokia Petrov defect from Canberra's Soviet embassy.
+ Bill Haley's 'Rock Around the Clock' kick-starts rock 'n' roll.
+ Roger Bannister breaks the four-minute mile.

New words: **discotheque, funky, junk mail, high-rise**

Not that might and majesty held any great allure for the 'gay personality', as royal-watcher Anthea Goddard described the princess in a media profile. The piece appeared in the *Sun-Herald* in the same year as the crossword coup, when Margaret was 23. 'She is less reserved than her sister and more vocal about her enthusiasms,' wrote Goddard. Cryptics, for example. A nameless court correspondent dubbed her the Puzzle Princess after the *Country Life* success. The crossword, the article continued, had been 'in the abstruse class, with a host of clues needing a knowledge of Shakespeare, Latin and other subjects.'

To refute any rumours of privilege, Margaret's entry was posted in a plain envelope with a 2½-shilling stamp, just like any other aspirant's. The princess had cracked any number of puzzles before then and had submitted earlier entries without much luck. All the same, the editor sniffed a hoax on seeing the sender's name, a plain 'Margaret P' from Clarence House, Westminster. She rang the royal residence to verify the claim and took delight in learning that *Country Life* had such a noble subscriber.

As for the abstruseness of the clues, Margaret knew her onions. Trained more in etiquette than Edmund Spenser, she still coped with allusions to the Bard and Wordsworth, anagrams and coins, botany and golf. Yet the clue that must have given the princess pause seemed seditious in tone: *It's a draw. 'Queen Anne's dead, chum!' (9).*

Queen Anne belonged to the House of Stuart, a dynasty ruling more than 250 years ago, and was of no direct relation to the royal solver. Childless despite a staggering seventeen pregnancies, Anne ruled Britain in the early 1700s. She died of gout complications in 1714, six months short of her 50th birthday, so ending the Stuart line.

Ages ago, in short. And that is the clue's gist. 'Queen Anne's dead' is an idiom for old news, in the same way Australians may say that Prime Minister Harold Holt is missing, presumed drowned, or

Americans could declare, 'The British are coming!' The newsflash has long been and gone; even the T-shirt is old.

Talk of a dead queen was therefore pure vernacular. No offence was meant, and none taken. The young solver at Clarence House was clearly alive to the slang of the outside world, leaping on STALEMATE and soon after completing the grid. To try her luck, she had resisted the palace's official stationery, as well as the franking of the Privy Purse Office. Instead she'd sourced a commoner's envelope, most likely from domestic staff. Whereupon she had licked the back of her sister's head and popped her entry in the post.

1955

How do you stop a taxi? (4)

DIM. One more clue to get in this crossword.

WIT. Read it to me.

DIM. *Postman complains about his daily burden.*

WIT. How many letters?

DIM. Too bloody many.

Boom-boom. So goes the ancient Dad joke, the punchline certainly applying to the Sydney Post Office in September 1955. The sorting room was pandemonium. Two major papers—*The Daily Telegraph* and *The Sydney Morning Herald*—had both taken a post office box for their crossword competitions, and half the population wanted a slice of the action. To aggravate matters, the box numbers were neighbours and the contests themselves had similar names—the

---

+ Disneyland opens—as Scrabble debuts.
+ Nabokov's *Lolita* is published.
+ The six o'clock swill ends in New South Wales pubs.

New words: surfer, karate, hot-line, Rastafarian

Telegraph's Teleword versus the *Herald*'s Findaword. Twin crosswords, twin guessing games really, both with fat jackpots, had triggered an avalanche.

'Crazy Words Jam Traffic in Sydney', ran a headline in *The Argus*, suggesting the bedlam at Sydney's GPO was mirrored by mayhem on the street. The same article claimed that a 'big traffic policeman hustled his way to the core of the hold-up' only to drop his Teleword entry into the slot and move on. Citizens jostled at suburban stamp counters to ensure their entries beat the deadline. Someone in the scrimmage, said *The Argus*, had openly asked, 'How do you stop a taxi? Do you CALL one, HAIL one, NAIL one, or what?' And let's overlook BAWL, WAIL, YAWL or RAIL.

Nor did the fever cool over time. Individual jackpots soared from £15 000 in September to £40 000 by early October. Meanwhile, a rival paper tried to deflate the hype, hiring an actuary to calculate the odds of guessing a perfect solution. The cold maths, read the article, claimed that a punter had one chance in 1 769 472 of scooping the pool. Such hostile odds encouraged hustlers to mushroom. Operators stalked the lanes of Kings Cross and Darlinghurst, their jackets lined with sealed envelopes. Not porn this time, but variant crossword solutions—one with HAIL, one with CALL, let's say. Or so swore the racketeers, handing out the sealed solutions and obliging clients to take them at their word, at one shilling a pop.

Every drinker at the six o'clock swill had his favourite answers to argue. The bug even bothered the country's highest paid broadcaster, Macquarie Network's quizmaster Jack Davey. In the course of 1955, if Davey wasn't quizzing a teenage John Howard (the future prime minister) on his *Give It a Go* game, he was a wretched Findaword victim at home: his wife, Dorothy, was hooked. For breakfast, she grilled her quizmaster for possible solutions. One clue, according to Davey's Hi-Ho! column, caused an eruption between the spouses. 'There was a grand ding-dong argument ending with my wife calling me a brainless nincompoop, and my shouting out that I could tell her where she could go, in four letters, ending in L.'

Eventually, when a jackpot did go off, the winners were multiple. One lucky lass, revealed *The Argus*, was Joy Trapp of Carnegie in Melbourne, 'a blue-eyed brownette with a beach-girl figure.' That she hailed from interstate is telling, denoting how widespread the attraction had grown. While I can't NAIL (or CALL) the exact sum Trapp snagged, I can tell you she sacrificed a teacup to the cause. The press article shows the 'brownette' dropping the crockery in pantomime shock for the photographer, just one more casualty in Sydney's Great Word War.

1956

Treacherous foe in bad or good faith (4,4)

Psst. Have you seen *The Hour*? No, not the time—the period thriller produced by the BBC. The reason I'm asking is that I don't want to spoil the suspense. Or tell you why a crossword is crucial to the action.

Oops, I've said too much already. As a spy I'd make a good chatterbox. It's probably best if I limit the damage by keeping this chapter brief: just long enough to tell you that the crossword in the *London Evening Standard* of 1956 may seem a bog-standard puzzle, but it's not when Freddie Lyon twigs to its secret code. Freddie, played by Ben Whishaw, is a new breed of television journo who becomes attached to a pilot show called *The Hour*, a news round-up 'you can't afford to miss'.

+ Pakistan becomes the first Islamic republic.
+ Elvis Presley first enters the charts, crooning 'Heartbreak Hotel'.
+ Grace Kelly marries Prince Rainier III of Monaco.

New words: glitterati, tranquilliser, jeans

Freddie's face is the first thing we see in the series, before he is hired by *The Hour*—before *The Hour* format is even hatched, in fact. A thick-maned leftie, Freddie is working on BBC newsreels as well as a crossword between dispatches. He solves in pencil, sucking on a fag between clues. 'I never finish crosswords,' he later confesses to Bel Rowley, his colleague-cum-love-interest.

You can tell Bel has the cryptic nous. There's something about those lambent eyes, the arch smile. Okay, maybe the actress, Romola Garai, is my love interest too. But when Freddie reads aloud a clue—*Treacherous foe in bad or good faith*—the leopardess leaps on the anagram like a piece of savannah manna.

'BONA FIDE.' (Sexily too, with that extra Latin syllable.)

Freddie's pencil obeys. Though this is not the crossword that really matters in *The Hour*. The real life-and-death puzzle is lurking around the corner, after the murder and before the crisis.

That's it. Do all you like. Flip on the bright light. Drag out the water board. Play the muzak at eleven notches. I'm not telling you anything more.

1957

(14)

Chances are you'd rather lose a game of Chinese checkers than Russian roulette. Or win a box of Turkish delight over a case of German measles. Every nation has its claim to fame, as paraded in the dictionary. Danes have their blue, and Spanish their flu. In Sweden the national possessions are massages and meatballs, or so Google Chrome insists, with the third string in the nation's bow being the Swedish crossword.

+ Egypt reopens the Suez Canal.
+ Sputnik enters the atmosphere, along with the frisbee.
+ Patrick White's *Voss* wins the inaugural Miles Franklin Award.

New words: holocaust, bonkers, growth industry

You've seen this style in untold magazines, in which celebrities have their pictures built within the grid, and arrows direct your answers. Most Europeans know the format as Swedish, using the term to distinguish from other styles such as British (with a waffle-like pattern), American (with every letter crossed twice) or the barred diagram made famous by Torquemada.

The breakaway Swedish style began in 1954, pioneered by the uncrowned king of Swedish puzzledom, Bertil Geijer. He called the style *kors & tvärs* (criss-crossing), a name that spliced two English ideas: hither and thither with across and down. The novelty appeared in *Svenska Dagbladet* (Swedish Daily), attracting over 15 000 entries hopeful of the prize.

Outsiders could be forgiven for thinking *kors & tvärs* a tame spin-off of Arthur Wynne's invention. You see a snap of Ingmar Bergman, and you bung the director's name into the squares. What could be easier? But Geijer's genius was far more twisted. While his diagrams carried four or five image-clues, these were not ordinary portraits. Consider this chapter's picture heading, for example: an orangutan masquerading as Sherlock Holmes. Safe to say the answer isn't BRIGITTE BARDOT or CHARLIE CHAPLIN. What sort of answer does this image expect?

Welcome to the hither-and-thither element of the Swedish revolution. While most picture compilations—those red-carpet pushovers found throughout the gossip mags—are exercises in the bleeding obvious, the *kors & tvärs* injected a second novelty into the mainstream: the pictorial cryptic.

To demonstrate the scope of Geijer's mischief, let's consider the orangutan. Notably it's not a name you're chasing, but a pun, a made-up phrase that occupies fourteen squares.

'Hang on!' you yell. 'Did you say *made-up*?'

I did, and you'll see why. There's a softer side to the Swedish style. A sprinkle of orthodox clues elsewhere in the grid ensures the solver has several cross-letters to enable some informed guesswork. Gaining as many letters as empty slots, you develop the courage to flesh out what the pun may be. In this case our Borneo ape is a PRIMATDETEKTIV. The setter has tweaked the word *privat* (almost the same term in English) to create the joke with *primat* (another close English cousin).

Hans Christian Nygård, my interpreter for this strange seam of Swedish culture, is a colossus of his local crosswording. I pity the bloke, as his has been the task of finding for me visual puns from the *kors & tvärs* backlist that not only work visually, but somehow work in translation. 'In English,' he confessed, 'it's hard for me to know what works, and what doesn't.'

His orangutan is a commendable choice, compared to the diabolic trickery of an Ainu playing a guitar.

An Ainu what? What's an Ainu? Is that Swedish?

Japanese, actually. Ainu is the name for the people native to northern Japan and parts of Russia. Ainu in fact is pure Japanese for man, or human. If you do enough quicks *per annum*, you'll recognise AINU as pure crosswordese, one of those words that recur often due to the convenience of its letter pattern. *Native of Japan*, the clue, crops up frequently in American fare, but this chapter is telling the Swedish story.

In Stockholm then, an Ainu playing guitar is a very different kettle of pickled herring. Picture the watercolour if you can: a Japanese man in traditional robes riffing on a Gibson. The image was sent by Nygård himself as an example clue for *Cluetopia*. (You'll see why I opted for the ape alternative in a minute.) The answer, in English, as kindly tailored by Nygård, has 12 letters. The image is all you get, an Ainu on guitar, and nothing else.

To shed a little more light, let me widen the camera angle. The Hokkaido dude was the fruit of my worldwide plea for exotic clues. As I was hassling media archives of the world, Barack Obama was being sworn in for his second term of office. The event inspired Hans to create his Ainu as a means of illustrating—quite literally—how sneaky a Swedish clue can be. Nasty even, which could partway explain why detectives like Kurt Wallander can handle such obtuseness in his fictional murder cases.

Anyhow, assuming you haven't leapt already, the answer to this Ainu on guitar is INAUGURATION, the covert anagram of a contrived phrase, saluting a major event on the world's other side. Even on learning the answer, it's confounding to think how Swedes can cope every day with such double-crossing criss-crossing. To make any headway in a *kors & tvärs* I swear you'd either need to be a native solver, or a primate detective.

1958

Lean man with bad feet; he's the greatest (7,4)

When you hear of a priest being headhunted, you may well imagine the Congo, or the Papuan highlands. Not even close. Try the shallow downs of Berkshire. The priest involved was Reverend John Graham, a chaplain at Reading University and a scholar of the classics. In the 1950s, Graham managed to win the prestigious crossword-setting contest in *The Observer*—twice—inspiring *The Guardian* to hunt down the stylist in 1958, offering him a slot on its crossword roster.

He accepted. Hence, for a decade the priest split his duties between the Bible and the *Oxford* under the radar, as *The Guardian* gig was anonymous and Graham wasn't one for flaunting his double life. His brother, also a priest, had no inkling that his older sibling

---

+ Mao Zedong launches the Great Leap Forward.
+ Hula hoops and Lego blocks dominate Santa's sleigh.
+ The initial Opera House lottery is drawn.

New words: autocue, tandoori, beatnik, modem

was moonlighting on the puzzle pages, despite the torment and delight the clues caused him.

Torment and delight were common responses to Graham's output. Belying his benign veneer, the priest embodied a new breed of setter, a rule-pusher, a scofflaw in some eyes, with clues that shone with apostasy. *He is loving and giving, which makes one shudder (7)*. This clue summarises its creator. The answer is FRISSON, its logic lying in the nursery rhyme in which Friday's child is loving and giving, therefore making a shudder of FRI's SON. Cheeky, no question, relying on the solver to make the leap as well as downsizing *Friday*. And if that's not enough, they also need to bestow a gender upon the infant. Yet the clue sparkles with play and originality—the reverend's signature.

Some 12 years later, the veil of anonymity fluttered. John Perkin at *The Guardian* wanted his contributors to forge pseudonyms. Graham went with Araucaria, after the monkey-puzzle tree: a subtle allusion at the time, though the priest later confessed in a BBC Radio interview, 'I was always an idiot to choose a name that people could neither spell nor pronounce.'

At least now solvers had fair warning. The minute they spied the name Araucaria, they knew to approach with an agile mind, a capacious vocab, an erudite sensibility. The man of the cloth had announced his presence in the cryptic galaxy. Over time, the alias became a beacon, and thousands of solvers were thrilled by his clues. Crime writer Ian Rankin, creator of Inspector Rebus, calls the monkey man the 'most infuriatingly ingenious setter working today.' Hugh Stephenson, John Perkin's eventual successor, had no qualms in calling the Big A the 'master compiler of his generation.' Prunella Scales, best known for her role as Sybil Fawlty, admits to Araucaria being her constant bedtime companion, despite what Basil might think.

Fandom is one yardstick. Yet the strongest proof of Graham's stature is the fact that his codename soon extended into an adjective.

Very soon one word—Araucarian—labelled the liberal school of clue-making, a nominal rival to the Ximenean, the more precise cabal of setting that we will meet in a year fast approaching. To the Ximenean camp, Araucaria remains a heretic. Quite the ironic verdict, given the reverend was eventually forced to leave his church and rectory due to a divorce, a few years after his byline arrived. Yet despite all the personal heartbreak, there was a silver lining for the solvers: Araucaria suddenly needed to craft more puzzles, as they were now his primary income source.

So then, to toast the game-changer, let's examine a fitting clue from the ex-priest's canon devised in the very year he adopted his botanical alias: *Lean man with bad feet; he's the greatest (7,4)*.

In one grab, three universes collide, which highlights the richness of the Araucarian mind. Firstly, the *lean man* is Cassius from Shakespeare's *Julius Caesar*: 'Yond Cassius has a lean and hungry look; He thinks too much: such men are dangerous.'

Secondly, the bad feet are planted in the Old Testament book of *Daniel*, in which Nebuchadnezzar suffers a strange vision. The Babylonian king dreams of a giant statue with a head of gold, a silver breast, and belly and thighs of brass. His feet are made of iron with clay soles, which are struck by a single stone, causing the whole statue to shatter. Hence, *feet of clay* relates to a person's hidden flaw.

Finally, Muhammad Ali rejected his birth name in 1964, when joining the Nation of Islam. The switch took a while to bite, as the catchiness of CASSIUS CLAY lingered in the public imagination. So too did the boxer's bluster: 'I am the Greatest,' a boast he'd yelled on dethroning Sonny Liston in that same year, chanting the claim to the battery of ringside journalists.

Boxers are drawn to showbiz strutting. It goes with the canvas, the silken robes, the swollen gloves. Crossword-makers, on the other hand, are modest by nature, often anonymous unless the page's policy demands otherwise. Made of different clay, the British priest was hardly susceptible to blowing his own trumpet, even if he was also the greatest crossword-compiler of his time. Yet thanks to the advent of *Guardian* bylines, the solving public was supplied a name to cherish or despise. Since then, plenty of worshippers have been trumpeting on Araucaria's behalf.

1959

Dumpynose, perhaps?! (9)

O kay, I won't lie—this is my cheat chapter. The clue above was fudged for the occasion, as now's the time to rejoice in crossword codenames.

In 1958 *The Guardian*, as we saw in the preceding chapter, conceded to the trend of naming its crossword-setters that was begun by *The Observer* in 1922, with the likes of Torquemada and later Ximenes, who became major drawcards for that paper. *The Listener* had followed suit in 1930, and then came other mastheads, with only *The Times* and *The Daily Telegraph* defying the urge to reveal the fiend responsible.

At least, that's the British summary. Elsewhere on the globe, the Hamlet-like dilemma (to be or not to be identified) has been treated by editors on a case-by-case basis. In America the tradition

---

+ Fidel Castro seizes power in Cuba.
+ Alaska is admitted as the 49th American state.
+ The first Snowy Mountains power station thrums into life.

New words: charisma, ombudsman, kinky, kooky

has been to reveal the setter's name, pure and simple. Rare exceptions have been the monikers adopted by *The Wall Street Journal*'s puzzle editor Mike Shenk, who, to dodge any rumblings that his work is being self-anointed, publishes under Maryanne Lemot (Not My Real Name) and Natalia Shore (Another Alias).

In Australia the trend is timid and relatively new; *The Sydney Morning Herald* plumped for the compiler's initials in the late 1980s. Regulars in the Italian weekly *La Settimana Engimistica* operate under the notoriety of Trick, Trip, Che, Woland and Anderson. *The Hindu* brags a mystic stable too, with Cryptonite, Spiffytrix, Buzzer and Textrous on its roster.

Great Britain remains the custom's focal point. So then, taking a halftime break from clue analysis, let's meet some of the Who's Not Really Who of British crosswords:

AFRIT
: This demon of Arabic folklore was the byline of Alistair Ferguson Ritchie of *The Listener*.

ALBIPEDIUS
: Latin for white foot was a natural fit for *The Listener*'s Richard Whitelegg.

ALCHEMI
: *The Independent*'s Michael Holmans found some old magic in his first name.

ARACHNE
: One day Athena, the Greek goddess of wisdom and weaving, turned the maiden Arachne into a spider, after the mortal had the chutzpah to challenge the deity to a weave-off. This *Guardian* codename is owned by Sarah Hayes, a former lecturer in Russian at Manchester University. For trivia hounds, Sarah also ran the Chester Marathon in 2011 dressed as a bottle.

BIGGLES
: A collective codename for four *Guardian* setters: John Graham, John Halpern, John Henderson and John Young. See the pattern? So did they, opting

for Biggles as their cover due to the flying ace's creator, WE Johns.

CHARYBDIS   The ship-eating whirlpool of Greek myth was the go-to byline of *The Listener*'s Chris Poole, or make that C Poole.

DINMUTZ   A random Scrabble rack that leapt out at Bert Danher, one-time setter at the *Financial Times*. The same man was once the great HENDRA in *The Guardian*, for manipulative reasons.

DOGBERRY   John Young picked the word-mangling constable in Shakespeare's *Much Ado about Nothing* for his *Financial Times* cameos. Dogberry is the same doltish cop to remark, 'Thou wilt be condemned into everlasting redemption for this.'

DUMPYNOSE   Byline of QC Chris Brougham, who wangled the letters of *pseudonym* for his *Spectator* alias.

HYPNOS   A tribute to *The Big Sleep* by Raymond Chandler, featuring the detective Philip Marlowe. As it happens, *The Independent*'s Philip Marlowe also creates under Shamus and Sleuth.

LOROSO   In Italian, *loro so* means they know. But do they know Dean Mayer chose Loroso for his *Financial Times* byline because he lives on London Road South?

MOODIM   Alex Jagger wished to commemorate her cats—Moo and Dim—for her *Independent* debut.

MORPH   Alias of *The Independent*'s Mick Hodgkin, former program editor on *More4 News*.

NEO   Part-time adman, part-time drummer Paul Bringloe declares his love of *The Matrix* franchise in the *Financial Times*.

PHSSTHPOK   This sci-fi allusion—a nod to the main character of Larry Niven's *Protector* novel—has bestowed a bonus nickname upon London lawyer Adam Sanitt. In the crossword realm he's dubbed the Unpronounceable One.

TERESMOS   The 'retro' alter ego of Derrick Somerset Macnutt in *The Listener*, the same man labelled Ximenes in *The Observer* after the severe Spanish inquisitor.

TRAMP   *Guardian* setter Neil Walker. Get it?

Now, back to the clue chase proper.

1960

Turning in big profits—slang (6,1,4)

In Crosswordville, Margaret Petherbridge Farrar is designated royalty. We've already met the veteran editor, her name now annexed by marriage to publisher John C Farrar in 1926. Plenty of history has flowed below the bridge, but the queen bee is still buzzing, 35 years after she'd been a co-conspirator with Messrs Simon and Schuster in producing the first crossword book. Now in her early 60s, Margaret cut a dominant figure in the black-and-white business, overseeing a constant stream of puzzles for *The New York Times*. More than overseeing—overhauling. She was the editor to oust many tired definitions from circulation. Rather than *Insect* being the hint for BEE, say, she insisted on other tacks:

+ Laser is invented.
+ The Beatles form.
+ The pill is released.
+ So too is Hitchcock's *Psycho*.

New words: cassette, consumerism, software

Nectar inspector?
Petal pusher?
Wax producer
Quilting event
Hum-bug?

Out with the rest, and in with the zest: the Farrar legacy.

She also installed the Sunday breakfast test, whereby the ghoulish entries of illness and atrocity were banished from the grid: the mood-shifters, the gloom-bearers. As she once wrote to an aspiring setter, 'Avoid things like death, disease, war and taxes—the subway solver gets enough of that in the rest of the paper.' The Sunday breakfast test envisaged Mum and Dad relaxing on the weekend having a moment of benign fun. To Farrar's way of thinking, these good people didn't need grim topics to accompany their cereal.

Another triumph of the Farrar regime saw a subtle and long-lasting change in the realm of a puzzle's theme. Compilers fresh after Wynne's breakthrough had been prompt to dabble in related entries. Six types of hats, for example, from DEERSTALKER to TAMOSHANTER, might line a typical diagram. This ploy was fair game between the wars—each hat-clue quite bald in its wording, so to speak, forsaking any attempt to camouflage the focal point.

Farrar changed this. She demanded more guile from her contributors. Not that the editor took all the credit for this added curveball. Indeed, she was keen to deflect specific praise onto a setter named Harold T Bers. In any piece you read about this velvet revolution, you will find the queen of *The New York Times* taking great pains to identify Bers as the father of the American theme puzzle.

Bers for his part was straight out of *Mad Men*. A jingle writer, a copy maestro, an amateur actor, the New York native worked for several agencies along Madison Avenue, including McCann-Erickson and Young & Rubicam. A few years on, in 1961, he died of a heart attack at the age of 47, while turning out taglines for Batten, Barton, Durstine & Osborn.

Amid all this campaigning, Bers injected cunning into the American clue, the art of the subliminal you could say. As Don Draper of *Mad Men* suggested, 'If you don't like what's being said, change the conversation.'

Before Bers arrived, a theme puzzle would entail SNAPDRAGON in the northwest quadrant balancing NASTURTIUM in the southeast. What you saw was what you got in many regards. The product was on the shelf and shouting at you in bold Helvetica. Bers however opted for a more covert approach. He preferred the tiptoe game, where the theme would gradually declare itself, the key entries carrying a more internal connection.

For example, in a giant Sunday grid called 'A Few Footnotes', each of the longer answers smuggled in a type of footwear: SANDALWOODS, BICYCLE PUMP, OXFORDSHIRE. The shoe link was there for the solver to spot, relying on the puzzle's title as the single wink to the theme. Perhaps this development seems incidental from a modern perspective, as this brand of wiliness is now default in American puzzles, but the ploy was a coup in its day.

Another example was named 'Full of Flavour'. The theme was a potpourri of tastes delicately infused through the ragout. ROSEMARY LANE was *One of a trio of Hollywood sisters*, BASIL O'CONNOR was *March of Dimes head* (a health program aimed at nursing mothers), and *Admission for all home games?* was SEASON TICKET.

As a creature of Madison Avenue, Harold T Bers quite possibly grabbed his chance at MAKING A MINT (*Turning in big profits—slang*). Be that as it may, the adman's rebellion as a puzzle-maker, combined with the editorial pizzazz of Margaret Petherbridge Farrar, have lent extra tang to an American solver's diet ever since.

1961

Leads to a point; such seems the purpose of this object (6,9)

Barely four, I could see an owl nesting in my suburb's name, Balgowlah, which made my heart go wow. The word wow was exciting too, a palindrome in league with race car or mega-gem. Even my birth year—1961—could do the same trick the moment you flipped the page.

Now a little older than four, I feel the same joy. The wow of wow and hidden owls has never quit my bloodstream. That mop-headed verbivore of Balgowlah is still alive and thriving in me.

I pity my parents in hindsight. Mum in particular copped the brunt of this craze, her yappy son an alphabetic fountain. My brain devoured knock-knock jokes, limericks, comic strips and puzzle

---

+ The Berlin Wall is erected.
+ Cosmonaut Yuri Gagarin is the first man in space.
+ American troops invade Cuba's Bay of Pigs.
+ The ABC news show *Four Corners* is launched.

New words: identikit, advertorial, biodegradable

magazines. I treated each word as a challenge, a test, seeing if I could find its inner secret, that hidden quirk which made it unique. Somehow the knowledge of good deed doer owning four doubled letters in a row was more fulfilling than helping old ladies across the road. And how cool to realise that lie lay central in believe, and that sneak was a mangle of snake. One word, in fact, was a new door, opening into another way of seeing.

No numberplate was safe. No road sign, brand name, Scrabble rack. Even reading a book became an exercise on two levels: enjoying the story and playing with the writer's words. Dustman, say, was a blend of mad and nuts, two diagnoses my parents obviously feared, until I discovered crosswords. Let me rephrase that: until I was introduced to crosswords. Mum played matchmaker. Her hunch was ulterior. She figured if she schooled me in cryptic clues, maybe she'd be encouraging a new companion in my life—and she was right.

I fell in love at 1-Across. With tricks like puns and anagrams, reversals and spoonerisms, the clues resembled riddles for adults. More and more I noticed people on buses and beaches locked in private devotion. The realisation was giddy. All of a sudden my owl-in-Balgowlah reflex had a future, a place to live, an occupation. Perhaps I could be that person of mystery behind the daily grid.

Looking back, I pity Lindsey Browne now, too. I bombarded the poor sod with puzzle drafts in my late teens. The man was my tutor in an organic version of Open University, marking my submissions and returning them with feedback. With good grace he elevated my gutter humour, sharpened my rebus reflex, fine-tuned my chicanery, ultimately prepared me for the grand debut, in 1983.

I still remember the day—6 August, a crisp winter morning. I was trapped in the tail-end of a communications degree, playing football, pulling beers, writing horror stories, living in a squat with a pinball machine beside my bed. But everything paled the minute I recognised my pattern on the puzzle page. I had to catch the morning bus, along with my breath, for no other reason than to spy on commuters grappling with my logic.

Bylines had not yet been introduced by the *Herald*. (LB was LB due to his moonlighting for a rival paper, *The Daily Telegraph*.) Hence, the '*Herald* Crossword Number 10 065' was anonymous, but mine. It was so mine. How I refrained from telling every stranger on the way to university I still can't figure out. Perhaps it was due to the amateurism of several clues. Try these for size:

Famous basset around one egg type = FRIED
Lustful man inside balsa tyres = SATYR
Irish town heads off mice and ground hogs = OMAGH

Yuk, in a word. These three clues are shockers in any era. As their author I can safely say they are rubbish. Their surface sense is nonexistent, their wordplay naked to a point of indecency. But for every mishap there was a clue I'd condone 30 years later, printed on the same puzzle page. Among them I'd nominate:

Zip through the air? = FLY
Clumsily insures this daily event = SUNRISE
Low automobile shows a football gash = SPORTS CAR

Time has flown, those 30 years zipping as I've been doing the job I love. I've since turned out half a million clues, if my maths is sound—cryptic and quick, themed and general, Across and Down, the general puzzles and the holiday puzzles. I'd like to think my clue-making has improved over that period, losing the surplus words, telling tighter stories and generally avoiding balsa tyres.

More than sources of pleasure, crosswords are also great teachers. Clueing over time allows you to refine your style and shed your rubbish. On some level, my pun clue for PENCIL SHARPENER—with its own semicolon—could actually be referring to the crossword as the object and me as the writer, becoming sharper with each turn: *Leads to a point; such seems the purpose of this object (6,9)*.

Or, then again, revisiting my maiden puzzle and encountering such oafishness as if for the first time, I'm grateful for a bout of 2-Down: *Seaman I wrecked before the loss of memory (7)*.

1962

Hymns? Hims? Bad! Try another way (10)

Len Deighton has only himself to blame. If you write a spy thriller in which the hero agonises over crossword answers amid the general cloak and dagger *and* you refrain from disclosing any clues, then readers will start filling the gaps for you. Or maybe that was the plan. After all, the hero has no name, despite being entrusted with telling the story, dodging the bullets and spending time in a Paris prison cell. The case deals with several eminent British scientists slipping from sight, a baffling matter that no doubt eclipses the niceties of providing a name for the narrator. Either that, or Deighton preferred to retain an air of mystery in his mystery, a-la the shadowy crossword that bobs up in three chapters.

To some degree, the hero of *The Ipcress File* was Deighton himself. 'Was it a depiction of myself?' he wrote in a confessional piece

---

+ Nazi Adolf Eichmann is hanged in Israel.
+ Marilyn Monroe is found dead in Los Angeles.
+ The crown-of-thorns starfish infest the Great Barrier Reef.

New words: auteur, glitch, tokenism

attached to a later edition. 'Well, who else did I have?' Both he and Mr X had spent some years in military service. Both were Londoners trained as illustrators with a penchant for cooking. And both had no clue what they were in for, be it writing a novel or investigating Ipcress. As Deighton admitted, 'Being unaware of what's ahead can be an advantage. It shines a green light for everything from enlisting in the Foreign Legion to getting married.'

The first mention of crosswords occurs midair, heading across the Channel to Paris. To pass the time the nameless man produces the nameless crossword (possibly from *The Statesman*) to cross out ROUNDELAYS and write in RONDOLETTO. Later, after a meal of frozen chicken and *pommes parisiennes*, the solver scraps RONDOLETTO to insert DITHYRAMBS.

Hang on a minute. If this was a cryptic crossword, there is no way that *roundelays*, *rondoletto* and *dithyrambs* could all be eligible for the one slot. While the musical terms each own ten letters, deeper problems exist—namely, semantics and associated word-play. Roundelays are cyclic songs; rondoletto is a symphony's third movement; dithyrambs are passionate Greek hymns. Each has its own musical pigeonhole, just as each term would invite separate manipulations.

Turning investigator for a minute, I'd say Deighton knew loads about MI5 and cadastral maps, plenty about air travel and French cuisine, but not so much about how clues work. Just a hunch. I may be maligning an elderly giant of the espionage genre. But in his tender years, 31 when writing *Ipcress*, Deighton perhaps had enough plot elements to fret over. Odds are the crossword aspect of Mr Anon's life was there as a nod to his intellect, despite the pot-shot guesses betraying otherwise.

What else can I presume, as the novel reneges on the clues? Later in the plot, another unstated clue has the hero vacillating between AWE and EWE. Seriously? Fear and a female sheep have little in common. On the same page is the three-way bet of EAT, SAT and OAT. While the options vary only by their initial, there's a vast difference between them as concepts. One measly clue would clarify what's what, but tellingly the reader is denied that glimpse.

Such an oversight triggered a clue-writing contest on my website. A clue needed crafting to compensate for the Deighton deficit. So it was a ring of mock-spies descended on the chatroom, bearing codenames such as Profumo, Emma Peel, Cone of Silence, The Saint and Double-O. Even Priceless Thief (anagram of *The Ipcress File*) had a burl. Each mystery setter did what Deighton had avoided, conjuring clues for ROUNDELAYS and RONDOLETTO, and that awkward AWE and EWE split.

Many clues were zingers. Mata Hari styled a gem for ROUND-ELAYS: *Broadcasts include uncovered hit songs* (RELAYS around POUND minus the P). While The Man From Unclue (sic) all but snared the prize with a devilish anagram for DITHYRAMBS: *Celebrating ARIAs, ripped shirt. My bad!*.

Ultimately, however, the winning entry was an alternative anagram for the same answer. On paper, the clue reads like a criticism: *Hymns? Hims? Bad! Try another way*. The clue was an elbow nudge aimed at the novelist, the so-called *Hims* responsible for reneging on his *Hymns*, a wry snub for writing a book full of crossword answers yet failing to declare a single clue.

Better still, the clue's creator matched this whole Ipcress impasse. Most weeks my site will run creative brainstorms, asking visitors to adopt suitable disguises to guard against partisan voting, but for this contest I played the lone judge. Naturally, there were high stakes, with a chapter title in *Cluetopia* up for grabs. I was hell-bent on picking the most fitting clue, regardless of its creator. Thus, when I chose Spyship's DITHYRAMBS, I had no idea of the author's identity. As fate would have it, the setter responsible was a newcomer to the website. When I let them know about the win, I learnt his (or her) name was Ulla. That's it—Ulla. No more, no less.

Even now, keeping with Deighton's incognito hero, I have no idea who Ulla might be. The confusion accords with the tale. Congratulations, madam (or sir): your brilliant clue has won a berth in 28-point type. Your anonymity warrants full disclosure, as your clue is a splendid thing. Who knows? Maybe Hodder & Stoughton can consider a few additions in future editions.

1963

Héroine pure? (12)

Thankfully the North Atlantic right whales were quiet in 1963. Not a splash. Not a moan. Not a ripple. Robert Scipion, the Paris journalist assigned to the write about the giants, was bored out of his skull. Even Ernest Hemingway, a writer he'd met, would struggle to write 2000 words about a boat seesawing on the swell, waiting for the world's biggest Godot to surface. At least the big fish in Hemingway's *The Old Man and the Sea* had the decency to turn up.

To ease his boredom, Scipion started drawing squares. He entered letters, wove words, invented clues. The pastime came easily, as the journo was a natural, like a fish out of water. His puns in particular were excellent, impressing the editor at *Le Nouvel Observateur*, who gave the reporter a bonus patch in the paper.

+ JFK is assassinated in Dallas.
+ Martin Luther King has a dream.
+ Lake Burley Griffin fills.

New words: bar code, ZIP code, promo, scam

Friends like Jean-Paul Sartre would hardly have been shocked by the added byline. Scipion was a regular at the Café de Flore, at which a scintillating assembly of minds was led by Sartre in politics and philosophy. Not that Scipion took an active part. He preferred to call himself Aramis, after the musketeer, defending his right to slouch at the table, vowing to be pun-full, poetic and lazy.

Before Scipion appeared, the French crossword was largely a black-and-white affair. In the early postwar period, most of the clues obeyed the dictionary, downright tame compared to the Scipion style. The emperor of the *double entendre* lent colour to the genre. The question marks that riddled his clues went to signal a more oblique approach. Consider this red duo, their humour largely intact despite translation:

Red light? = STALIN (think a leading light of communism)
Cellar full of red? = VEIN

Though my favourite Scipion clue meddles with another colour, a pun that works as well in English as in French: *Héroine pure?*. Straightaway your mind turns to drugs, the prank the setter intended. For the answer's domain is the pinnacle of innocence, with *héroine* in French, as in English, being both smack and a story's lead female. Here, that female is BLANCHENEIGE (as in Blanche-Neige, or Snow White). With clues like that, no wonder France was hooked.

1964

She hasn't made a catch drop a catch (4)

Love is seldom easy. Ask Elspeth Knox. I'm sitting in her Sydney kitchen, sharing a pot of coffee, as she talks about her great escape to Brisbane in 1963. 'I was offered this fabulous job as a social worker attached to the University of Queensland, and I took it.' There is a light shimmer in her eyes as she recalls the episode of half a century ago. The last few years have been tough on the wiry woman. Lately, she's weathered two bouts of severe pneumonia, and a pulmonary embolism for good measure. An oxygen tube attached to her nose is her latest hospital souvenir, but she's still fighting, still regaling her guest with colourful stories.

'I'd been working at the Women's Hospital on Crown Street [in Sydney] for four years, which was very stressful and challenging.

+ Nelson Mandela is given a life sentence for inciting civil unrest.
+ Japan's bullet train zings into action.
+ Dawn Fraser wins her third straight 100-metre freestyle gold at the Tokyo Olympics.

New words: quasar, sitcom, water cannon

I thought, one day when I'm 60 I'll wake up and they'll press a gold watch in my hands and I won't remember what happened in the intervening years.'

It made the idea of campus life in the lower tropics appealing. On top of that, the move north would grant her some extra space from the flurry of various friendships, give her the luxury of distance to help get a bit more perspective. One of these friendships was with a bloke called Lindsey, a journo with *The Sydney Morning Herald* and prolific crossword-maker.

Of course, we've met Lindsey before now. His full name was Lindsey Browne, alias LB of the puzzle page—or Lin, as Elspeth knew him. The pair had met on a Double Bay tennis court in 1961. ('I'd been roped in as they needed an extra woman.') Lindsey was badly hungover from covering the federal election the night before. Indeed, that's how Elspeth retrieves any date from her past: as the sister of Sir William Knox, once a prominent Liberal politician in Queensland, she can recall the nearest election of any given period, working to and fro from there.

Lin was on his own by the time of the tennis match. Despite a mercy flight to Sweden to seek help from an oncology expert, the man had lost his great love, Nancy Moore, to a brain tumour in 1959. The tragedy turned Lindsey into a workaholic, squeezing shifts at a foundry in Willoughby between journo rounds and the crossword load. Hard work was how he kept his four children fed, though the house felt empty without an adult companion.

Elspeth's eyes are glowing as she recounts the raffish charms of LB. In spare moments, which were few, Lin would call her at home or the Women's Hospital, trying to find a window to catch up with this feisty social worker some years his junior. 'It was getting too much,' says Elspeth, drawing deeply on her airtank. 'I needed some space.'

So she flew the coop. Gave notice at the hospital and packed her bags in December 1963. The Brisbane job was perfect, not least the timing. But Lin was a stubborn bugger. You get that impression when you see his copper-press portrait on the wall above us. Crafted by a fan, the tribute depicts a defiant-looking gent with a cartridge pen as walking stick, standing on a crossword grid much as a captain commands the bridge. *Man seeking to confuse horribly*, reads the caption at his feet.

'Lin was always persistent,' says Elspeth, with a girlish wag of her head. 'One day he rang me when I was in Brisbane and told me to buy *The Bully*. He told me to do the crossword for that week.'

The Bully is a nickname for *The Bulletin*, a magazine that has also cropped up already in our clue quest. Despite making crosswords for the *Herald* and the *Telegraph* almost every day, Lindsey had chosen *The Bulletin* because the weekly was national: he knew his handiwork would reach his beloved fugitive.

'I remember solving it,' the runaway recounts. 'At first I didn't know what he was going on about, but then I saw the pattern in the right-hand column.'

Without any warning to the general solver, the lovesick Lindsey had buried a serenade into his solution. Reading down the grid's eastern edge, clusters of letters at the tail of each answer, was a plea from the heart:

CALENDAR

STARTLING

ASTROPHELS

MORPETH

PECCAVI

MISS

BAYOU

CARUSO

The clue for MISS underlined the setter's solitude, a wistful double-meaning: *She hasn't made a catch drop a catch (4)*.

Elspeth unpicked the message—'Darling Elspeth, I miss you so'—and still didn't budge from Brizzie. Not immediately. Why would she? The uni job was a breath of fresh air, and she wasn't quite ready to be the automatic stepmother of four young children. But half a bottle of single malt with an old girlfriend while debating the pros and cons of a lovable man called Lin saw her make a late-night phone call.

'Another coffee?' she asks.

I pass. There's still some in the plunger.

'What about some tea?'

I'm glancing at the dictionaries still stacked on the kitchen shelves, where most homes would carry cookbooks.

Elspeth laughs. 'Tea reminds me of our honeymoon story. We went to Tasmania, a driving holiday. And one day we were passing a small café beside the road when Lin said 'overshined seats'. When I asked him what he was referring to, he pointed to the sign outside the door that said Devonshire Teas. He never stopped playing with words.'

The 'he' is LB, the man captured in copper above us. Elspeth studies the caricature for a moment before exhaling a sigh of borrowed air. She misses Lin, she says. The lovable curmudgeon died in 2003, after spending 37 lively years, and fathering three children, with the woman who nearly got away.

1965

Exhausted at reports (9)

When you write a book like this, your social life tends to dry up. Every day there's a new excuse to stay at the desk, on the web, in the library. The price you pay for this kind of project is exile.

Friends stopped asking me out. My wife watched season 5 of *West Wing* before I realised I was stranded in season 4. Now and then I felt like Rip Van Winkle after a power nap, emerging from my office with three-day stubble and wondering what breed of psychopath had kidnapped my family.

So when a mate rang mid-manuscript to say let's drink, I had to agree. Science tells us there's only so much diligence in the human system. We started slowly, as George and I often do, two kids playing with matches in a beer garden. Pretty soon the spree was ablaze. We climbed up narrow stairs and somehow drank below street level.

+ 3500 US marines land in South Vietnam.
+ Nicolae Ceaucescu rises to power in Romania.
+ Roma Mitchell becomes Australia's first female judge.

New words: kaftan, meltdown, unleaded

We toasted absent friends in a bar where ice hockey beamed from a no-volume television. We ate noodles down an alley and found ourselves in a car park where a barman served Stellas from inside a shipping container. Eventually, we ended up with whiskies in an Irish bar with harps and Cabbage Patch Leprechauns bolted to the walls. James Joyce and Samuel Beckett were also there, riveted to a column. They stared like gunslingers at the posse of writers opposite.

'Flann O'Brien,' George read aloud. 'Sounds like a pastry chef.'

I got to my feet to stare at the photo, going nose-to-nose with Flann the man. 'I'm onto you, you crafty bastard.'

George was disappointed. 'He can't hear you.'

'Wasn't even his real name,' I rambled, the alcohol making my research bubble to the surface. 'He was actually born Brian O'Whatsit. Man loved a drink.'

'Let's text him. Have him join us.'

'Changed his name again, he did. Tried out Myles na gCopaleen. How's that name strike you? That's what he chose to write a column with.'

'Perfect,' thought George. 'Given where he is.'

'The what?'

'Nailed to a column. Being a columnist.'

Of course I get it now, but I didn't get it then. Instead I said the Gaelic ballocks meant Myles of the Little Horses, but George wasn't listening anymore. He was back at the bar, telling the Belfast backpacker she had a fetching lilt, and asking if she knew why river dancers didn't move their arms.

I drained my glass and eyeballed the author. 'I'm onto you, you little brimming jug, you.'

Crúiscín Lán (Little brimming jug) was the name of the weekly column overflowing with sozzled brio that O'Brien wrote for *The Irish Times*. For more than 20 years he served up tales of wayward sprees in Dublin, the dives and denizens of downtown badlands before ice-hockey television was invented.

'I know your game, Brian of the Shetland feckin' ponies. Changing your name to protect your skinny arse, am I wrong? Making money for your ten stranded siblings by day and writing unbridled by night. Drinking and scribbling. Your comical novels. Those free-wheeling diatribes. The odd serenade to locomotives. Not forgetting your darkest confession, hey? You know what I'm talking about. Don't act all noble-faced with me, you felon. I'll give you a clue if you can't remember: crosswords.'

'Megan's starting to worry about you,' said George, two whiskies in his paw.

'Who's Megan?'

'Not *Mee*-gan—Megan. The Irish way.'

'Listen, you know what this bloke Myles did?'

George frowned. 'You getting enough sleep?'

'This little brown jug was nothing but a scam artist, saying as much in his column. One time he rode his bicycle down to *The Irish Times*, three in the morning we're talking here, just to get his hands on the early edition.'

'Coincidence,' said George, consulting the shamrock above the bar. 'It's almost three in the morning now.'

'Getting home, he dragged out a dictionary, his almanacs, whatever it took. He'd smoke a pipe, kick the dog, stare at the wall . . .'

'What say we make this drink our last?'

'He set aside the entire morning to solve the crossword. And when it was cracked, you know what he did?'

George's face was the type you give to old men screaming at pigeons.

'He shaved, didn't he?' I turned to Flann, who remained tight-lipped. 'You shaved, didn't you? You headed down to the golf club, all innocence and purity, and sat at the members' bar, waiting for your mate to drift over.'

George sucked an ice cube. 'I've got a staff meeting, first thing.'

'Guess what the topic was?' I said.

'I don't know,' said George.

'The *Times* crossword. *The Irish Times*. How hard it was. That's all his golfing pal could say, only for this little pastry chef to play all promiscuous with the truth, say he didn't do it any more as the clues were too easy.'

'I'll get Megan to call us a cab.'

'But the friend turned sceptical. Of course he did. Wouldn't you? He fished the paper from his jacket and read a clue aloud. That was the game, the great con, with Myles or Brian or Flann acting dumb, as if he'd never clapped eyes on the puzzle, shameless as he was.'

George was moving his tumbler on the table, turning it like a steering wheel.

'Do me a favour, mate. One favour is all I'm asking.'

'Me?' asked George.

'You say, "*Exhausted at reports*". Say it for me. That was the clue his friend at the golf club mentioned. Which is shite, when you think about it, because it's only half a clue.'

'That's what I was thinking. Not the full quid.'

'No definition, is there? Just a tarted-up anagram, really. But say it. Pretend to be my drinking mate at the golf club and call my bluff.'

'Say what?'

'*Exhausted at reports.*'

'*Exhausted at reports*,' said George.

'More like a question. Like you don't believe I could be such a Jedi of *The Times*.'

'*Exhausted at reports?*'

'PROSTRATE,' I managed to utter, if only just, landing face-first on the emerald carpet. Flann O'Brien, I swear, never batted an eyelid.

1966

I am in the plot, that's clear (5)

Genealogists come to blows with phrases like 'father of the crossword' and 'father of the cryptic' and 'father of the modern cryptic crossword'. This last epithet sits most comfortably on the shoulders of Derrick Macnutt, alias Ximenes, owing to the rulebook he drafted. When I say rule, I really mean principle, as that's the word Macnutt preferred.

Macnutt was the heir of Torquemada, another feasible father of the cryptic. You may recall those prototype clues that Torquemada (whose real name was Edward Powys Mathers) pioneered in *The Observer* 40 years earlier, those early experiments locked inside the giant weevil. The alias Torquemada, of course, was borrowed from a sadistic cardinal from the Spanish Inquisition, and Macnutt adopted his colleague in torment, Francisco Ximénes de Cisneros.

+ Decimal currency is introduced in Australia.
+ Indira Gandhi is sworn in as India's PM.
+ Botswana achieves independence.

New words: kung-fu, centrefold, Jacuzzi

But getting back to that rulebook—sorry, those principles—they appeared in official fashion in 1966, as the gist of *Ximenes on the Art of the Crossword*, a momentous book that became a cruciverbal Bible. Red in colour, the book had all the Maoist potential to create a revolution, as came to pass in the decades that followed. Thanks to the musings of this lecturer in classics, the crossword campus is divided into two schools: the Ximenean and the libertarian (also known as the Araucarian). To understand the schism, we need to understand the nature of wordplay, and how it sits inside a clue.

Put simply, as we've seen, a cryptic clue fuses two parts: the definition and the wordplay, or vice versa. Both pieces need to be present for the clue to work. As for the wordplay, this can take multiple forms, be that anagram or reversal, homophone or charade, or maybe an amalgam of several. The key roles entrusted in this element are twofold: to tell a persuasive tale, and to deliver the answer. All compilers subscribe to that plan, though some (the Ximeneans) subscribe more bindingly than others (the libertarians).

Let's focus on a clue that Ximenes himself handpicked from his own back catalogue: *I am in the plot—that's clear (5)*. The answer is plain to anyone raised on a cryptic diet. That is, the answer is PLAIN full stop. The clue relies on the container recipe, also known as the sandwich formula, where X goes in YY to make YXY. Or, in this case, I perches in PLAN (*plot*) to render PLAIN (*clear*).

For me, the clue is hunky-dory. Perhaps I'd pare the needless *the*, as excess words are undesirable in the clue racket, but the overall deception works. It's not brilliant—but it works for me, a card-carrying member of the libertarian league.

By contrast, a man like Macnutt would gnash his teeth at this clue, despite the phrasing being drafted by his younger self. In seven short words it symbolises the rift between the looser Araucaria mob and the precisionists. (I thought I'd made up the word *precisionists*, but the spellchecker didn't blink.) The crux, as expressed by an earlier setter, Alistair Ferguson Ritchie, is that 'you need not mean what you say, but you must say what you mean.' The surface meaning of the clue, the so-called tale it tells, is believable and succinct. Read it again: *I am in the plot, that's clear.* But if we examine the clue's elements in a harsher light, as Ximenes does in his little red book, we find a technical flaw.

Warning: you'll need to minimise all distractions for a moment, as this next paragraph gets down and dirty with the nitty-gritty of clue-mechanics. If you bought *Cluetopia* for a few laughs, rather than the lab analysis of dual-acting grammar, then make for the chapter's punchline, and hasten on to 1967. No harm, no foul. Though if deep geekery is your kind of pleasure, then continue with caution. Bear in mind the clue under the microscope: *I am in the plot, that's clear.*

As Ximenes argues, the clue tells a sound story. Yet when we view the clue as command—the how-to manual that allows a solver to build the answer—there is a breakdown. To quote the X-man, 'we really mean I [the letter] *is* in the plot, so we aren't saying what we mean.' The clue's *I*, in other words, is treated as a pronoun in the clue's *story*—given the verb form of *I am*—yet is treated as a letter in the container formula, which demands the verb form *I is*.

As a narrative, then, the clue is seaworthy. In contrast, the clue as instruction owns a hairline crack. To Ximenean eyes a fairer casting of the wordplay would be *I must be part of plot* or *I can be part of plot*. Both these versions work as a grammatical unit, and as a persuasive tale. They say what they mean twice, both as a manipulation device, and as a surface narrative.

As petty as this detour may seem, the sticking point was a big issue in the evolution of crossword-making. Supreme clues, from the purist angle, had to function on both levels, telling you a story as well as imparting the wordplay, both impeccably. Our search for clues was obliged to take this sojourn, with 1966 the year the line was drawn. Pretty much the moment the manifesto hit the shelves, every setter had to decide on which side of the line they belonged.

The gospel according to Ximenes juggles other hot potatoes in its 170 pages, yet this notion of dual-acting grammar is the keystone. Can *earthquake*, say, fairly lead to HEART, the anagram, or should that be *quaking earth*? Which anagram fragment is flawless in both modes? For what it's worth, I'm happy with either option—both versions imply a shifting of the correct letters—though the X-gang would only consider the second for reasons of unimpeachable grammar.

Gladly, both camps can agree to disagree. On paper, we're not so different. Libertarians may well take greater latitude, but in the end both camps love to meddle with words, suggesting we have more in common than not. Solvers likewise revel in wordplay, whichever school of setter they select. Thanks to a milestone paperback, those schools in 1966 were given labels, the contrasts increasingly plain for insiders and outsiders to see.

1967

In difficult times a match calls for science (11)

Alfred Bately was packing up his chalk for the last time. After years of teaching maths to spotty boys in Essex, the moment had come to leave the school for good. Enough Venn diagrams. So long, long division.

On the quiet, the other staff had tried to settle on a gift. They'd pondered the man's hobbies. Did he golf? Garden? Would he try either, now that he had the extra time? Might he travel? Play guitar? Then inspiration had struck. Their colleague was a crossword whiz, solving *The Times* as if the clues were basic algebra problems. Every day Alfred conquered the puzzle in the staffroom as others lost their heads around him. If the kitty couldn't spring a watch, then what about a conspiracy as a farewell present?

+ Harold Holt vanishes.
+ The first heart transplant is performed.
+ *Born Free* tops the box-office charts.

New words: groupie, cursor, dork, gofer

A few months before Alfred's final day, a staff member had contacted the crossword editor at *The Times*. Nobody expected miracles. Maybe just a clue, a few answers hinting at the feature's biggest fan. The best part was that Alfred would never suspect a thing. He'd sit in his favourite chair at lunchtime, working his methodical way through the puzzle, when suddenly the tribute would whop him on the head. The gotcha moment was sure to make his day—his last at Westcliff High.

The editor had rained on the parade, however, explaining how *The Times* crossword was not a place for messages. 'Try the personal column,' was the likely suggestion. And there the matter had stalled, obliging Alfred's cohorts to price a range of wristwatches.

With Plan A scotched, and Plan B on the drawing board, the day was no doubt shaping as an anticlimax. Alfred himself packed up his set squares and left a few days short of the scheduled date anyway. The party seemed pooped before a balloon could be blown, leaving the usual knot of Westcliff teachers (minus Alfred) to convene at lunchtime to tackle *The Times*.

An early warning of something extraordinary was found at 1-Across: *Roman vale booked . . . (7)*. The answer is GOODBYE, translating *vale*, the Latin for farewell. The *booked* element of the clue bled into 5-Across, which mentioned a carpenter, namely MR CHIPS, a book by James Hilton. The 1934 novel follows a beloved teacher of Latin retiring from a boys' school.

Despite the editor's rebuff, the *vale* was a veiled homage to Alfred Bately. So too were the four smallest answers in the grid: ALF and RED, plus BAT (*Blind cricketer?*) and ELY. The entire puzzle was littered with accolades. There was even EDUCATIONAL: *A variety of aid—not a clue?*. And a glimpse of the blackboard jungle: *One subject school?* (GRAMMAR).

But where the hell was Alfred the man? Did he do *The Times* in his new downtime? A copy was fetched and sent his way posthaste.

How wonderful to think this beloved teacher could inspire the paper's first possible Nina, or secret message.

Before I reveal the final gotcha, I should explain Nina, a term belonging to a second heart-warming story, a journey back in time to the late 1950s, when a cartoonist named Al Hirschfeld ruled America's glitterati. In a subtle way, to make the grade on Broadway or Tinseltown, you needed to be the subject of a Hirschfeld portrait. To have your features depicted by his concise and fluid lines was deemed a rite of passage, a standard of success. Hirschfeld worked for *The New York Times*, and his portfolio included every jazz great under the sun, along with Cole Porter and Papa Hemingway. He later penned The Beatles, Dylan, Jagger, Springsteen. Lean and eloquent, the caricatures were doubly notable for Hirschfeld's ability to insinuate a signature into their lineaments: the upper-case letters of *NINA*, honouring Hirschfeld's only daughter, born the year World War II ended.

You had to look closely to find the treasure. The name might be laced within a shawl, planted in a window box, etched in an earring, arrayed inside a hairdo. The joy for Al rested in the embedding, until he realised that viewers were sifting his artwork more for hidey-holes than for appreciating the execution. Thence, he gave the custom a miss. For a time.

Crossword historian Peter Biddlecombe believes that the incognito theme devoted to Alfred Bately was *The Times*'s first Nina, and I'm inclined to trust his delving. As for the impact the gesture had on the feted retiree, we can only guess. One thing we do know, however, is the puzzle combined the teacher's two passions, namely anagrams and 11-Across. For, unlike Mr Chips, Mr Bately taught MATHEMATICS—*In difficult times a match calls for science.*

1968

Successor to The Sound of Music *(4)*

For the tactic to work I needed to shout at full pitch. So I filled my lungs and bellowed, 'HEDONISM!' across the foyer. The silver-haired man looked around. His entourage turned my way as well. As did a chaperone, in combat stance. But the gentleman's smile was the magic ingredient. Suddenly, a path opened in the tumult, my invitation to stroll into the company of Stephen Sondheim. We went to shake hands before the composer remembered his right wrist was broken, an injury sustained from a recent fall at home. In the end we settled for a fist bump, gangsta-style, me and the S-dawg, homies from the west side.

'You must do crosswords,' he figured, harking back to the anagram I'd yelled, the nerd's equivalent of Open Sesame.

+ Czechoslovakia breaks Communist shackles.
+ Lionel Rose beats Masahiko 'Fighting' Harada.
+ The Tet Offensive begins in South Vietnam.

New words: aerobics, pager, paparazzo, unisex

'And so do you. Or did. Make them, I mean.' I was nervous. In my pocket was a grainy printout from 1968, Sondheim's debut crossword. 'Your cryptics, I'm talking about.'

The tumult had shushed by this stage. Even the minder was listening, as few people in the theatre ever guessed the lyricist behind *West Side Story*, the creator of *Sweeney Todd* and *Into the Woods*, once made crosswords. For two years he did. Cryptic—they had to be cryptic.

Stephen made his penchant clear in a feature accompanying his maiden puzzle: 'The [crossword] familiar to most New Yorkers is a mechanical test of tirelessly esoteric knowledge. *Brazilian potter's wheel* or *East Indian betel* are typical definitions, sending you either to *Webster's New International*, or to sleep.'

Gloria Steinem, the era's leading feminist, had been writing for the *New York* magazine, and she knew her musical friend had a bent for games. Would he consider a challenge to distinguish *New York* from the pack? Sondheim had leapt. He loved the 'bafflement' of the British-style clues, and the gig provided him with a chance to play with words in another way.

Good as his lament, not a single lousy betel nut appeared in the librettist's first hit-out. Instead, a melody pervaded the clues. One double-meaning seemed a recap of his collaboration with Leonard Bernstein: *Write for someone else with spirit* (GHOST), while another could serve as an accolade for the imminent *Company*, the setter's own musical on the horizon: *Successor to* The Sound of Music (HEIR, which sounds like *air*).

By celebrity alone, Sondheim was the man to introduce the cryptic to mainstream America. Others might argue Frank Lewis to be that pioneer, a wartime code-breaker we'll meet around the corner, a man whose playful clues ran in *The Nation* prior to the Sondheim series, but don't discount the sizzle of a famous name, be that on Broadway or a puzzle page.

Chances are that Sondheim's two-year stint at *New York* influenced the future duet of Emily Cox and Henry Rathvon, two fine successors in America's cryptic relay. As a gift of sorts, standing in reach of Stephen Sondheim, I quoted a clue from this pair that praises the lyricist's name: *Sondheim's ultimate song!*. The clue type is dubbed an &lit, or a literal clue, in which the wordplay acts as the definition. To make MARIA from *West Side Story* you combine Sondheim's ultimate letter (M) with ARIA.

Meanwhile, back in the foyer, the night was getting on. The show was over—*A Funny Thing Happened on the Way to the Forum*—and the Princess Theatre was winding down for the night. My audience with Sondheim was borrowed. I rummaged in my jacket for his crossword for the man to sign, the favour feeling more awkward by the minute. The icon was 82, with one arm, jetlagged from his flight, the Roman carry-on, and probably done with crossword trivia too, let alone fawning word nerds who yelled anagrams across a crowded room. Besides, if the minder didn't bar my request for an autograph, Stephen himself was hardly eligible for the task. His southpaw squiggle would only spur jealous musical friends to accuse me of forgery. Forget it. I plumped for my other pocket.

'Here,' I said, handing over a copy of *Puzzled*, my first crossword escapade. 'I want you to have this.'

Stephen glanced at the cover's chequered pattern. He noticed the photo of me on the inside flap, which caused a double take. 'So you're a composer?' he asked.

No, I told him. I make crosswords. 'You, sir, are a composer.'

1969

For effeminate lays? (4,4)

Tom Driberg lived large before the phrase was invented. He counted Evelyn Waugh among his friends, along with the poets WH Auden and Allen Ginsberg. He was on drinking terms with Lord Beaverbrook, the first baron of Fleet Street, and waltzed around Knightsbridge with mystic Aleister Crowley and critic Edith Sitwell. Over the years he was close to Gore Vidal, Mick Jagger, the Kray gangsters, Prime Minister Harold Wilson—and a nameless Norwegian sailor whom Tom fellated in Edinburgh.

A constable caught the pair *in flagrante delicto*. The liaison's setting was an air-raid shelter, the seaman in full repose as Tom rummaged between his legs.

'Och, ye bastards,' yelled PC George Crowford. 'Ye dirty pair o' whoors . . .'

+ Neil Armstrong and Buzz Aldrin walk on the Moon.
+ Woodstock concert is held in New York State (as *Hair* is staged in Sydney).
+ Rupert Murdoch buys the UK's *News of the World*.

New words: pixel, jet lag, hands-on, ego-trip

Homosexuality was an offence in 1943, putting the issue of public decorum aside. The cop kept his torch fixed on the men while fishing for his manacles. But Driberg had a better idea. He volunteered his name as William Hickey, being partly true, as that was the alias he assumed to write a gossip column in London. He also said he was a serving MP, which was 100 per cent the case. Indeed, that mantle accounted for his Scottish jaunt, as journalist Francis Wheen explains in the uproarious biography, *The Soul of Indiscretion*. As the sitting member of Maldon, Driberg was there in the Scottish capital to support an associate in a coming by-election.

The Scandinavian was last seen running into the night, while Tom, thanks to clout and quick talking, defused all charges. He also showed some politesse. From London he sent PC Crowford a collection of William Blake poems, plus six guineas' worth of book tokens. Such was the Driberg charm, and paradox—a model of fine breeding with a lust for rough trade.

The Edinburgh episode was not in isolation. Naked in his feelings as much as his nocturnal life, Driberg was dubbed the queers' Casanova, a pouncer in the alley slang, a reprobate. At his death, in 1976, keeling sideways in a taxi, the columnist-cum-polly was the first individual to be cited as homosexual by *The Times*, an organ for whom he freelanced.

Yet the periodical to win him greater notoriety was *Private Eye*. In 1969, hard up for cash, Driberg was on retainer with the satirical biweekly, relaying gossip from the underpasses and the House of Commons. The service, however, proved erratic, as recounted by his editor, the same Francis Wheen. Soon the retainer was ditched for a fiver-per-rumour system. But Driberg needed something more bankable. Living large came at a cost. As Wheen remembers, '[Tom] proposed that he should compose a regular prize crossword whose main characteristics would be extreme difficulty and moderate obscenity.'

The magazine capitulated. The puzzles appeared in 1969, under the alias of Tiresias. According to legend, Tiresias was the blind transsexual Theban with the gift of prophecy. You can meet the 'old man with wrinkled female breasts' in *The Waste Land* by TS Eliot, another passing acquaintance in the Driberg social circle.

To underline his intentions, the new setter loaded his maiden challenge with smut. The diagram included ERECTION, PROSTITUTE and PERCY, the last the Australian slang for penis. Before too long the crosswords had garnered a reputation for being both slipery and obscene. To a casual observer his clues seemed orthodox cryptics, yet orthodoxy was hardly the Driberg way. *A nude poet*, for example, was how he denoted his dear mate AUDEN, despite the lack of anagram signpost. What matter? The puzzle revelled in naughtiness. Driberg spent his life testing the boundaries, and his crosswording merely upheld that habit. In the same AUDEN puzzle, the filth flowed:

Surely one doesn't store haemorrhoids? = STOCK PILES
For manual rubbings, not the scrotal therapy you hear of = HEELBALLS
Seamen mop up anal infusions = ENEMAS
Sounds as if you must look behind for this personal lubricant = SEBUM
Run amok with order to strip = UNROBE
For effeminate lays? = CAMP BEDS

From 1969 until that fatal taxi ride, the Driberg canon was brazen. Even though the man's output was not the first collection of filthy puzzles around the traps, its sequence was prominent. Proof was delivered every fortnight, as readers jammed the *Private Eye* mailbag in hope of the £2 prize. Winners were announced in each issue, including Mrs Rosalind Runcie, who conquered the puzzle we've just sampled. The name was familiar to anyone who followed the society pages, not least Tom Driberg, as Mrs Runcie happened to be the wife of the Bishop of St Albans. An outrage to most, though not to Tiresias: Britain's first official homosexual was shockproof.

1970

Fejtsünk alumíniumot! (6-7,18)

Hungary was the salami in the sandwich for most of last century. Early in World War II, the landlocked nation joined the Nazi push to conquer communist Russia, but a series of heavy losses convinced the prime minister Miklós Kállay to negotiate an armistice with the Allies. Hitler went ballistic. He sent troops over the border, reducing Hungary to a German protectorate, yet the arrangement was short-lived. Soon the Nazi empire fell to the Allies, creating a vacuum in Budapest which the Russian army quickly filled.

The puppet in charge of the new regime was a former grocer's boy from Ada, now in Serbia. His name was Mátyás Rákosi, better known as Stalin's disciple, a tyrant to his bootstraps, as evidenced by the secret trains that freighted dissidents to Siberia, by the subversion of the courts—even by the crosswords.

+ West Gate Bridge collapses.
+ The Beatles dissolve.
+ Stricken Apollo 13 is safely returned to Earth.

New words: Exocet, epidural, ecofreak

The rules for correct puzzle-making in Hungary were simple and unwritten. No abbreviations relating to fascism were allowed. No mention of religions. No use of leaders' names—from either Hungary or Mother Russia—unless the leader had moved on to the great Kremlin in the sky, in which case he could be included, but only in glowing terms. Hungarian crosswords came with fancy titles too, many yelling loyalty to state ideals. Try these for size: 'Let's Get to Know Tikhonov' (a Soviet Army hero), 'The Machinations of Imperialism' and 'Mátyás Rákosi: The Wise Leader of Hungarian Workers'. You get the picture.

Fun was in short supply, like meat and vegetables in the market-place. Even when Rákosi was ousted by the 1956 revolution, the new Hungary succumbed to a milder strain of Russian rule (or *goulash communism*, as it was known). Yet still the crossword-makers of Budapest were denied free expression.

That said, the odd breach did occur, like when the daily paper *Népszabadság* (The People's Freedom) ran a swastika in its pattern. The matter was reported by 'watchful comrades'—as snitches were dubbed—obliging the minister of the Interior to investigate. No charges were laid. However, the greatest outrage took place in August 1970. The alleged culprit was László Tiszai, the editor-in-chief of Hungary's favourite crossword magazine, *Füles*. Rain or shine, every issue of *Füles* carried a donkey on the cover, the magazine's totem. But on this bizarre day in crossword history, snitches wondered who was attempting to make an ass out of whom.

The puzzle in the spotlight was a government commission. The compiler was obliged by dint of state powers to plug the Hungarian-Soviet aluminium treaty, a trade deal displaying every symptom of colonial pillage. Russia was an overlord seldom given to compromise, as implied by the propaganda demand. In Hungarian, the trade deal was called the Magyar-szovjet Alumíniumegyezmény, and all 31 letters were poised to occupy two edges of the grid. The puzzle's title was 'Fejtsünk Alumíniumot!', a difficult phrase to render into English, even for my valued insider, Valéria Szeli, the head of reference at Hungary's national library. On one level the phrase can mean 'mining aluminium'; on another, 'let us solve aluminium'. But the real scandal was lurking deeper in the magazine.

You see, in Hungary, when a solver confronts an unbarred diagram, the crossword's title plays a pivotal role. Often this banner will double as a clue, a nudge towards the puzzle's general theme. Budapest biros slowly worked out the 31-letter phrase, despite its lack of listed clue, using the letters of transecting entries to creep closer to the trade deal. Yet four unchecked squares remained, requiring a modicum of intuition to reveal the final answer. When every T was crossed, solvers then dived down the back of the magazine to see whether their guesswork had prevailed.

Maybe it did, though I'll guarantee nobody considered that MAGYAR-SZOVJET ALUMINIUMEGYEZMENY could be construed instead as MASZAR-SZOVJET ALUMINIUMEGYEZMENY. Notice the difference? It's only slight. The first word, MAGYAR, meaning Hungarian, has altered into MASZAR, which seems small beer to a foreigner, but the difference is dynamite to a native speaker.

A typo in the solution grid? That was the editor's plea, as the head of *Füles* was dragged before the politburo to face charges of sedition. Not that any Siberian train was summoned, since the goulash regime failed to carry enough iron in its fist, but László Tiszai must have spent the best part of a day explaining to his masters why an aluminium treaty with Russia was identified as *Ma* (today) *szar* (shit).

1971

Near-saint heading without direction and confused (6)

haturvasi was on his honeymoon when his eyes fell upon tempta-
tion, a grid in *The Hindustan Times*. The adjacent caption read,
'Daily Crossword Puzzle No. 1'. 'My bride excused my engagement with the puzzle for a few minutes,' Chaturvasi remembers
with fondness. The day was 15 February 1971, an auspicious date
on the calendar. Not only were two newlyweds footloose on the
Malabar coast, but one of the nation's largest papers had launched
a crossword puzzle. Gita understood her husband's diverted gaze.
The moment provided further evidence that he'd married the right
woman—gorgeous *and* understanding.

UNDERSTANDABLE, in fact, was the maiden answer: *Easy to
comprehend, and provides a bundle and a rest.* The clue type was an

---

+ Neville Bonner becomes the first Indigenous parliamentarian.
+ The Doors' singer Jim Morrison is found dead in a French bathtub.
+ VCRs go on sale.

New words: chairperson, passive smoking, gonzo

anagram, asking for ABUNDLEANDAREST (the fodder in crossword-talk) to be rearranged. A sly clue, too, as it wasn't understandable if you lacked the rudiments of a cryptic education. Growing up in Madras, now Chennai, Chaturvasi had received that schooling from an older cousin while dangling in midair. He and a bunch of other children were sitting on a narrow plank suspended high on a colon-naded veranda. 'We were escaping the heat,' he explains. 'My oldest cousin mentioned a clue for ACID. He told us how it worked. Yes, even though it was years ago, I still remember the wordplay—*Bitter account I had* (or AC plus I'D). That piqued my interest.'

Alas, Chaturvasi could not share the pastime with his cousin for long. The young man joined the air force, 'and soon after that visit he became a martyr in a border war with China.' You might see Chaturvasi's crossword passion as a silent tribute to that loss, as, even into adulthood, he shows no signs of relinquishing his devotion.

Meanwhile, back in the honeymoon suite, Chatuvarsi suspected the debut *Hindu* puzzle to be home-grown product. *The Times of India* ran the *Daily Mail* puzzles from Britain, yet this new puzzle murmured home. Aside from a cricket reference—that other British legacy—there was a salute to India's greatest hero:

Near-saint heading without direction and confused (6).

Another anagram, but this time with a twist. Subtract a direction (E) from HEADING, then jumble the fodder, and GANDHI will surface. This crossword had to be locally crafted.

The groom was right. The setter was Admiral Ram Dass Katari, the first naval chief of India. Retired from active duty, the Hyderabad philologist didn't hesitate to become the paper's sole puzzle-maker, despite having been nothing but a keen solver until then. What was the fuss? He knew the language and the architecture from a lifelong *Times* habit. Besides, navigating a submarine through the

Atlantic was far more difficult than coordinating letters in a box. Or so the veteran believed, aged 60 by then but rejuvenated by his fresh calling. Yet in those early days, practising with pencils and blank pages, making word lists and countless false starts, Katari soon found himself at sea.

In the end a strategic mind won out, the admiral handwriting over 1400 crosswords. For many years he was the paper's single setter—anonymous, inventive, tireless. Sadly, however, the incipient signs of motor neurone disease plagued his once-steady hand, obliging him to pass command to Commodore Bernard Warner, an expat officer serving with the Indian navy.

This naval club persisted on the puzzle page for some years, eventually gatecrashed by some dazzling civilians in the 1980s. Among the non-naval arrivals was Chaturvasi himself. The young journalist and editor was born to be a puzzle-maker, which accounts for the alias he chose. You see, Chaturvasi was not the groom's real name. The camouflage appeared in 2009, when *The Hindu* introduced bylines for all its setters. Coimbatore Gopal Rishikesh—better known as Rishi to his friends—devised the colloquial term for one who dwells in a grid—Chatuvarsi—though physically he lives in Chennai, where the crossword romance began, on an airborne plank.

1972

(45)

Three quid was a fair amount back in 1972. You'd hope so, as that was the potential reward for solving a Jac crossword in *The Spectator*. Each week there was a different mountain to climb. Once or twice nobody managed it, not a soul across Britain, causing the £3 to double for the next week's so-called Jac-pot. Themes were eclectic—a polite way of saying haphazard and bloody hard. Jac was not a setter for the meek. During the man's ten-year tenure, in which he single-handedly created more than 500 puzzles, he asked solvers to inscribe Leinster counties and Japanese divinities of happiness. To boost the degree of difficulty, the challenge was often double-edged. First a solver had to deduce the theme, and then determine what subjects within that theme had been recruited, despite the absence of relevant clues. These might be Shakespearean lords, French wines

---

+ The Watergate scandal is uncovered.
+ A siege occurs at the Munich Olympics.
+ Gough Whitlam is sworn in as prime minister.

New words: detox, gentrify, flexitime

or a Horace quote in Latin. Like I say, eclectic. And for all your Herculean labours (another theme) you stood to win £3.

But the joy for many lay in the treachery. Jac was the genius of the barred diagram. He pioneered the 14 by 14 frame that still distinguishes the *Spectator* series today. His clues were crisp, scholarly and misleading—ANTIOCH, for one, merited the clue *Detour to Chinatown*. Meanwhile, the rarities that marbled his grids, such as KILLICK (a small anchor) and MULUNGU (the divine creator in Bantu), received fair and lucid treatment.

Jac stood for John Adelmare Caesar, a private man who lived in Weymouth, Dorset, on England's south coast. In 1971, to secure his post at *The Spectator*, he sent the magazine a stream of unsolicited puzzles good enough to catch the editor's eye. The man's house, according to one acolyte who made the pilgrimage, was a puzzle museum, half-crumbling in the salty air. Grids and graph sheets littered every available surface. Upstairs, the office symbolised the retired town clerk's intellect, a crammed space groaning with reference works. Bear in mind his 500 themes preceded modern search tools; everything he meshed he found buried in his tomes. Including, perhaps, his most ambitious stunt, in 1972, a puzzle he labelled 'Breathless'.

The crossword's instructions were a puzzle in their own right. *Lights*, I should explain, is British parlance for a grid's solutions—what most other nations label as the answers. (The term is something of a lyrical conceit, where answers go to illuminate the path among the shaded squares.) Anyhow, Jac's breathless wording went this way: 'The six unclued lights (not all of them being complete words), when joined together in correct sequence, illustrate a 40-Across 36-Across.'

In Jac fashion, these last two lights also lacked any accompanying clue. A solver had to rely on any cross-running entry they could grab. Oddities ranged from a grass spikelet (PALEA) to the Spanish word for stop (TERMINAR). Sorry, did I mention that a Jac puzzle would often resort to other languages, aside from classical Latin and opaque English? Anyhow, once you gleaned these neutral lights, you might have unveiled the key entries at 40-Across and 36-Across: RESPIRATORY DISEASE. This phrase served as your clue for the mega-light that Jac had obscured, its six fragments spread through the diagram in morphological piecemeal. Find those, and then your challenge was sussing out their sequence. This feat was accomplished by Mrs R Bett of London, who relinked the pieces to make PNEUMONOULTRAMICROSCOPICSILICOVOLCANOCONIOSIS, the longest word listed in most dictionaries, and now sitting inside a national crossword. The bearer of the title is a curse that besets asbestos-miners, fibro-workers or anyone standing too close to that Icelandic volcano Eyjafjallajökull when it blew. Needless to say, for her troubles, Mrs R Bett won £3.

1973

The Partridge Family's favorite record company (4)

Before the *Idol* franchise, before the shiny-floor genre of dance shows and talent quests, there was *The Partridge Family*. This Friday night experiment was launched by America's ABC network in 1970. Classed as light drama with songs, the show was an early television bid to crack the Billboard charts, as *The Monkees* had done a few years earlier. Every week a few million viewers around the world followed the covey (the true collective noun of partridges). The nest included mum Shirley (played by Shirley Jones, a former Miss Pittsburgh), eldest son David (the teenybopper pinup David Cassidy) and four other siblings. To all intents and purposes, Mr Partridge did not exist.

+ The Sydney Opera House is opened.
+ Papua New Guinea achieves self-government.
+ *The Godfather* wins Best Picture at the Academy Awards.

New words: junk food, prioritise, streaking, action replay

Needless to add, the covey could sing. Imagine *The Brady Bunch* with a rhythm section. Shirley took lead vocals, but all her fledglings had musical chops, and the band did the variety circuits and jail visits in a hippie-themed minibus, first according to the script, and later for real.

Part of the global push was a string of vinyl releases, starting with the smash single 'I Think I Love You' and trending downhill after that. By the time the make-believe family's eighth album hit the stores the partridge was one weary bird. Maybe in a bid to add value to the product, the marketing division at Bell Music stuck a crossword on the yellow cover. The pattern was all over the shop. One clue, in fact, yields SIX—*The Partridges in all (number)*—but the answer doesn't connect to any other entry in the shambles.

Though the clue to jump out asks for *The Partridge Family's favorite record company*. Given the tracks were cut by Bell Studios, the puzzle concept was born of Bell PR, and the album was distributed and promoted by Bell, the answer should be within your powers of deduction. Tellingly, this low-ranking compilation was close to Bell's bell lap, the label swallowed by Arista a year after *Crossword Puzzle* was released, the six songbirds likewise flapping off to the four winds.

1974

The beautiful one (7)

The Māori alphabet has eighteen letters, plus two paired letters that act as their own sound units. Next time you need to pen a postcard in Pohutukawa, those letters are A, Ā, E, Ē, H, I, Ī, K, M, N, NG, O, Ō, P, R, T, U, Ū, W and WH. The language is reluctant to cluster its consonants, meaning many Māori words have surplus vowels, as well as a steady alternating pattern. The first six months of the Māori year will give you the drift: *Kohi-ātea*, *Hui-tanguru*, *Poutū-te-rangi*, *Paenga-whāwhā*, *Haratua*, *Pipiri*. Reliable spelling and a riot of recurring letters mean the language is custom-made for weaving. Though a Māori crossword is only as good as its proofreader, something the editor of *Te Ao Hou* (The New World) discovered in 1952, in the first edition of the magazine's existence. Issue 2 carried the following apology:

+ Richard Nixon resigns.
+ Cyclone Tracy devastates Darwin.
+ Molly Meldrum's *Countdown* blasts off.

New words: Silicon Valley, retro, food processor

'Everybody connected with *Te Ao Hou* must offer his profound apologies for our first Crossword Puzzle—the proofreader did not notice the misprints, the artist failed to black one square and put one numeral in the wrong position. It was all a terrible flop. This time the crossword has been really well checked. Readers can have a try at it with renewed confidence.'

As promised, the in-house team beat the bugs. Indeed, they oversaw a succession of high-quality English–Māori crosswords that lasted all 26 years of the magazine's life. (A reverend named Hohepe Taepa was the setter credited with some of these puzzles, though the majority lacked any byline.) To quote Rangi Faith, a contributing poet, 'The crossword went on to become probably the most popular part of *Te Ao Hou*, the first page readers turned to when they received their copy.'

Rangi's own grandmother—Hinekerangi Gordon—was proof of that. A former teacher and a well-read lady, Hinekerangi had lived in a small fishing port in the South Island called Moeraki. 'As a small boy,' recalls Rangi, 'I remember going to watch television at her house as she was one of the first to get this newfangled invention!'

Much more than telly, the Moeraki house offered kinship. The hub was the family's *tūrangawaewae* (standing place). When the TV went off the singsong followed, led by Nana on the piano or her trusty accordion. In warmer months she joined husband Jim chasing whitebait and salmon on the Opihi River. Now and then Rangi would go with them, the lean poet growing into a man, spending weeks with his elders in their simple *bach* (beach hut).

A summertime memory he cherishes is the sight of his grandmother crouched close to the hurricane lantern, glasses balanced on her nose, a Māori dictionary at her elbow, solving the *Te Ao Hou* crossword. 'She always did them in capital letters,' says Rangi, a former teacher himself, now dedicated to tramping and fly-fishing in the wilds of South Island. 'She also liked to add to her vocabulary of Māori words.'

Words like *ike* (high), *oha* (generous) and *maia* (brave): three of the solutions inside 'Crossword 59', sitting near the back pages of an old *Te Ao Hou*. This was the puzzle found on a fireside table in the empty *tūrangawaewae*. The crossword was the final whirl for Hinekerangi, before she'd been taken to hospital for last-minute care, passing away not long after. 'Out of the 122 clues, she only managed 30,' says Rangi from his home in Rangiora. 'She was suffering from arthritis at that time, and I imagine it would have been quite painful to hold the pen.'

So Rangi took up the pen on her death, composing a poem that was too late to find its home in *Te Ao Hou*. The friend he mentions in the opening verses is the crossword itself, the shivery writing in the grid 'reminding me of my grandmother. She had that quiet grace and strength that held the family together and will never be forgotten.' Here is an extract of the tribute, 'Unfinished Crossword', composed by grandson and fellow word-lover Rangi Faith:

If they say:
you may find a friend
in the least likely places,
I have, here—
fifteen across, *ataahua*, the beautiful one;
and here—six across—*aperira*,
the month of the leaf fall;

here—eleven down—*aue!*
and all the gods crying
in all the places
that ever were & still
      & still do;

and here—five down—*atua*,
the gods calling your god,
like the candle flame
and the star in the wide night—
a beckoning.

1975

Sales decoration of old? (John's country relative had one, in other words.) (7)

Mix up Lewis and you get Wiles, the perfect surname for a cruciverbalist. Even better if your first name is Frank, as in easy to read, which a Frank Lewis clue seldom is. One clue, in fact—this chapter's heading—was so evasive that his editor at *The Nation*, where his crosswords appeared, made a world precedent.

The Nation is a leftie flagship based in New York. Established in 1865, the weekly blend of essays and columns is recognised as the oldest of its kind in America, a platform for luminaries such as George Orwell, Jean-Paul Sartre and Gore Vidal. If radical politics was not enough to distinguish *The Nation* from competing titles at the newsstand, then its other distinction was the crossword.

+ Gough Whitlam is dismissed as prime minister.
+ Pol Pot ravages Cambodia.
+ Hobart's Tasman Bridge is struck by a bulk carrier.

New words: drive-time, Post-It, bean-counter

By and large, across America, the clue of choice at that time was the orthodox. Compare this to the British style, as the cryptic was labelled, which turned language inside-out. Jack Barrett began *The Nation*'s crossword in 1943, the first mainstream cryptic in the country, 25 years before Stephen Sondheim entered the spotlight. The curio found an audience from the start, the riddle-like clues refreshing for a swelling band of solvers jaded by plainer hints. Sadly, though, Barrett lost his life in a boating tragedy four years later.

The contest to find a successor was more like a taste test, with two secret compilers—Mr X and Mr Y—presenting their puzzles in *The Nation* for three months, giving readers a chance to select the preferred candidate. Mr Y won, and so the public was introduced to Frank Lewis, though there was plenty in his recent past that he couldn't discuss, owing to issues of national security.

As a bright lad with a gift for language and music, Frank had been whisked from the Department of Death Benefits into the brainy aspects of war. He was trained in code-breaking and sent to Bletchley Park, near Oxford, where he helped to defy the Japanese navy, cracking the Purple Code, which relayed coordinates across the Pacific. Or so I can glean. Frank never shared too much intelligence, owing to the gag rule of Public Law 37. We do know two things about him, however: the young 'cryppie' returned home after the war to receive two Exceptional Civilian Merit Medals for efforts in code-breaking; and he adored British crosswords. When he wasn't unravelling Japanese map references in the Bletchley mansion, he was in the mess picking over gobbledygook on *The Times*'s puzzle page.

His reign at *The Nation* as America's newly crowned cryptic king began in 1947. Hallmarks of a Lewis puzzle are humour and an insouciant sweep through high and popular culture. The man could crack wise about John Keats or Buster Keaton, Latin or slang, and always in his loose-limbed, self-made style. Swank Filer—the anagram he conjured—became a cult figure, attracting such Frankophiles as avant-garde novelist Kurt Vonnegut and composer Leonard Bernstein.

Numerically, his career was no less impressive. The Lewis reign stretched over 60 years and 2962 puzzles, from 1947 to 2010; he penned his last at the age of 97. Mind you, in those twilight years, *The Nation* relied on Frank's golden oldies to supplement his new supply, including a puzzle containing the clue that enforced the aforementioned precedent.

The puzzle hailed from 1975. The sticking point was the clue *Sales decoration of old? (John's country relative had one, in other words.) (7).* Judith Long, the editor who managed Lewis's output for half of his time at *The Nation*, recalls in our interview, 'The clue seemed impenetrable. Nobody in the office could parse the clue, even when we knew the answer.' Which was LUNETTE. But how?

Time can wield a strange effect on language, just as brilliant crossword-makers can lose their mental acuity in their final years. In 2010, when the puzzle was to reappear, Frank was almost 98 and beyond consultation. This left the editors a dilemma. Did they run the flashback despite the clue's mystery or pick another puzzle from the vault? Then a third solution was suggested—publishing the stumper with an open plea for help: 'If you "get" the first part of clue 9, please write. We don't!'

'We got a barrage of mail,' recalls Judith, 'but the explanations did not agree.' Opinions split down the middle. One half favoured a mystical figure of Catholic history, Saint Francis de Sales, the patron saint of journalists and deaf people. The second half adhered to a public toilet. I should explain in greater depth.

According to the saint-pushers, the LUNETTE was the fingernail moon you see in the heraldic shield belonging to St Francis: *Sales decoration of old.* The evidence seemed sound, though the toilet lobby queried the logic. If the clue's opening was indeed an allusion to this holy gentleman, then who the hell was *John's country relative* in the second part of the clue? What made far more sense was a vaudeville reference, argued the lavatory mob. Charles 'Chic' Sale was a comedian during the 1920s and 1930s, his persona a yokel modelled on the backwater types he met on tour. Eventually, Chic moved to Hollywood from Urbana, Illinois, and won a place in the Ziegfeld Follies, plus several movie roles. Yet most of these achievements were eclipsed by an outhouse builder named Lem Putt, a comic character Chic invented in 1929 for the play *The Specialist*, a latter-day *Kenny* from Australian cinema. The comedy dwelt on a hayseed carpenter and his misadventures in the toilet game. The show was a smash, almost too successful, as the name Chic Sales soon denoted a stand-alone outhouse. Tragic when you think about it: a comedian longing to emulate WC Fields only to leave the stage as shorthand for a WC.

As for the LUNETTE, it's a decoration common to most dunny doors, in particular the country cousin of the urban John. Of course, the saint-pushers resented the toilet humour, insisting the religious path was the way to the truth, rather than the well-worn trail to the backyard convenience. 'Never the twain would meet,' laughs Judith. The two parties tiffed on the Letters page for weeks, with the fragile word-juggler once called Mr Y incapable of adjudication.

Frank Lewis died three months after the LUNETTE kerfuffle. His passing prompted obituaries in all the major papers. A cryptic god had fallen from the American sky. For editors at *The Nation* there was only one solution: this time they invited five contestants, each equipped with an alias, for a crossword taste test.

1976

Four-legged creature (9)

Alfred Guttman had rules: no plurals, no abbreviations, no slang, no gerunds (all those ugly -ing words like solving and setting), and no past participles (making ban okay, but banned, well, banned). Cynics scoffed. How did an Israeli migrant from Switzerland hope to build a puzzle empire in Britain with so many restrictions? It was ludicrous.

The launch issue of *Puzzler* came out in 1972, a milk-skinned female solver on the cover hemmed by chequered squares. The layout was clean, the paper stock decent, and every page carried a conundrum. Most formulas were familiar: word searches, arrow-words (in the Swedish style), pyramids and ladders, codewords, spot-the-difference cartoons. Others took a fresh approach. One

---

+ Vietnam's first boat people arrive in Australia.
+ The ebola virus breaks out in Zaire.
+ Nadia Comaneci scores a perfect 10 on the uneven bars at the Montreal Olympics.

New words: bulimia, stakeholder, minibar

puzzle I adored as a kid entailed a detective with trench coat and pencil moustache who ambled through a crime scene, often in a triptych of panels, requiring solvers to deduce the culprit.

Val Packer, my godmother, subscribed to *Puzzler* in its second year. I was a tween at the time, merrily lazing in Val's dusty library in Artarmon, northern Sydney. Whenever I stayed overnight I would lose an entire Sunday in her cartoon shelves, a tallboy barely taller than me loaded with *BC*, *Wizard of Id*, *Peanuts*, *Punch* and *New Yorker* collections. She even had a gumball machine with trinkets in capsules. Plus a growing pile of *Puzzlers*, which I devoured.

Honeycomb, another word game in the magazine, was invented by a language teacher named Tom Johnson. Picture a bed of crammed flowers, each flower owning six petals. So tightly are the flowers planted, they share their petals with their nearest neighbours. These same petals await six-letter answers, clued by each flower's hint, printed in the corona. As you complete the pattern, the letters mesh clockwise or anticlockwise with their companions. Thus HERESY (as clued by *Blasphemy*) could share its ES with SECTOR (*Segment*), the adjoining plant spinning the other way. Johnson was paid a £5 bonus for his brainwave. I won't say that's tight on Guttman's behalf, as £5 was a hearty meal in 1976, but solvers could win ten times that if they unravelled the magazine's prize crossword.

Unabashed, Johnson supplied more than 2200 puzzles over the ensuing 40 years, from honeycomb to the orthodox stuff. 'Guttman established a brilliant magazine,' says the setter, a man we'll meet for grisly reasons later in *Cluetopia*. 'I'm chuffed to be part of the setting stable throughout its many years.' Not that Guttman allowed words like *chuffed* or *setting* or *years*, being slang, a gerund and a plural in a single quotation. But who could deny the recipe? The puzzle emperor had clearly drafted the right manifesto, ensuring his magazine's crosswords were less trite than those in rival titles on the rack.

Since Guttman's time, the new regime of Puzzler Media has modified the recipe slightly. The magazine still flourishes, enjoying a loyal readership, though plurals and participles have snuck through the gates. Nevertheless, if you compare issue number 500 with issue number 1, you'll still find the zestful, middlebrow magic that Guttman created.

As visionaries go, however, Alfred was a hermit, seldom leaving his north London home. In the words of Tom Johnson, 'Our work was conducted by post. In all the years I've worked for *Puzzler*, I've only had one five-second phone call with Mr Guttman, back when he was the editor-in-chief.'

The controversy that necessitated the phone call was a four-footed animal, a QUADRUPED, in fact: one of the answers in Johnson's giant crossword. No good, said Guttman, owing to the past participle taboo. The setter was flummoxed. Let's be clear: quadruped is *not* the past participle of *quadrupe*, which may well sound like a verb, meaning to droop four times worse than normal, but it's not a word. Not even close. Still and all, Johnson felt like sagging past his knees when he heard the boss's veto over the phone, but he didn't flinch. The job was too much fun. Besides, in the end, the so-called QUADRUPED breach was explained in good spirit, the boss assured no *Puzzler* commandment was broken, the jumbo puzzle proceeding unscathed into my boyhood. As for Johnson, he smiles to think that the only time he heard his employer's voice was prompted by a four-legged red herring.

1977

Yiddish for bedbug (5)

Mobile Army Surgical Hospital is the mouthful behind *M*A*S*H*, the sitcom that ruled the sitting room for most of the 1970s. Families across suburbia watched Hawkeye Pierce and his comrades stay alive and keep others alive while the Korean War raged off-screen. Nominally the enemy was North Korea, though the greater foe was boredom. Dreaming up ways to maintain sanity was the prime source of comedy. In various seasons the ploys numbered table tennis tournaments, poker schools, joke embargos—and the burning quest to identify a Yiddish bedbug.

'Five letters,' says Hawkeye in the mess tent. 'Starts with v.'

The crossword he's solving is a windfall. Major Frank Burns ordered a pornographic ball game, the type where you tilt a picture so that captive ball bearings roll into their designated holes. This

---

+ Elvis Presley dies.
+ *Star Wars* blitzes the cinema.
+ World Series cricket swings into action.

New words: user-friendly, supermodel, quality time

is Frank's bid for sanity, while Hawkeye and his pal BJ Hunnicutt prefer *The Times*, which came as the plaything's wrapping. Every soldier who arrives for lunch is bugged for their Yiddish lore. The conundrum looms larger than a peace treaty, and Hawkeye pesters the padre about his grasp of Semitic insects. The cleric ponders, 'The Bible has hosts of locusts, plagues of vermin and hordes of scorpions . . .' But no bedbugs.

Desperate, the medics conspire to ask a naval pal, Tippy Brooks, who's a crossword demon. Unfortunately, wires get crossed by Radar the radio operator, who makes the emergency seem medical, not cruciverbal. As a result, Tippy lobs via cattle train and jeep from Pusan Harbour, accompanied by Admiral Cox.

Fun and games follow. The men and women of the 4077th M*A*S*H do their best to camouflage the true purpose of the call-out, except for Corporal Klinger, who eats a jeep in the hope he may be discharged for insanity. In the end the truth wriggles free. After several cover stories fray, Cox stands to his full height and booms, 'You dragged us all the way up here just to get the word VONTZ?!'

1978

Small breed of chicken (6)

Christine Evans wandered the red-light district of Sydney, carrying her ironing board under her arm like a two-metre Malibu. Mid-morning, but already disco music pumped from doorways. The bouncer at the velvet rope saw the British nurse and laughed. 'Ya lost, love?' Other men leered. Where was James? He said he'd be here when the bus arrived. William Street crawled with strangers, and no boyfriend in sight.

A woman in hotpants and fishnet stockings took one look at the ironing board and almost choked on her cigarette. A car slowed beside the kerb, shadowing Christine's steps. She kept walking. She had a number in her head, the house where James was living, and she'd be safe there. The car was drawing level now. The driver had the window open. 'You like a lift somewhere?'

+ In Greater Manchester, Louise Brown is the first in-vitro baby born.
+ The Sydney's Gay Mardi Gras is hatched.
+ The hit film *Grease* is released.

New words: BMX, megastar, me generation

She turned and realised the car was a cab. 'I'm fine,' she lied. Three long days on a bus, from Cairns in the far north to Gomorrah in the south—it was only adrenalin that kept her moving.

'Where you heading?'

'William Street—I'm here.' But Christine stopped, her heart sinking. The number on the iron fence belonged to an office building, not a residence, and tears began to trickle. 'My boyfriend is expecting me,' she heard herself say.

The driver gave a crooked smile. 'Which William Street you talking about?'

'I don't have much money.'

'You English, eh? I like the English.'

Crazily, Christine trusted him. She put her suitcase in the boot and the ironing board beside her in the backseat like a dummy chaperone. William Street in Kings Cross was not the same as William Street in Paddington, the man persuaded her in the mirror. Too far to walk, he promised. 'That's why you needed me.' The young woman perched on the seat's edge, watching the colours of Sydney blur, the uncertain image of James Lovatt in her mind.

He'd worn a rollneck jumper despite the Cairns heat, and sunglasses that turned darker when he went inside. Not a shadow of doubt, James was the thinnest person she'd ever met outside a hospital bed, but there was an easy intelligence about him. He played guitar. Drove a double-decker bus with another British bloke called Ivan, and they knew how to have a good time, continually playing tricks on each other. So was this whole rendezvous a joke, the address in her hand one more prank?

'This is it,' said the driver, outside a terraced house. Christine fished in her purse, but the man didn't want a cent. Instead, he wished to see whether this girl found her boy, or at least if somebody answered the door.

Eventually, after a minute of ringing and knocking, a figure appeared in underpants, pallid to the point of ghostly, all 57 kilos of him. 'Oh no!' yelled James, seeing his visitor. 'What's the time?'

Anticipation had tormented the poor lad all night, counting the hours until Christine arrived. In all his nervous energy, James had barely slept, until dawn came around and he blacked out with exhaustion, missing the alarm.

'Best get some clothes on,' teased Christine.

'Any chance I might use your ironing board?'

All was forgiven, despite the reunion almost never happening. Soon, in fact, the two expats tied the knot and rented a place to live in Bondi. By then, Christine was nursing at St Vincent's Hospital, while James was subediting at *People*, a racy lowbrow magazine boasting a bikini girl on the cover and a UFO sighting somewhere inside.

Around the late 1970s, the letter P tyrannised the cheesecake subgenre of men's titles, with *Australasian Post* joined by *People* and *Pix*, each title vying to flood the limited market. To fight for space and score a coup, the people behind *People* wished to construct the nation's biggest crossword—every week. Curiously, they turned to James.

In his favour was Christine, who had grown up with the puzzles, cobbling together her own as a twelve year old in south London, appeasing a work-weary and verbal dad most evenings. Touch wood, she still had the knack. Making the Colossus ('the BIGGEST crossword in Australia') was a different ball of wax, however. The major rival in the game was Mr Wisdom's Whopper, which appeared every week in the *Post*. This involved quick clues attached to a 37 by 37 grid rife with words like ELEMI and ADIT and ORIBI. The British newlyweds wanted to up the ante, to refresh the language, and to inflate the box to 47 by 38 dimensions.

'James filled in all the black squares with a felt-tip pen,' Christine tells me. 'I'd made the grid quite difficult for myself, and I spent three weeks fraught with despair, headaches and frantic searches through the dictionary for impossible words. James would help me in the evenings when his day job was over. That dictionary fell apart before the next crossword was due.'

This flurry of graph sheets, word lists and box files marked the outset of the Lovatt puzzle empire. Their maiden clue—*Small breed of chicken*—was the egg that hatched an enterprise now spanning 20 separate puzzle titles around the world. The BANTAM, you could say, had laid a golden egg.

1979

Giggling troll follows Clancy, Larry, Billy and Peggy who howl, wrongly disturbing a place in Wales (58)

As good as its word, Ironbridge in Shropshire has an iron bridge, the world's first arch bridge to be made of iron, no less. The feat was accomplished in 1779, with many of the bridge's joints and ribs fastened in carpentry fashion, a clue to the new ground the engineers were breaking.

Two hundred years later, to commemorate the achievement, the Queen travelled to Ironbridge, 250 kilometres northwest of London. Naturally, the local council was eager to make a splash. Not in the Severn River below, but with a bicentennial publication detailing the bridge's history.

+ Margaret Thatcher becomes the first female British prime minister.
+ Mother Teresa wins the Nobel Peace Prize.
+ The Walkman wires the world for sound.

New words: downsize, karaoke, couch potato

Yet, to paraphrase Alice before she fell down the rabbit hole, what is the use of a commemorative book without a crossword? The problem was remedied by Roger Squires, an Ironbridge local, whose puzzles run in most major mastheads around the country. Roger is Rufus to *Guardian* readers and Dante in the *Financial Times*, among many other incarnations. Fittingly, the puzzle he made for Telford and Wrekin Council was an engineering feat of its own.

For starters, the grid was 58 squares wide, custom-built for the single entry that spanned the design, much as the iron bridge extends across the gorge. Instead of a phrase, or a chunk of industrial history, Squires selected one name, the longest name in the atlas and destined to become the longest intact entry in a crossword puzzle, as recognised by the *Guinness Book of Records* some years later. The town is Welsh, 200 kilometres from Ironbridge as the crow flies, and the clue presenting the nuts and bolts of LLANFAIRPWLLGWYN-GYLLGOGERYCHWYRNDROBWLLLLANTYSILIOGOGOGOCH was a recast anagram complete with eleven LS, seven GS and far too few vowels: *Giggling troll follows Clancy, Larry, Billy and Peggy who howl, wrongly disturbing a place in Wales (58).* A little arch, don't you think?

1980

Not a brief innings for a cricketer but perhaps it wasn't really cricket to bring the team from Samarai and patronise them although at least it was the first time men appeared in any way equal which was more than you can say for the way they were treated at Kwato which was miles ahead of its time especially industrially but still left Charles Abel enthroned while the natives squatted on the verandah which is unfair seeing it's based on only one photograph in the New Guinea Collection and was probably due to the fact that the poor missionaries only had one chair anyway and he was reading to them from the good book and they couldn't read but it looks more impressive if you do it like a guru and squat on the floor, on a floor-mat or a doorstep or a foot-stool or a packing-case and other hyphenated words (4–4)

+ John Lennon is shot.
+ Azaria Chamberlain goes missing.
+ Pac-Man and Rubik's Cube compete for our attention.

New words: download, phwoar, NIMBY

Trekking in Papua New Guinea in 1988 I met a man called David with a cassowary bone through his nose. He lived deep in the Simbu jungle and had never seen blond hair before. Or glass. (The former was on my head, the latter in front of my eyes.) His bare feet were so wide they seemed webbed, the better for gripping the log bridges that spanned the gullies. His arms were scored with initiations, bulging from a tangerine T-shirt promoting video rentals—a freebie from the aid workers who visited the Highlands. He called me *wannem*—which is Tok Pisin for namesake, as in one-name. He called my corkscrew a *santu tel bilong pik*, which means a sacred pigtail.

That story is your clue to Papua's bewildering effect. I didn't take photos on my trip, as every day brought a fresh barrage of the strange, an onslaught that still pulses in my memory. Cloud forests. Landslides. A python strangling a goat. Wallpaper made out of a Myer catalogue. Blood-red pineapple. This is a nation that recently lived in the Stone Age, an island of 600 languages, wifi and barter, Catholicism and cannibalism: Australia's nearest neighbour.

In three weeks of hiking I was bewitched, as John Collier had been 30 years before me. Collier first went north in 1956, working as a medic for the Australasian Petroleum Company. The trip ignited an obsession, and the Sydney bloke returned in 1960 as a teacher. He later completed a PhD in Port Moresby, studying Papua's dense oral history. In 1976 he became a naturalised citizen, and at about the same time he ditched his stuffy surname, mutating into Dr John Kolia, academic, lecturer, writer.

This chapter's title, in fact, is a sample of his prose. The chunk is an extract from a story he wrote called 'A Crossword Puzzle'. Over 10 000 words, the premise hinges on a newspaper scrap that wraps 'a hygienically-baked loaf of bread left standing on the dirty pavement outside a Waigani shop'. The paper has a crossword, and Kolia's story is an opaque rave in which every paragraph sprouts from an undisclosed clue, an anti-clue, if you like, heavy on conjecture and light on punctuation. You may be relieved to hear that the chapter title is the shortest example among eighteen slabs of prose. Even now, at my umpteenth glance, I still have no inkling what the answer could be. WELL-READ? HOLY-BOOK? BACK-REST?

Charles Abel, as suggested, was a missionary to the shores a century earlier than Kolia. He set up Kwato Mission on an island in Milne Bay, an indentation on Papua's eastern tip. The Englishman was big on cricket and dairy farming, and hell-bent on erasing paganism through the three Bs: bat, ball and Bible. Traces of that story underpin Kolia's riff. Indeed, much of the man's writing centred on traditional values and colonial supremacy—and not always lucidly, I might add. The author revelled in evasion, the postmodernist of Port Moresby. Most stories in *Without Mannerisms*, the collection in which 'A Crossword Puzzle' is found, delight in scorning Western imports, including crosswords and, quite possibly, literature. At one point in this anti-crossword, a chink in the extra-long ramble that is 19-Across, Kolia writes a self-effacing barb. 'Go back to your own country and be artistic there. You think you're aiding our culture but you are not.'

By way of postscript, another memorable moment during my Papuan holiday was the conversation I had with a village elder out of Mount Hagen. When he heard I made crosswords for *The Sydney Morning Herald*, he told me on good authority that the paper was considered the best around. I was flattered. I promised to tell my own elders, once I flew back to Australia. Until I twigged the gentleman meant the best paper for rolling wild tobacco.

1981

Geschriebenes (7)

His mum dressed him warmly: a blue-green coat with brown fur hat, a white jumper, black pants. His older sister walked with him halfway down the street. This was a big occasion. Lars was only seven. The walk had been his long-held wish. As a *Jungpionier* of the Free German Youth movement, the boy felt himself old enough to walk to the nearby cinema to see *Thumbelina*.

It was winter, mid-January. His mum agonised as the sky darkened, the matinee long over. She called friends and relatives to see if Lars was there. Nothing. She grabbed her jacket and walked to the cinema, then through the other roads and lanes of Halle-Neustadt. At eight o'clock she filed a missing person report with the *Volkspolizei*. A sergeant told the woman to relax. 'Children can forget the time,'

+ Prince Charles marries Lady Diana Spencer.
+ Irish prisoner Bobby Sands goes on a hunger strike.
+ Trevor Chappell bowls underarm to Kiwi Brian McKechnie.

New words: gridlock, infomercial, tough love

he said. 'They usually turn up.' He'd send out a few cars to see what they could find.

By noon the next day the mood had changed. Every phone call was a dead-end. Police checked the ponds to see if the ice was broken. They combed parks and derelict buildings. By afternoon the Socialist Unity Party in the twin city of Halle became involved, the case assuming a political edge, as often happened east of the Berlin Wall. A major party congress was coming up. The socialist anthem was bound to lose its lustre if a *Jungpionier* had vanished.

Cabbies and bus drivers were interviewed by a special taskforce. Canals were raked, the banks of the Saale River searched. Stray tickets and a handkerchief were found. The lead investigator exerted pressure on Lars's estranged father, an alcoholic with an unconvincing alibi, but that also came to naught.

Two weeks later a suitcase was found on the Halle–Leipzig line. Inside was a series of thick plastic bags wrapping the hunched naked body of a boy. Lars Bense had been found. The autopsy confirmed he'd been bashed with a blunt instrument and stabbed several times. He'd also been sexually molested.

The sole consolation was the amount of evidence the suitcase contained. The case itself was cardboard with unusual basket-weave lining. The plastic bags were imprinted with 'Euvetes Nederland' and had once been packaging for a bedspread of spun rayon and acrylic. Also in the bags were balled-up sheets of magazines and newspapers. Police discovered that several pages contained the half-completed grids of German crosswords.

The suitcase was placed in the window of Halle-Neustadt's main department store, accompanied by an appeal for anyone who knew its owner, or had noticed someone carrying it, to contact the police. Dozens of people came forward with accounts, yet none led to a result. The bedspread angle was no less futile: the items were imported in large numbers, with more than 1000 recent sales in the district.

The ultimate key could lie in the periodicals. The titles were diverse, from *Junge Welt* (Young World) of the East German Youth Movement to a women's magazine, *Für Dich* (For You), as well as several tabloids. The crossword-solver also had peculiar handwriting. It was distinct: the N in ARENA, for example (the answer for *Kampfplatz*), had a preliminary downstroke, making the N seem w-like, and the R had a loopy junction in the word SCHRIFT (uncannily, the German for handwriting, as clued by *Geschriebenes*). The word *Uta* was also found, a woman's name. Could the script belong to a female hand?

The Ministry for State Security joined forces with the crime squad. Together, they drafted a table of the solver's writing quirks. The next step was door-knocking Halle-Neustadt, asking residents to copy down a customised writing test. Most complied, and the police gathered over 21 000 samples in one operation. Abstainers were secretly registered and covertly checked by the ministry. Deep in the civic vaults, other writing sources were harvested: apartment applications, car registrations, ID card paperwork and telegram forms. On the quiet, police commissioned a crossword to run in the city's local paper, *Freiheit* (Freedom), the solution built around the mystery solver's more distinctive letters. Generous cash prizes helped to entice another 11 000 samples for the forensic team.

Despite every effort, however, the killer's identity remained a mystery. The writing samples yielded little but the valuable siphoning of man-hours. The party congress came and went, with police no wiser to the circumstances surrounding the child's death. In the following weeks the taskforce was culled. Months passed. The hunting fever, as the Germans called it, cooled the longer the stalemate continued.

Then came the break, in mid-November. One writing sample was discovered that matched the script. The writer was a waitress working in a health resort on the Baltic Sea, 360 kilometres north of Halle. She was 50. Her work was seasonal, requiring two addresses during the year—one for her summer job, and the other in Halle-Neustadt. Police paid her a visit in Ostseebad, on the coast. They showed her the series of crossword puzzles, in which she recognised her own handwriting. Next they showed her a photo of the battered suitcase. The woman was baffled: it was her luggage. And yes, she did once buy a Dutch bedspread. That's when the police requested her whereabouts on 15 January, the day Lars Bense had gone missing.

The woman had not been in the Halle region at the time. She'd moved to the Baltic earlier in the year. Her last night in Halle had been 11 January, four days before Lars disappeared, and this was verified by witnesses. But her daughter had been staying at the apartment, she believed. The girl was eighteen and also a waitress, working two hours southwest of the city, in the Thuringian Forest. With a solid workload, the girl headed back to the apartment only now and then, to check that everything was secure.

Police learnt that the daughter was friendly with a boy her own age who worked as a janitor at the Thuringian venue. His name was Matthias. Occasionally, the couple had headed back to Halle-Neustadt together, staying at the women's apartment for a few nights if time allowed. In mid-January, in fact, just after the mother headed north for the Baltic, the two lovers had taken their chance to stay over. The girl soon had to return to work, but Matthias was able to remain a few more nights, so she left him the keys before she went.

Back at Halle-Neustadt, detectives spoke at length with the girl, keeping her for several hours at the station. From the interview they learnt how Matthias had expressed some strange sexual fantasies during their relationship, relishing scenarios of abuse and cruelty. Police wanted to hear more in person and took the youth into custody.

With unkempt hair and pallid skin, Matthias was verging on catatonic. Police doubted the interview would elicit much with the teenager in such a state, but the moment they moved to set up the recording apparatus, the confession came out in a torrent. The suspect admitted he'd seen the boy outside the cinema that day and had convinced him to abandon *Thumbelina*. He had led Lars to the apartment, where the rape had taken place, and then the panic, and the hammering. Matthias said he'd bundled the body into the old case and jammed the gaps with newspaper and old magazines to stem any blood. Come dark, he had walked to the station and caught the Leipzig train. As soon as the carriage was empty he'd tossed the suitcase out the window. When he arrived in Leipzig he had caught the next train back.

As for the tools—the hammer and knife—Matthias had dumped them in one of the many bins outside the apartments. A few days later he had caught a train to Thuringia to join his girlfriend at work. Enough time had since passed to make him think he'd go unpunished.

'Here,' said an officer, sliding a paper across the desk, 'sign here, and here.' The resulting tangle of letters formed the final entry in a ten-month puzzle the newspaper archives call *Der Kreuzworträtselmord*: the Crossword Murder.

1982

Last finish on river (6)

Pat Clark and John Gillishan were boilermakers—or platers in the dockside slang. Both men worked on Glasgow's Clyde River, sealing the hulls and cabins of ocean liners and freighters, as well as gas rigs for the North Sea. One morning, the pair were busy doing a training course in how to use a lance-like welding rod, a tool essential for building the ocean platforms. At least, they were busy for a spell, until the power was cut to enable some repair. The rods sat idle. With nothing to do, Pat retrieved the half-done crossword from the tea break. His mate joined him, reading the clues. One jumped out: *Mammal and insect used for waterproofing (7)*. That was a doddle for two platers trained in the shipping game: SEALANT.

+ The Falklands War erupts.
+ ET lands—in cinemas.
+ The first bionic ear is implanted.
+ The 'computer' is *Time*'s Man of the Year.

New words: AIDS, EFTPOS, spreadsheet, yuppie

Presently, the instructor appeared at their bench. A senior foreman on the dock, Eric Clark was no relation to Pat, and no ally either. He advised the men to put the paper away. But why? they argued. Power was down. Work was on hold. As shop stewards in the plater crew, Clark and Gillishan knew where they stood within the workplace rules, and they fanned the debate to flashpoint. Before the day was out, both boilermakers had been suspended pending a disciplinary hearing.

The tribunal was ruthless. Gillishan copped a month minus pay, while Clark was sacked outright. To quote the offending crossword, number 4980 in the *Financial Times*, the verdict was *A file to irritate one's senses* (RASP). The plater crew met *en masse* the next day and voted for union officials to negotiate with management, rather than opt for a flat-out strike.

Before we continue, the story may benefit from a full description of the Clyde shipyards. The industry had been Glasgow's lifeblood for centuries. Forges and foundries jammed both banks. At their peak, early in World War I, the yards generated 370 ships in a calendar year. If every horse is nominally born on 1 August, then every giant ship at one point was hatched on the Clyde.

Comedian Billy Connolly is a second product of the place, himself a welder during the early 1960s. 'The great thing about Glasgow,' he once said, 'is that if there's a nuclear attack, it will look exactly the same afterwards.' Harsh but not untrue: the city was built for building. If you wanted pretty photos, then piss off to the lochs. Work was hard, the unions pugnacious. If safety was compromised or workers' rights abused, the smallest dispute was sure to gather steam.

A prime example was our Great Crossword Walkout of 1982. In late September, as negotiations stalled, 300 platers downed tools and walked off the job, demanding the return of the two banished solvers.

Gossip was rife. Management at the company accused the strikers of being minions of the Red Army. They said the building of *British*

Spirit, a jumbo tanker, would be further delayed, attracting needless penalties and cancelled contracts. Clark, they said, had already had a black mark against his name, the shop steward having been caught selling *Hammer and Tongs* (a direct action rag) on site a few years earlier.

For their part, the platers painted the crossword as a distraction. The real issue, they claimed, was the cloud that hung over the yards. Work had tapered in recent years. The ousted workers were mere scapegoats, an excuse to incite the entire stand-off, a bogus impetus to close the yard for good.

If nothing else, this theory threw the emphasis onto 8-Down in Clark and Gillishan's puzzle, another charade built for the occasion: *Last finish on river*. The clue was easy pickings for an Anglophile, and anyone familiar with the River Ure in Yorkshire, running not so far from Scotland. The laws of probability suggest that Clark and Gillishan had nailed the solution, yet as the strike persisted, days becoming weeks, the word ENDURE was slowly wearing thin as platers awaited the solution they craved.

Newcastle became involved, the headquarters of British Shipbuilders. Gillishan's suspension was softened to a week, but then discussions sputtered. Clark remained in exile. Leaflets were printed on both sides of the schism, each camp accusing the other of producing propaganda. The clock was ticking. The tanker lay in pieces, in jeopardy. All the while the *Glasgow Herald* and Scotland's *Evening Times* filled their pages with Crossword Walkout updates.

After three weeks of argy-bargy, the platers met in Greenock Town Hall, a short stroll from the Clyde. When the question was put to the crowd, a dominant show of hands decided to return to work. The strike was over. The next day the gang picked up torches and went about salvaging the *British Spirit*. As for Pat Clark, the long-time plater joined the welfare queue, perhaps with a crossword to help pass the time.

1983

CARDIAC

Right away, this chapter is a misfit, the heading displaying the answer versus the clue. The reason is simple, since the best way to sample the clue is not by sight—but sound. Yes, that's the other distinction: 1983 is buried in song.

Flick through any vinyl stack and you're bound to find a song that mentions crosswords. By my latest reckoning the total stands at 30 or so. Taylor Swift goes there in 'Red', along with XTC in 'Millions' and INXS in 'Simple Simon'. Dead Kennedys, The New Pornographers, Tori Amos: the list is scattergun. Eerily, the day I wrote this chapter, my radio delivered a haunting tune from an album called *Crosswords* by Melbourne's own lo-fi garage girls, Super Wild Horses. But doubtless the stand-out track in this cruciverbal

---

+ Soviets shoot down Korean Air Lines Flight 007.
+ Bob Hawke is sworn in as prime minister, pledging to spare the Franklin River.
+ Bjorn Borg retires on winning five straight Wimbledons.

New words: cyberpunk, safe sex, CD-ROM, liposuction

subgenre is 'Cardiac Arrest' by Madness. The song was composed by Chrissy Boy, the band's guitarist, and Chas Smash, the trumpeter.

Chas, in fact, stars in the video. (Check out the retro antics on YouTube for the madness in general.) Poor Chas is the commuter in bowler hat who suffers a seizure on the morning bus. The gent is running late, the bus packed, the traffic heavy. Though the morning's real bugbear for Chas is the crossword. Cue Suggs, aka Graham McPherson, who leans across the seat and tells us the frustrating clue that is on Smash's mind, a letter-juggling quatrain that paraphrases the clue on the commuter's lap.

The beauty of this ploy is twofold. 'Cardiac Arrest' becomes the only chart-reaching song to cite a cryptic clue, despite the lyrics failing to quote the clue verbatim, and, the greater joy, we need to solve this verse, converting CADILLAC (the big American car) into CARDIAC, to match the song's title.

Importantly, nowhere else in the song do you find the words cardiac or cardiac arrest; instead, the name is encoded in a rhyming piece of wordplay. And, just like Chas, you need to figure out the partial clue—ideally with fewer side-effects.

1984

Asthenopia (14)

I spy with my little eye something starting with b. Go on, take a wild stab—I'm standing in a library. All right, well done: books. But wait; this is no ordinary library, and these aren't your average books. Examine the spines and a theme will emerge: *Anterior Chamber Surgery, Journal of Cataract and Refractive Procedures, What You Need to Know about Endothelial Keratoplasty* . . . Welcome to the Ronald Lowe Library, an archive of medical history and practice hidden inside the Royal Victorian Eye and Ear Hospital, in Melbourne. I'm here on eye business, in fact. Imeri, the Fijian curator, checks the pass around my neck before surrendering the book I've reserved. After all this time trawling catalogues, sending emails, making calls, the volume feels disappointing in my hands, almost too flimsy to rate as treasure. 'Best place to read is the museum,' says Imeri.

+ Bob Geldof organises Band-Aid.
+ Toxic gas leak devastates Bhopal in India.
+ 'Advance Australia Fair' is declared the national anthem.

New words: spin doctor, glass ceiling, A-list

'Where?'

She leads me past the shelves into a sunlit room. The main window faces the spire of St Patrick's Cathedral, but my eye is distracted by the showcases along the walls. Inside are tubes and scalpels, mini-callipers, toy hammers. Some carry labels that make no sense, like 'Trephine' and 'Erisophake' and 'Maklakov tonometer'. The only item of comfort is a deep transparent vase—until I go closer and read the tag: 'Leech jar, circa 1912'.

Time for the comfort of puzzles. Brief comfort, as the crosswords are also dedicated to eye surgery. Eric B Keates of Columbus, Ohio, was a man dedicated to the eyeball, compiling 30 surgical stumpers for his *Ophthalmic Crosswords*. An early clue in 'Puzzle 2' sets the tone: *Wideness of palpebral fissures in goiter (sign)*. The answer is DALRYMPLE, apparently after the ophthalmologist John Dalrymple. If you need more information, I recommend a specialist. Other clues seem equally foreign:

Carbonic anhydrase inhibitor = ACETAZOLAMIDE
Paratrigeminal syndrome = RAEDER
Circumscribed bulbar elevations = PHLYCTENULAR CONJUCTIVITIS

As I goggle over the answers, I realise the language animates the gadgets around me. The ERISOPHAKE is an *Instrument to remove cataract*. The TONOMETER is a *Device that measures intraocular pressure to check for glaucoma*. TREPHINES? You don't want to know what trephines do—believe me.

Once upon a time, trainee surgeons and future eye doctors may have solved these puzzles, accumulating jargon to match their fees. Though there comes a time when jargon begets jargon, seen in a clue like *Asthenopia*, the answer to which is OPHTHALMOKOPIA.

The room is warm, but still I persist with the ocular vernacular. Even when words are familiar, the clues find a way to shut out the lay person. TOBACCO? That's a *Toxic amblyopia.* USHER? Try a *Syndrome of pigmentary degeneration of the retina.* After fifteen minutes I am in no danger of contracting LAGOPHYTHALMOS, the *Inability to completely close the eyelids.*

1985

Stone found in Queensland (7)

'**M**agnum is caught up in intrigue when a lady who believes her life is in danger involves him in her affairs.' The episode teasers in the TV guide, beside the crossword page, capture the era better than the date printed in the corner. Welcome to the four-channel days, when cable was something a ship used, and televisions sat in rooms like cardboard boxes instead of wall hangings. *Hey Hey* ruled the weekends, plus formulaic cop shows in which Magnum was punctually misled by intriguing women every Saturday.

I'm only guessing, but that same summary would probably have covered most episodes. The recipe was time-tested, audience-approved, in the same way a reader of *The Courier-Mail* could rely on the crossword page to carry a general quick and a slippery *Guardian* cryptic. Some things never changed. Until Australia Day 1985.

+ Mikhail Gorbachev dismantles Soviet Russia.
+ The *Titanic* wreck is located.
+ The *Rainbow Warrior* is sunk in Auckland.

New words: gobsmacked, Semtex, air-kiss

The catalyst was Shirl O'Brien, a Brisbane mum of seven. Growing up in Herston, in the city's heart, a teenage Shirl had won five shillings for solving a *Telegraph* puzzle. Fancy that, she thought, getting paid for doing something you love.

Teaching was another joy. After the war she shared a nomadic life with Jack, the young man who saved her from keeling over on a Brisbane train. Together they gained their teaching degrees and headed north to work in Rockhampton, Gladstone, Mount Morgan and Townsville.

Eventually, the family relocated to Brisbane. This was the early 1980s, when *The Courier-Mail* first began importing the *Guardian* puzzle, presenting Shirl the chance rekindle her girlhood passion. A day felt incomplete without tackling the crossword, yet somehow the challenge itself felt imperfect. Her grievance lay in the British skew—the Sussex villages and London motorways, the Whigs and Tories. The ex-teacher was all for learning. She thrived on musical and literary allusions, but the fact that such gifted setters were oblivious of Indooroopilly and Woolloongabba and all the other suburbs surrounding her home was, well, a pity.

There was only one way to fix it, Shirl reckoned. She bought some pencils, mapped some squares, and gave this puzzle-making a bash. Friends encouraged her to send the grids in to David Smith, *The Courier-Mail*'s editor. In her letter, she made a gentle push for more local content. She must have been persuasive, as Smith signed up the 58-year-old for a year's trial. If the readers responded warmly, then the gamble was a win.

January neared. Australia Day shaped as the ideal kick-off. Better still, the national holiday fell on a Saturday, Shirl's new niche. Fair to say, her start was cautious. The Queen was mentioned rather than Queensland, with the letters ER indicating Elizabeth Regina, just as the RAF, not the RAAF, was cited in a clue for AIR MAIL. Yet among the *Guardian*-esque clues there were some home-grown touches. SLICE, say, invoked a chunk of Norman Lindsay pastry: *Portion of 'The Magic Pudding' sampled on the golf course?*, while the poet hiding in the grid was MACKELLAR: Sydney-born and female, just like Mrs O'Brien. It was subtle, but the Australian element had arrived on the puzzle page.

Shirl learnt her craft as the weeks progressed, and the local references increased, kept in check by an empathy for expats who might find COOLIBAH, HOOP PINE and BLUE WREN as evasive as LEIGHTON BUZZARD had once struck her. Come her tenth puzzle, however, a flag was hoisted. By then the feedback was strong and positive, giving Shirl the heart to show her true colours. A precious green, in fact, as the setter's first state mention was a little gem: *Stone found in Queensland* (EMERALD). For non-Australians, Emerald is a coal town. The secret was out. *The Guardian* had a local rival.

Shirl's one-year contract lost its expiry date, as Southern Cross, Shirl's alias, went on to fashion 1223 puzzles, from general to themed, from global to provincial. Indeed, if a subbie ever needed a précis to prelude Shirl's work, they might take a leaf from the *Magnum* file: 'The solver is caught up in intrigue when a charming lady involves him in her affairs.'

However, we can't leave Shirl's story without a sweet postscript. So bright was her dazzle, Southern Cross was also noticed in the northern hemisphere. There, John Perkin, a British editor, hired the antipodean grandmother on his compiling team, and she turned out clues every month or so for a British audience. Shirl was flattered, and thrilled. The byline she chose was Auster, Latin for the southern wind. And the second home for her crosswords? *The Guardian*.

1986

The young couple desired intercorse (11)

It was an advencher story.

He was a medic with the army kor.

She was a singer in a quire. She had a nice natcher. She suffered badly with asma. 'I carnt go out tonight.'

He had to tred carefully. He made a sign with too fingers. (It was my duty to condem him for what he did.) He was a nawty boy.

For a woman she was tawl. 'Wi did you do that? Where are yoo going?'

He sed nothing. He put a hat on his hed.

The nite was dark because there was no moon. It was so cold he felt num.

The car was fitted with noomatic tyres. (Too much licker can

+ The Space Shuttle *Challenger* explodes.
+ The Chernobyl Nuclear Power Plant explodes.
+ *Crocodile Dundee* rules the box office.

New words: glasnost, Internet, shock jock

cause accidents.) The sine indicated a level crossing. It was a garstly mistake.

The explosion made a loud noize. He suffered a great trorma after the accident. The doctor said he had concushun.

He gave a last garsp before dying. It was a very sollum occasion. Deth is the end of life. At the funeral service we sang a him.

I told the story trooly. There is no dowt about it. English is a difficult langwidge.

Peter George Hannan was convinced. With Joe Thornton, he produced the booklet *Spelling Wen Yoo Dont No How Crosswords*, in which every sentence in this chapter's opening soapie, along with the chapter's title, was a clue in one of the 30 mini-puzzles. After serving as an honorary probation officer across Victoria, Hannan had seen how literacy went hand-in-hand with opportunity. As a means of eekwhippping those in need, thairfor, the jent made a peckyulier book ov crosswords.

1987

One to whom an accession is made (Law) (7)

Cornelius van Broek was frail and terrified. He hated to think his six surviving relatives might inherit his fortune without raising a sweat. So the plutocrat devised a plan, composing five crosswords instead of a will. The person who could solve his endgame stood to win his fortune.

The six contestants, so to speak, assemble in the Cruciverbal Club in New York. Picture the scene: the sextet of relatives arrive eager to hear the will's announcement, only to be told there is work to be done. Crossword work. A challenge to ensure the business empire will land in worthy hands.

This drama opens *Crossword Legacy*, written by Herbert Resnicow. A retired engineer with a fetish for games, Resnicow wrote several

---

+ Colonel North stands trial in the Iran-Contra Affair.
+ Australia's first mobile phone call is made.
+ U2 releases *The Joshua Tree*.

New words: virtual, empty nester, biodiversity

whodunits in the crossword vein—or *cluedunits*—from *The Crossword Code* to *Murder Across and Down*. The genre bloomed in the 1980s and was later sustained by a husband-and-wife team, Steve Zettler and Cordelia Frances Biddle, who wrote under the guise of Nero Blanc.

Yet the real coup achieved by the Resnicow series was the recruiting of Henry Hook, one of America's finest puzzle-makers, to design the stories' crosswords. With due respect to the novelist, that's the equivalent of the Moreland Zebras recruiting Lionel Messi as their striker, or Mighty Mouse getting Spiderman as a sidekick. Hook was picked up by *The New York Times* as a teen and later secured a gig as contributing editor to the legendary *Games* magazine, though for my money his genius shines brightest in the cryptic sphere, a style he developed in a series of Simon & Schuster books, *Hooked on Cryptics*. Like the best in the game, Hook can make you look at any word afresh, seeing COURTHOUSE as THOU in COURSE, or IMAGINARY as a woman nursing a drink (I and MARY around A GIN). For all that, the puzzles scattered through the Resnicow novels are quicks, with a Hookish bent.

At face value the clues are a snap, dictionary definitions, in fact, where *Twinge of pain* is PANG and *Prolonged struggle* CONFLICT. Now and then the heirs (and readers) need to forage for a more elusive answer, such as CAROM (*Strike and rebound*) or GRANTEE (*One to whom an accession is made (Law)*), but the wannabe millionaires aren't fazed.

The game's real grief lurks beyond the solutions. With a completed bunch of grids, the treasure-hunters are left to stare at each other. Now what? What's the point? And where's the money? This is where the Hook–Resnicow combo excels. Without betraying too many details, since the dime novels await all crossword sleuths, the main three puzzles hold more than the solvers first think. Put it this way: if you had $18 000 000 to offload, would you be happy to sink your fortune into a simple acrostic in which every first letter (of the clues or answers) tells the solver where to dig?

1988

'You're Only Old Once!' *author (5)*

The Gotcha Club is home to an elite group. These are the hawk-eyed solvers who spot errors in the *New York Times* crossword. A LION, say, could never be crowned *The king of the jungle*, as one clue vouched, since the king of beasts prowls the savannah. Old Leo would snarl his mane if he ever took to skulking the Congo. Likewise, a *Tuba's sound* could never translate as OOM-PAH-PAH, owing to the PAH-PAH part sounding more like the tuba's higher cousins—namely, the clarinet and trombone.

Both observations arrived in the mail during Eugene Maleska's term in office. Graciously, the overseer conceded his bungles. Human error was bound to creep in to his role, he knew: it was guaranteed if your job entailed proofreading 2.8 million clues per year, as his obituary claimed in 1993. Yet taking the rap was only part of

+ Australia's Bicentenary is celebrated.
+ Pan Am Flight 103 disintegrates over Lockerbie, Scotland.
+ Salman Rushdie's *The Satanic Verses* is published.

New words: lambada, road rage, crop circle

Eugene's ritual. Whenever a slip was singled out, the man would find time to turn to his desk drawer, pull out his best cartridge pen and a printed sheet and, in his elegant schoolteacher hand, inscribe the sender's name along the certificate's dotted line and so induct the reader into *The New York Times* Gotcha Club.

Hundreds of readers aspired to get through the Gotcha doors, but most fell short, landing in the Leaper basket. As the name suggests, Leapers were solvers who jumped the gun: 'those who grab their pens or rush to their typewriters to chide me for a mistake I haven't made,' as Maleska wrote in his memoir, *Crosstalk*. Such reader mistakes often involved booby-trap clues, in which *Food for hogs* seemed certain to be MASH but was actually MAST, a kind of acorn pulp. Or the fabrics TULLE and TOILE became muddled in the solver's mind, or two words unified, making a Leaper understand a phrase incorrectly—thinking MAKE A GO OF, for example, was MAKE A GOOF, which Eugene seldom did.

Be that as it may, he did finish 1988 with a gaffe. The clue was 'You're Only Old Once!' *author*, a pushover for any child of the 1960s or any parent roped in to story-time duties. The writer is Dr Seuss, of course, the pseudonym of Theodor Geisel. (As a tangent, I'll bet you a plate of green eggs and ham that how you say Seuss rhymes with *goose*. Am I right? Don't worry. Most of us say Seuss that way, despite the author stating his pen-name rhymed with *voice*. Which leads us back to Maleska's slip, though I'll need to escape these damned brackets before I can proceed.) You may know a person well, but that won't save you from making false presumptions. Setters and editors can be so familiar with a name that they don't feel the need to look twice. In fact, they overlook. A reader identified as LM of Kew Gardens, New York, caught out Maleska on this score:

On Monday, December twenty-eight,
While doing the puzzle rather late

And filling in on Thirteen Down
My forehead suddenly starts to frown:
ABOU and SOIE, it all fits well,
But Author SUESS, that rings no bell.
The E is preceded by the U,
While just the opposite is true:
It's Dr SEUSS not SUESS, you know,
Oh, *Times*, how could you blunder so!!

The gotcha was a piece of Seussian joy, and Eugene headed for his drawer. He fetched his pen and a blank certificate. Afterwards, by way of cover note, the editor attempted a rhyming reply:

Oh Dr. Seuss, you cooked my geuss.
But what the deuss,
A rare mistake was deu me;
So seu me!

The perfect ending, you'd think. An upbeat note to conclude the Maleska melody. But there remains one more exquisite irony to report, which relates to Eugene's 1993 obituary. I'm not sure who noticed the gaffe—perhaps an in-house staffer did the maths, or a number-crunching reader sent an email to the paper. Either way, a correction appeared in the following days: 'An obituary ... about Eugene T. Maleska, crossword puzzle editor of *The New York Times*, miscalculated the number of clues he sifted in reviewing puzzles submitted for publication. It was 40,000, not 2.8 million.' Rest assured, if it was a reader who spotted the oversight, a Gotcha Club membership was on its way.

1989

Bradman's famous duck (6)

If this clue works, you'll be thinking about Sir Donald Bradman and that grainy footage of the master batsman watching his bail dislodge. Depending on your colours, the day is (in)famous in cricket history. On that bright August morning in 1948 the crowd rose to applaud the Australian captain as he strode onto the Oval. This was his final Test, his ultimate outing in the baggy green. The man had faced down every challenge. His batting average was a tick below a ton, only needing four runs to create the three-figured precedent. Yet two balls later, misreading a googly from Eric Hollies, Bradman was heading for the gates, the crowd rising almost on the rebound and clapping him back to the sheds.

'I saw Bradman at the Oval in 1948,' said Waggy Greenaway, a patient at the John Radcliffe Hospital. He was speaking to the

---

+ The Tiananmen Square massacre occurs in Beijing.
+ The *Exxon Valdez* gushes oil into Alaskan waters.
+ The Berlin Wall comes down.

New words: d'oh, eco-friendly, fatwa

Oxford cop, Inspector Morse, who lay entangled in tubes on the parallel bed, also nursing an ulcer. 'He got a duck then.'

The inspector shook his head. 'I shouldn't worry too much about cricket,' he told Waggy. 'Just think about Walt Disney.'

The answer is DONALD, if you heed that advice: a clever splice of namesakes into one red herring. Beginners like Waggy Greenaway tend to fall into traps like that, convinced there's only one story on offer. Police inspectors, on the other hand, are trained to mistrust what they are told. Morse's ability to see through witness statements was matched only by his knack of plumbing a cryptic clue.

The duck deception appeared in *The Wench Is Dead*, the eighth novel in the Morse series. While the clue was crafted by Don Manley (ironically, known as Bradman in the *Financial Times*), the crime writer was not incapable of doing the composing himself. Solvers at *The Listener*, in fact, knew Colin Dexter as Codex. For quarter of a century the ex-teacher juggled the roles of writer and compiler. His thirteen Morse books, whose hero is a believer in the powers of real ale and quality solving time, bristle with clues of the crime and crossword variety.

Morse is a Wagner fan too, like Dexter. Both author and character live in Oxford. Both find time for single malts and double-meanings. As for the Morse name, I'd always suspected the label was a wink to Dexter's days in the Royal Corps of Signals, where morse was an obligatory skill. That theory was dashed, however, when I discovered the crossword connection.

Sir Jeremy Morse, the former chair of Lloyds Bank, was a gifted clue-monger in his day. Occasionally, he constructed puzzles under the obvious alias of Esrom. In the early 1950s, Morse was also Dexter's nemesis in the *Observer*'s clue-writing competitions. Another rival was Mrs B Lewis (whose real name was Dorothy Taylor.) Readers and viewers won't need to be reminded that Inspector Morse's sidekick in the mean streets of Summertown, north Oxford, is the loyal, no-ballocks, contrapuntal Sergeant Lewis. And the deviant killer in the first Morse adventure, *The Last Bus to Woodstock*, is a third clue-making champion from those formative crossword days. You'll need to read the case yourself to unmask the wordsmith—or see if you can decipher the clues before you get there.

Which leads us to the most enduring mystery at the heart of the series, namely the first name of Inspector Morse. For most of the copper's caseload, the detail was shrouded in speculation. Nobody could blame fans for starting to suspect their hero's birth name may have been Inspector. Despite the pressure, from readers and fellow characters, the two crossword-lovers (that's Dexter and Morse) remained tight-lipped. Until the penultimate book—*Death Is Now My Neighbour*—when cop and author combined to divulge the holy grail of trivia in the guise of a cryptic clue:

My whole life's effort has revolved around Eve (9)

Readers of *Cluetopia*, or those game enough to adhere to the timeline, will know the answer already, an eerie bit of voodoo back in 1945. While the clue's surface could be telling us about Morse's troubles to unmask the killers of women—both in *Wench* and *Woodstock*—the plainer truth lies in a letter shuffle. When those last two words are spun, the answer is ENDEAVOUR.

Though as your final Morse morsel, there awaits the surprise hiding in the character's full name. The man to stumble on this miracle was David Bourke, a stellar contributor to the website Anagram Genius. Encouraged by the name's letters, Bourke did a spot of scrambling to learn that INSPECTOR ENDEAVOUR MORSE was a blend of SO, REPORT: NAME IS UNCOVERED. Surely that result is almost as jaw-dropping as Sir Donald's swansong duck. Well, almost.

1990

Персонаж из Мертвых душ Гоголя (7)

Believe it or not, this clue promises a murder, a scandal, two novelists, a catwalk of gorgeous models, a bunch of dead slaves, a television show and a puppet, not to mention the social turmoil of modern Russia. To start, let's turn on the telly. Channel 1, if you don't mind. Time to watch an episode of *Polé Chudes*. The game will seem familiar at first. You may recognise the spinning wheel, the letter-picking, the Hangman-style word-filling on the bright and shiny board. That's right, *Polé Chudes* is based on the American franchise *Wheel of Fortune*, where contestants need to guess consonants to fulfil a mystery name or phrase, banking whatever money the wheel decrees if their stabs are successful.

+ Tim Berners-Lee creates the first web server.
+ Nelson Mandela is freed.
+ Lech Wałęsa is made Poland's first president.

New words: Generation X, prenup, feminazi

At least that's the version most of us know. The Russian variation is a different beast. The title alone—*Polé Chudes*—translates as Field of Wonders, which slang-wise means a place where people get scammed, a kind of clip joint, but on a grander scale. Social critics say Russia can be its own *polé chudes*, the age of glasnost inviting an epidemic of corrupt business dealings to fill the Soviet vacuum, but that's getting ahead of the story.

The title's purer reference is to a popular children's story. The hero is Buratino, a wooden puppet with a long nose. As you may suspect, the toy-boy is a rip-off of Carlo Collodi's *Pinocchio*, which was remodelled by Aleksey Tolstoy, a distant relation of the great Leo. Aleksey remixed the fairytale in 1936, his story selling in the millions across the Soviet Union. The plot proceeds along similar lines to the Italian version. Naïve as they come, Buratino falls in with a bad crowd, a *polé chudes*, if you like. Karabas Barabas, the evil puppeteer, cons the wooden child to join his show. But pretty soon the crook wants to cut his hostage's wooden throat, as his string-free antics are forever disrupting the performance.

Anyhow, getting back to the game show. When *Polé Chudes* began, in 1990, the host was the charming Vladislav Listyev. Gangly, bespectacled, with a shock of black hair, Listyev was loved throughout Russia, his spinning wheel and winning spiel drawing over 100 million viewers. He was also the man responsible for the format's eccentric Russian touches, like the lavish plates of food placed on the wheel. Drop-dead-gorgeous models would plant bowls of beluga caviar and smoked pork on the surface to make the whole thing resemble a gourmet lazy Susan. He was also instrumental in having the wheel spin more slowly than its American counterpart, meaning a game might uncover two letters in fifteen minutes, but five or six conversations.

As for the contestants, they hailed from all corners of the country. Every applicant had to complete a crossword to be considered.

A cakewalk for any citizen of mid-range education, the puzzle had lots of common geography, a teaspoon of Tchaikovsky, and some literature for good measure, including the clue Персонаж из Мертвых душ Гоголя *(7)* (*Character from Gogol's* Dead Souls).

The answer is MANILOV: a stretch for most non-Russians, no doubt; but bear in mind the classic novel was part of the national canon. The plot deals with squires who own serfs as much as they own cutlery or horses. Even in death, when the serfs transmute into souls, they remain the gentry's chattels. Manilov is one of these toffs, a maudlin landowner with a gang of dead slaves on his books.

If solvers knew this name, as well as the bespectacled snake of India, for example, they stood every chance of completing the puzzle. Later, if they were lucky, they might get the call from VID, the production company in charge of *Polé Chudes*. A new player in Russian media, VID was a game show specialist. Its logo alone was controversial, depicting a mask of Taoist philosopher Guo Xiang—hardly the hero you'd associate with a former communist stronghold. But that was the point. VID was the new breed, like its owner, the selfsame Vlad Listyev—a fresh talent with radical ideas.

Listyev was ambitious, as well as versatile. Not only did he host *Polé Chudes,* but produced the show into the bargain. Indeed, VID was the licensee of several franchises, including talent quests, a dating game and a local spinoff of *Name That Tune*. The company was a growing democratic force in modern Russia. So much so that Listyev moved to change the way advertising revenue was handled by media companies. Instead of relying on countless agents in the middle (operators gouging huge profits from their deals), Listyev switched control to the hosting channel, thereby governing the cash flow from client to network.

This perhaps was the fatal move. Nobody knows for sure, as police never found Listyev's killer. In 1995 the television darling was shot dead at the foot of his apartment building, with valuables and cash left on the body. Russia was outraged. No common crime, the murder had the whiff of assassination. Calls of corruption—financial or political—were heard across the country. The man was adored, as vouched by the silence observed by several channels the day after the murder, network bosses refusing to broadcast anything. Instead, they ran a simple message across the screen: 'Влад Листьев был убит' (Vlad Listyev has been killed). Even in death, the Russian public would not let his soul rest.

1991

Zulu for gatecrasher (7)

Doug Files longed to be a doctor but hated the sight of blood. Aged eleven, the poor guy fainted when getting a needle from the local GP. Graphic stuff on the television made him bury his face in the couch. Open cuts would set off dizzy spells. Career-wise, he loved the idea of medicine, but maybe medicine didn't love him back.

At high school, Doug was good at maths, but numbers left him flat. Words, on the other hand, possessed a pervasive charm. 'I loved languages my entire life, for the same reason I loved codes,' Doug is keen to tell me. 'They were secret at first, but once deciphered, new languages open up new worlds.'

That inborn appetite ushered him towards a linguistics major at Michigan State University. This was 1998, the year he met Tim Pulju, a brilliant student with a knack for parody. Tim, in fact, was

---

+ Operation Desert Storm is fought in the Middle East.
+ The Soviet Union crumbles into fifteen republics.
+ Paul Keating replaces Bob Hawke as prime minister.

New words: babelicious, carjacking, SMS, FAQ

pivotal in launching *Psammeticus Quarterly*, a mock-journal dedicated to highbrow ridicule of the linguistic kind. Imagine Monty Python let loose in the alphabet, or *National Lampoon* with diphthongs and phonemes. *Psammeticus* was all about exposing the pseudo. Articles ranged from 'Dolphin Linguistics' to 'A Stratificational Approach to Making Macaroni and Cheese'. Charles the Bald and Jakob Grimm were among the contributors, along with Xerxes, King of Persia (retired).

In the tradition of campus satire, the enterprise fizzled after four issues, though Tim and his co-editor, Keith Slater, were having too much fun to let the dream go. Two years on they created *Speculative Grammarian*, or *SpecGram* for short. To jazz up the mix they commissioned a crossword, knowing Doug Files was their go-to setter. Just one snag: Doug had quit the linguistic life and moved on to medicine.

'But what about the blood?' you ask. Before entering anatomy classes, Doug volunteered at a local emergency room. With scrubs and gloves, gore-mopping and body-bagging became the new normal. 'I also carried amputated limbs from the operating room to the pathology department,' he boasted in one email. Lastly, to prove he'd outgrown that woozy kid, Doug took to donating blood every month. The qualified linguist was determined to try a different path.

But before jumping the divide completely, Doug did his semantic mates a favour, observing one last goodbye. It took the shape of a 19 by 19 grid with 120 extraordinary clues. The puzzle's title, 'Crossword for Linguists', was redundant the moment you read 1-Across: *Ndonga for man's apron made of the first stomach of a ruminant*. The answer is KOPEKA, which must be spurious, surely, as *SpecGram* dwells entirely in the specious. If stories about elevator English and bee grammar fill the pages, then why would the puzzle be authentic? Clues like *Russian for wow* and *Zulu for gatecrasher* surely stemmed from in-jokes. How could any mortal know the *Ligurian word for valerian* unless they happened to come from Liguria and knew a valerian from a turnip? For the record, this herbal sedative is SALIUNCA in northwest Italy, while a wowed Russian is prone to yelling AX, perhaps on seeing a TONSELA invade a Zulu soiree.

Yet the biggest surprise of Doug's farewell, perhaps the greatest twist in the annals of speculative grammar, was to forget whether the multilingual puzzle was 100 per cent authentic or partway bogus. To quote Tim Pilju, 'No doubt it took Doug a very long time to make the puzzle, looking up words in dictionaries. In that sense, it's a testament to his dedication and skill.'

To quote Doug himself, 'I cannot even recall if it was a real crossword or just a spoof. A lot of water has gone over the dam since that time.' By water, he means a medical career in the United States Air Force. He has served in war zones like Bagram airbase in Afghanistan. The runaway linguist has flown in choppers as rockets zipped around him. Working in field hospitals camped on the edge of conflict, he's also seen his share of blood.

Did he cope? YA (*Malay for yes*). Did he ever faint again? NE (*Serbo-Croatian for no*).

1992

Is this your average icebox? (3,6)

The terrace house at the leafy end of Carlton in Melbourne is a private museum. Walk inside and the relics engulf you: painted plates on the sideboard, ornate mirrors over the fireplace, one whole wall of Chet Atkins's guitars. Nearby shelves hold more silver than Bolivia could unearth in a year: spoons and lanterns, platters and gravy boats. And, standing amid the clutter, almost 2 metres tall, is Patrick Street, the honorary curator.

We shake hands. He leads me to a dining table prepared for a feast—of crosswords. Stacks of glossaries and old magazines compete for space. 'You're looking at the history of the Australian Crossword Club,' says Patrick, a former magistrate and now a professional hoarder.

+ The Los Angeles riots are triggered by the beating of Rodney King.
+ War breaks out in Bosnia.
+ Native title is secured by Eddie Mabo.

New words: digerati, Photoshop, grrl, on-message

Precise to a T, my host has piled the magazines in chronological order. The topmost is the first issue of *Crozworld* that Patrick edited, back in 2000. The font is Bookman Old Style, clean and crisp throughout the 12 pages of original puzzles, each one crafted by an ACC member. Patrick is the volume's publisher, designer, editor and distributor—a collection of hats to go with his silverware and Gretsch guitars. He's also the ACC president.

He tells me the club started in 1988 as a group of cryptic-lovers. A Greek general in the Persian Wars led the charge. Aristides, alias Alan Eason, was a Fairfax compiler who produced *Crossworder* magazine, the prequel. An issue from 1989 is also on the table, stacked in its logical pile. I flick through its inkiness to find 'Roundabout', a carousel grid of criss-crossing letters built by someone called Stroz.

'That's me,' confesses Patrick. 'Street from Oz. Not very exciting as aliases go.' Perhaps not, though the byline adds a fifth hat to the man's collection. 'Roundabout' was his ambitious debut as a setter, made while he was still wearing the magisterial suit by day. The grid alone is noteworthy, based on Patrick's fetish for the intricate constructions found in *The Listener.* Yet the Stroz puzzle that caused the greatest stir appeared a few years later, after Eason's experiment sputtered and the ACC arose from the ashes.

Before we meet one of Stroz's outrageous clues, I need to teach you another language. Strine is the comical dialect collated by Afferbeck Lauder, whose real name was Alastair Morrison. The lingo captures the Australian gift for tamping sounds into minimal syllables, which linguists know as syncope. When Strine is in full flow, each sentence is a glued mumble that only a practised native can unstick. *Strine* is Strine for Australian, for example, a condensation that reduces four syllables into one. Meanwhile *baked necks* are a popular choice at breakfast time. And in case you haven't twigged, *afferbeck lauder* is Strine for alphabetical order.

Patrick gestures to the room we are in. 'I've been living here for more than 25 years, which is why my favourite Strines are terror souse and Gloria Sarah Titch.'

Even Stroz the alias had a Strine ring, thought Stroz. 'Aorta make Strine puzzle,' he reckoned.

Fare nuff, he did, calling his crossword 'The Strine Slengwidge', which appeared in issue 26 of *Crozworld*. What might have seemed your average animal at first glance turned out to be a savage mongrel of Australian syncopation. SINNY was the opener, *A city with a harbour*, followed by fifteen more bewdies in every Across entry. Consider an ARKELLERY, *Where pictures are hung*, or WOSKOANON?, a *General inquiry*. There was also the question *Is this your average icebox?*. The answer on paper looked anything but: AIR FRIDGE.

Reaction to the edition was largely positive. Some members despaired for the damage inflicted upon the Queen's English, but most responses entered the Aussie spirit, resorting to general gobbler mince: 'Doing Stroz's puzzle gave me a split nair dyke', 'Your Strine Slengwidge almost brought on a nerve sprike tan' and 'Quite enuf to strine the brine'.

The club continues to grow. Subscriptions have climbed above the 250-mark, with a raft of encoded members, such as Praxis and Timid Terrier, Zinzan and Raoul, keeping the innovation rolling. To any Australian with a care for crosswords, the omens are airspley fair billis.

1993

Mad poet mugged by banjo player sees red while eating pickles (3,4)

The name, Victor, is ironic, as this bloke seldom triumphs. His full name is Victor Meldrew, a retired security guard and principal clown on the BBC sitcom *One Foot in the Grave*. The part is played by Scottish actor Richard Wilson, who happened to be born in foghorn range of the Clyde shipyards we roamed in 1982. The show ran throughout the 1990s, racking up 40 episodes plus a few Christmas specials. Victor is central to most of the show's mishaps, like being shed-bound by marauding bees or scoring a ventriloquy gig at a death metal concert. In 'The Trial' he is stuck at home, waiting to see if he's required for jury service.

+ Bill Clinton becomes US president.
+ Stephen Hawking's *A Brief History of Time* is published.
+ Two heroic medicos—Weary Dunlop and Fred Hollows—check out.

New words: netizen, e-commerce, food porn, V-chip

He's not, but wet weather and a sense of duty see Victor powerless yet again. The episode is essentially a 26-minute monologue, written by David Renwick, in which Victor navigates his boredom with distraction and hypochondria. He measures a wall crack with his fingernail, fiddles with a radiator, picks a scab and even tries a crossword—the cryptic, of course, as Victor sees himself as a superior chap. This conceit is part of the hilarity as he reads aloud the first clue: *Mad poet mugged by banjo player sees red while eating pickles (3,4).*

Victor sucks his biro. He reads the clue more deliberately. A good tactic under normal circumstances, he isolates each word in his recital, though a larger problem for Victor is the blue ink escaping the pen and staining his lips and chin. The final straw is the last clue: *Elk's ego gets my goat. Head of MI5 upset the French by reversing into Dad's underpants. It's a doddle.*

David Renwick is having fun. The writer has a long history of zany wordplay. His script credits include sketch shows with Spike Milligan, Alexei Sayle and the Two Ronnies. But *Elk's ego* gets the gong for most preposterous, a deliberate poke at the nonsensical imagery some cryptics can generate. Now blotched in blue, Victor tosses the paper to the floor. 'I don't seem to be able to do the crossword today, as I appear to be temporarily out of mind-bending drugs!'

1994

Expert craftsman (6,7)

Roger Squires was the David Copperfield of his day—the illusionist version, not the Dickensian. He could make your pocket produce an ace, pull a coin from your ear: precisely the reasons his mates in the Fleet Air Arm banned him from the card table. I mean, seriously, would *you* bet big on poker if your opponent was a magician? Didn't think so. When rain was heavy and flying lessons were cancelled, the card games helped to pass the time.

Banished, Roger found another hobby, as he admits via email: 'I used to commandeer the wardroom papers to spend the time solving puzzles instead, attempting up to twelve newspapers on very wet days.' This was during the early 1950s. Newsprint was loaded with Soviet blocs, iron curtains, the looming Suez crisis, and puzzles. Roger feasted on the last of these. Little did the

---

+ The Chunnel opens.
+ Nirvana's Kurt Cobain is found dead.
+ *Schindler's List* wins seven Academy Awards.

New words: cybercafé, mwah, mouse potato, golden goal

crewman-cum-magician know he was laying the groundwork for a third career. More than a career: a trajectory.

After a decade of flying from the navy (yes, that heavy rain eventually relented), Lieutenant Roger Squires metamorphosed into El Squalido of sorcery, performing comedy and magic tricks in hospitals and nightclubs as far-flung as Rio and Singapore. He became a regular on British TV, boggling audiences at home and in the studio, on several variety shows. On late-night films you might still see him playing a chauffeur in *Licking Hitler*, or a ballroom extra in *War and Peace*, twirling in the background as Anthony Hopkins rules the screen.

However, his sharpening focus in civvy street was crosswords, a new challenge he tackled with typical zeal. His maiden puzzle appeared in Wolverhampton's *Express & Star* in 1963, and he made the national stage with a *Radio Times* crossword in the same year. The magician was an *Expert craftsman*, to quote his own *Daily Telegraph* clue of 30 years later.

By that stage—the mid-1990s—Roger was on his way to becoming the most prolific cryptic-setter on the planet. Keeping tabs on the tally is almost impossible. At last count the puzzle number verged on 75 000 and was still rising. To muddle the audit, his byline differs from paper to paper. He is Rufus in *The Guardian*, Dante in the *Financial Times* and Icarus in *The Independent*. He's also part of the *Times* and *Telegraph* stables, not to mention a welter of other periodicals from the *Daily Mail* to the *London Evening Standard*.

Should you visit the setter's home in Ironbridge, Shropshire— where there's an arched iron bridge that's older than colonial Australia—you will meet a spry man in his early eighties, kept in trim by regular swimming sessions. He's nimble-minded too, as he continues to fill his days with black-and-white squares, salting away his million-plus clues in parallel cabinets to guard against an entry receiving the same clue twice. This makes the task of choosing a single Squirean clue a special kind of lunacy.

Among the more memorable candidates—for sinister reasons—is the clue that appeared in *The Daily Telegraph* on 24 September 1994. Maritime buffs may register a faint bell in the distance, though when Roger set the puzzle some months in advance there was no bell to hear. How could he know an Estonian ferry would sink in the Baltic Sea, becoming Europe's worst peacetime shipwreck, in the same week the puzzle ran? He couldn't, which accounts for the hapless motif of sea life (and sea death) that pervaded the clues. As 852 lives were destined to be lost on the MS *Estonia* during a night crossing between Tallinn and Stockholm, the paper ran several uncanny entries:

Expert craftsman = MASTER MARINER
The stowaway won't be found on it = PASSENGER LIST
Master pleaded for change of ship = PADDLE STEAMER
Cover used by an American gangster = HOOD
Land on a site needing development = ESTONIA

In case you're wondering why HOOD made the list, let me remind you of the British cruiser which sank during World War II, just a few years before Boy Seaman Squires joined the ranks, consigning some 1400 men to the Atlantic. As for ESTONIA, the eeriest of the quintet, the setter recalls, 'I had ERITREA inserted and only changed it in the very late stages to complete the puzzle.'

No less spooky, however, is the fact that Roger Squires was alive to create this gruesome coincidence in the first place. You see, the compiler is intimate with life-and-death events at sea. In Cornwall, after the young Roger passed his Air Arm test, he added observer to his list of credits, acting as navigator and radio operator for various squadrons. During that time he flew to more than 50 countries and always touched down safely on the airstrip or carrier deck. Except once.

In 1961, when Lieutenant Squires was 29, his role was fighter-controller on a twin-engine Gannet over the Indian Ocean. The plane was in sight of HMS *Hermes* just off Ceylon, modern-day Sri Lanka. Approaching its base, the aircraft stalled 100 metres above the ocean. The plane plummeted, smacked the water. A wing broke loose. The fuselage flipped, and the Gannet speared deep into the blackness.

Roger yanked the lever to open the compartment door, but nothing happened. Water was gushing in. Thinking quickly but clearly, he removed his parachute, finding the last pocket of air near the ceiling. He hoarded his last breath. That's when the water pressure levelled, matching the ocean pressure outside. Five seconds later the door slewed off and floated away. As Roger recalls:

'Once free of the aircraft I inflated my Mae West and rapidly moved up in darkness. I recall a huge feeling of delight as the light became brighter and brighter. I popped up so fast, only my feet didn't leave the water. On the surface my eyes were suddenly blurred by aviation fuel. When I wiped them clear I could see the rescue helicopter hovering above me. Two minutes later I was back on board. Sadly the pilot had been killed.'

As a crash survivor at sea, Roger became an automatic member of the Goldfish Club. 'Before the accident I was a bit of a worrier,' he confesses. 'But since then I have taken life far more lightheartedly.' He's been more productive too, puzzle-wise. But the near-fatal episode remains fast in his memory. It's why he chose Icarus for his alias at *The Independent*, saluting the moment the magician almost vanished. Sometimes, in the local pool, the feel of the water evokes the memory of the cold sea. Other times, like on 24 September 1994, a dark coincidence does the remembering for him.

1995

What's this all about? (2)

Socrates will forever be tied to his cave idea. Life, said the Greek, resembles a parade of shadows projected upon a cave wall. We, the watchers, are trapped inside the cave—our skulls, in a sense—and we cannot face the light to see what creates the images in the first place. So it is we build our notion of the world on ethereal forms and suppositions.

Swiss giant Carl Jung used a different analogy. He likened all of human consciousness to a high-rise building in which every storey is a different era. Humans currently alive are in the penthouse, surrounded by the trappings of now. Downstairs we find our earlier selves, from earlier centuries, each floor less vivid in the mind's eye. As we descend, our consciousness blurs, and we sink to the Roman ground floor, then the Neolithic cellar. We have little access to these

---

+ Qantas is privatised, as Telecom becomes Telstra.
+ Oklahoma City is bombed.
+ OJ Simpson is declared not guilty.

New words: alcopop, Britpop, ego-surf, wiki

storeys, the foundations of our animal selves, despite the whole building being leased in our name.

Whether God is a watchmaker (William Paley) or dead (Friedrich Nietzsche), we are what we think. For more up-to-date ideology we can turn to the musings of Susan Haack, an Oxbridge professor of philosophy and law, more recently tenured at the University of Miami. She's also recognised by the *Sunday Independent* as one of the most important women philosophers of all time. Throughout her writings, her most enduring analogy is the crossword. The crux of Haack's metaphor is truth. What is right? Usually this question belongs to the ethical brigade, the moral philosophers, but Haack lives among the epistemologists, those concerned with how we know what we know. Her booth in the great expo of the mind is labelled *foundherentism*, a blend of two schools: foundationalism (dealing with the relevance of your own experiences) and coherentism (the basis of what you believe).

I'm being a tad cursory in my summaries, as this is dense stuff. For evidence, look no further than Haack's landmark work on the subject, entitled *Evidence and Inquiry: A Pragmatist Reconstruction of Epistemology*. Not a title you'll find at your nearest airport bookstore. The 400 pages pulse with intellect, a vast analysis of Western thinking, and sitting plumb centre in the work is a crossword puzzle.

To a trained eye, the puzzle betrays Susan's own background, the two continents she calls home. A dozen evasive British clues sit beside a grid as American as McDonald's apple pie. The crossword's purpose is to illustrate our mind flow when we are asked to determine the truth of something. Our brain flits between what we know and what we believe. Most philosophers of Haack's calibre will turn to a mathematical proof as a way of seeking certainty, but Haack found more substance, more metaphorical mileage, in a crossword. So ha ha, Sudoku—you dipped out!

Sorry, couldn't resist. Let's give the mike to Susan: 'The clues are the analogues of the subject's experiential evidence; already filled-in entries, the analogue of his reasons. The clues don't depend on the entries, but the entries are, in a variable degree, interdependent; these are the analogues of the asymmetries ... between evidence and reasons.'

In lay terms, you enter the answers you know, then you surmise the remainder from what you're told (the clues you need to grapple) founded on the intersecting letters you've established (a factual claim). This is the pattern—our proven knowledge serving as the basis of what correlates and connects, the whole system furthered thanks to the 'persuasive mutual support' of fact and evidence interacting.

The grid in Haack's opus is pocket-sized, just 6 by 5, with only a handful of white squares uncrossed by a second answer. Usually, when you solve any puzzle, you sift the clues and seize what is guaranteed to be true. When I see *She's a jewel (4)*, I quickly think of RUBY—a girl, and a gemstone. OPAL, you could argue, is a remote possibility, while ROSE applies to a crimson quartz, but RUBY seems the obvious truth, epistemologically speaking. That's how a solver operates. Humans in general process this way, maintains Haack. We ricochet between experience and reason. Piece by piece we tend to the 'integration of our web of empirical belief'. We might use the Y of RUBY to feel sure about YARD (*A measure of one's back garden*) or muse other answers elsewhere by measuring the hard evidence of RUBY against iffier bits of new data.

Ten years before this breakthrough treatise, Haack showed signs of a crossword bent. Or so runs my tenuous reasoning, based on the evincible fact of the professor's earlier paper '"Know" Is Just a Four-Letter Word'. Not that KNOW managed to squeeze into Haack's one and only published crossword. Yet a clue that goes close to the mark must be the refrain uttered by every lay reader (like me) who wanders into Haack's web of *Evidence and Inquiry*. I refer to

6-Down, a two-lettered answer with the clue *What's this all about?* The answer is RE, the common word meaning concerning, or in reference to. At least, I think it's RE, a form of the Latin word *res*, meaning thing. I'm pretty certain it's RE. Give me a moment. Let me double-check the other letters . . .

1996

Lead story in tomorrow's newspaper (!)

Will Shortz calls this crossword his all-time favourite—quite a claim for a man who has overseen two decades of the world's finest, working at the puzzle helm of *The New York Times*. So let's take a look at the clue lying central to the celebrated scheme, including its peculiar *(!)*.

Screamers, as printers know exclamation marks, are rarities in American crosswords. By contrast, cryptic-setters exploit them. Typically, an exclamation mark signals a clue known as an &lit, in which wordplay literally doubles as the answer's definition. For example, SEMESTER could be clued as *Sees term in translation!*. The anagram, coupled with a mixing prompt, reads like a straight-ish definition. Next time you see a screamer in a cryptic, you may be facing a literal (or &lit) clue. However, on election day in America,

---

+ Mad cow disease breaks out in the UK.
+ The Spice Girls and Oasis jostle for top chart position.
+ Ted Kaczynski, the Unabomber, is nabbed in his Montana cabin.

New words: chick lit, tamagotchi, McMansion, screenager

5 November 1996, this rare punctuation mark was alluding to an altogether different term.

Two candidates vied for the White House—the incumbent Democrat, Bill Clinton, and the Republican, Senator Bob Dole. Lead-up polls had tipped a sizeable win for Clinton, yet no sane editor would dream of pre-empting the result. That boo-boo had already been committed, in 1948, when the *Chicago Tribune* trumpeted victory for Republican Thomas Dewey over the incumbent Harry Truman, despite the fact Dewey didn't. For years the *Trib* dined on crow for its banner heading 'DEWEY DEFEATS TRUMAN'. A cautionary tale, one closely heeded by *The New York Times*—on the front page, anyway, though it seems the puzzle section had greater chutzpah.

The clue *Forecast* at 17-Across fired a warning shot, yielding PROGNOSTICATION. Then came the doozy a dozen Acrosses later: *Lead story in tomorrow's newspaper (!)*. The answer was entered in two blocks of seven letters each. Solvers hesitated. Could this be happening? Had Jeremiah Farrell, the grid's engineer, forecast the result of a presidential race? Why did Will Shortz allow this propaganda to cheapen such a reputable broadsheet?

Cross-letters affirmed that ELECTED was the closing word to occupy the second block. Thus the first block had to be the showdown's eventual winner, the showdown still raging in the streets! With timid pencil, most solvers wrote CLINTON in the squares. To vindicate their guess, every Down solution clicked. Below, with the letters of CLINTON in bold, are those seven answers, beside their accompanying clues:

Clue							
Black Halloween animal				C	A	T	
French 101 word (French for him)				L	U	I	
Provider of support, for short (Individual Retirement Account)				I	R	A	
Sewing shop purchase	Y	A	R	N			
Short writings		B	I	T	S		
Trumpet			B	O	A	S	T
Much-debated political inits (National Rifle Association)				N	R	A	

All day the phone rang off the hook. This was a crossword first: a foolhardy tip parading as truth. Depending on your point of view, Jeremiah Farrell was a prophet or a gambler. Somehow, this retired maths professor from Indiana, also the home state of Shortz, had called an election result 24 hours before the concession speech.

Or had he? When you look at zebras, do you see black horses with white stripes, or white horses with black stripes? If you focus on OPRAH, do you see Ms Winfrey or HARPO backwards? Contorting the art, Farrell had made a möbius strip, in which one clue could accommodate two sides of politics, playing on the bias of your average American solver. While it's true that CLINTON did the trick, so too did his rival, BOB DOLE. Take a second look at those clues, this time with alternative answers:

Clue							
Black Halloween animal				B	A	T	
French 101 word (French for yes)				O	U	I	
Provider of support, for short				B	R	A	
Sewing shop purchase	Y	A	R	D			
Short writings		B	I	O	S		
Trumpet			B	L	A	S	T
Much-debated political inits (Equal Rights Amendment)				E	R	A	

Farrell had done the impossible. In a refreshing take on black-and-white politics, both candidates were fit to serve their role, once installed. Republican solvers no doubt deemed the puzzle to be gallantly wishful, putting Dole in power—and sadly wrong. Meanwhile, few in the Clinton camp realised their darling Bill had as much right to occupy the squares as Bob.

Farrell himself had a history in such duplicity. In 1980 the professor had meshed two other aspirants, CARTER and REAGAN. Again, the relevant squares could hold whichever of the two surnames solvers chose. It was a brilliant sleight of hand, but Eugene Maleska, the puzzle editor of that period, whom we met earlier, was less smitten. He refused Farrell's draft because of the frail chance that John Anderson, an independent in the race, might reach the Oval Office. Crestfallen, the setter took his paperwork to *Games* magazine, a hotbed of innovative puzzling at the time. The editor was wowed by the construction yet had to knock it back due to the magazine's long lead time: the election outcome would be a *fait accompli* by the time the next issue hit the stands. The editor's name was Will Shortz.

A week, they say, is a long time in politics. Plausible as that sounds, this milestone crossword proves that a dazzling idea is timeless.

1997

Small bomb which temporarily dazes its victims (4,7)

Where were you when Kurt Cobain died? Michael Jackson? Amy Winehouse? I still recall the day when Princess Di breathed her last. I was sitting in a football stadium watching the Kangaroos wallop the Magpies, just minding my own beeswax. The news came courtesy of another spectator, a stranger sitting a few rows down. He had a pocket radio pressed to his ear, yelling the grisly newsflash as a town crier might broadcast a public lashing. The death felt wrong. Surreal. At first I suspected the stranger of committing a sick joke, until more fans around me relayed the bulletin. No question, the calamity stole the purpose from the football game, though I do recall

---

+ Hong Kong returns to China.
+ Princess Di is killed in a Paris tunnel crash.
+ Tony Bullimore is found alive in his capsized yacht.
+ Comet Hale-Bopp crosses the sky.

New words: e-tail, muggle, manbag, shagadelic

one wag replying to the first announcement, 'You got the progress score from Geelong?'

Tom Johnson heard the news on BBC Radio 4 just after waking up in his Cheshire home. 'From that moment on,' he told me, 'Jean and I were glued to the television reports and speculation for the rest of the day.'

Johnson goes by many names. One is Doc, in homage to the father of lexicography, Dr Samuel Johnson. Doc is the alias linked to *The Spectator*'s puzzles, in the deviant tradition of Jac—the pioneer we met in 1972. Johnson's other crossword nickname is Busman, due to his 'anorak affair' with vintage coaches of every stripe. Indeed, Anorak is a third pseudonym, which labels his work in the *New Statesman*. And readers of the *Financial Times* know the man as Gozo, also the name of a small island off Malta, where many quaint buses operate.

But getting back to limousines—the Mercedes-Benz carrying Princess Di into that French tunnel—the news was a violent slap across the face of Britain. Thousands left flowers and cards at the Spencer family estate. Mourners kept candlelight vigils outside Kensington Palace. Elton John retoggled his Marilyn Monroe tribute. And in the market town of Nantwich, a pretty Tudor settlement on the River Weaver, Tom Johnson scrambled for his eraser.

Only days before the crash, the setter had submitted a general knowledge crossword to *Prospect* magazine, as he did every month. (Just to clutter the CV, Johnson creates these large brainteasers under yet another pen-name, this time Didymus, after the querulous disciple Thomas.) To give you some bearings, *Prospect* contains a suite of essays and analysis, and boasts a strong suit in fiction and cultural matters. As part of the blend, the Generalist puzzle is a mammoth diagram testing solvers' grasp of literature and nature, sport and geography, and doses of current affairs.

Affairs like Squidgygate are a case in point. This cutesy name had been coined by the tabloids as a label for a phone-tapping scandal in 1990 involving Princess Di and her close friend James Gilbey. The Squidgy element denoted the nickname that Gilbey had used for Diana. Their chats revealed all manner of private anxieties, touching on the princess's exclusion from the palace circle, her deep unhappiness in her marriage, her fondness for clairvoyancy, her possible pregnancy.

In September 1997, only days after the primary speaker in the affair had been killed in a high-speed smash, any crossword reference to SQUIDGYGATE would have been far too much for a solver to bear. Johnson moved quickly. He dug out pencils, booted the computer. The mission was clear: camouflage SQUIDGYGATE at 28-Down in the *Prospect* puzzle or risk the ire of every reader. But the turnaround time was brief. Only a few days lay between proofing and publishing. How to remove the grid's new flaw and still save the crossword?

'The solution was fortuitous,' recalls Tom. 'For a change, for this issue, I had happened to devise a grid based on mirror-symmetry [where only the vertical axis of symmetry applies], and the very nature of the pattern lent itself to an easy edit.' As fate would have it, SQUIDGYGATE occupied the least frantic corner of the mesh. The most immovable letters—for reasons of lengthy crossovers—were the s, u, a and e. With clammy fingers, Johnson tapped those letters into his crossword software arrayed amid a series of question marks implying gaps: 's ? u ? ? ? ? ? a ? e'. If no other word fitted the sequence the entire creation was doomed, his name would be mud, and *Prospect* stood to inherit a blank page for a puzzle.

Bingo. A match surfaced on the screen. Creepy, in light of the Parisian shockwaves reverberating across Britain. Johnson could not believe his luck, not to mention the uncanniness of the last-minute substitute. He penned a new clue: *Small bomb which temporarily dazes its victims.* STUN GRENADE.

1998

Kind of artistic craving causes interference (8)

Every weekday, twice a day for six years, Andrew Gangoiti rode the school bus, watching the wires of the high-tension cables dip and climb against the sky. Closer to earth, the wires of the fences ran like music staves across the paddocks. 'In a sense I have been seeing lines forever,' he says. In his family line too, which traces back to the Basque Country. His father, Nicolas, worked with fishing lines as a younger man, the reason the family settled in Lakes Entrance, a fishing port four hours east of Melbourne. Andrew's mum was Australian, the wordy one in the house. The Gangoitis lived on the town's outskirts and had four kids, with Andrew third in line.

+ Bill Clinton is impeached.
+ Australia stages the first National Sorry Day.
+ Google is founded.

New words: Bluetooth, Viagra, senior moment

At trade school in 1977, when Andrew was sixteen, he refined the art of drawing lines, working with T-squares and French curves, slide rules and drafting tables. He calibrated angles and created depth.

After school the obvious path was engineering, but Andrew wasn't convinced. 'I took a few years off, trying to decide what I wanted to do,' he told me down a crackly phone line. 'I laid carpets for a while, worked for an uncle who had a repair shop. I waited tables, picked up work on building sites. I guess you could say I was slow out of the blocks.'

The strangest job was also perhaps the most dangerous. The Gangoiti name had a good reputation on the water. Andrew's dad worked as a cook on the trawlers, 28 days at sea feeding the fishermen, then home for twelve. Lakes Entrance was a small world, and talk said that work was going on the barges, so Andrew applied. He wanted the money to travel. That's how he found himself cleaning the decks and cabins of a giant construction barge in Bass Strait. 'The work was pretty mindless, and noisy. Two weeks on, two weeks off—seven till seven, day or night. But you made good money.'

The barges dragged the scaffolds, or jackets, of the strait's oil platforms into their drilling location. At the critical moment, the vessel would half-sink into the ocean, immersing the jacket as the engineers adjusted the ballast. An onboard crane hoisted the whole rig upright, enabling steel pipes to be fed down the jacket's legs. Tonnes of cement and grout were next poured down the legs, ready for the pile-driver which walloped the monstrosity into the seabed.

Day in, day out, nobody could escape the noise, but Andrew found a way to float above it. His secret lay in chalk. Not just any chalk, but the durable limestone type the welders used to mark their lines. 'The crews would leave large clumps behind in the locker room. I'd put them in my pocket. I had a tiny hacksaw blade, and when the cleaning was done, or I was trying to sleep in my cabin,

I started carving the chalk, made these little amulets and figurines, no bigger than your fingertip.'

Another relief was crosswords. A chopper delivered the *Herald Sun* every day, along with fresh food and supplies. The paper in the mess room was open to everyone on deck, assuming you could find the downtime. 'Night shift got pretty boring, so we started filling in the crossword—me, the other cleaner and the laundry guy. The paper lay open on the table. If you were passing or grabbing a coffee, you filled in another answer.' It was just the quick, but that was perfect. One guy's breakthrough would lead to someone else's. By dawn the puzzle was usually complete—a team effort.

'I tried doing the cryptic as well. It was in the same paper, but it made no sense.' More appealing was *Time* magazine, also on hand, in particular the art pieces by Robert Hughes. 'I remember he wrote about Velázquez, the Spanish painter: his precision, his control of light. I still have that article somewhere.'

After the barge, after Europe, after a bash at guitar-making, art became Andrew's calling. At 28 he won a place studying the subject at the Royal Melbourne Institute of Technology, in one part thanks to his technical drawing, and the eloquence of his chalk scrimshaw. He revelled in the work of Henry Moore and Herbert Ferber, the master sculptors, though he couldn't stand the French thinkers. 'Everyone at college was quoting them—Barthes and Derrida and Lacan—but nobody was reading them with any understanding.' The density of their work rang a bell, reviving a memory of opaque sentences on an ocean barge, an image of language running in severe lines. For his final honours project, Andrew built a cryptic crossword.

Or a retable, to be precise. Scrabble players will know the word, though Andrew had to explain to most people that a *retable* is the same as a *reredos*. 'A what?' they asked. An altar screen is the simplest way to put it, a triptych structure that often serves as a frame for icons behind the communion table. In Andrew's case, the icon was a crossword—one of mine, in fact.

I remember the phone call. It's not every day a sculptor rings your home to ask you for a tough crossword. 'No,' he added. 'Better than tough—make it *dense*.' He fleshed out his reasoning. It was all about Marcel Duchamp, the archpriest of postmodern art. The Frenchman's most notorious piece is *Fountain*, the snapshot of a porcelain urinal. Andrew resented the reams of twaddle devoted to that single image. His altar screen was a form of artistic payback. The ideal puzzle would seem almost solvable, but not quite. Like a tease, a false promise, with a hidden message: knowledge is power—ignorance is bliss.

Instead of making a puzzle from scratch I thought I'd sift my backlist to find an appropriate head-scratcher. Was that okay? Perfect, said Andrew. After all, just like the welders' chalk, or the window sashes for his retable, the practice of finding and reusing objects was central to Andrew's work.

One crossword jumped out. Not sure why. According to solvers' feedback, it was tough, which helped. In fact, FEEDBACK was the first answer, which appealed to the artist in Andrew—the constant craving for peer acknowledgment. Better still, running off the E and B of FEEDBACK was another artistic allusion: EMOTIONAL BAGGAGE (clued as *A sad case?*). Good as done, though the secret message was ticklish to retrofit.

Thankfully, the clue tally fell into our hands. With 16 Across clues and 15 Downs, the clues' first letters could be easily doctored by a subtle manipulation to spell out a message when read vertically. Somehow we managed to rope in Duchamp and Lévi-Strauss, while FEEDBACK's clue became a forlorn double-meaning: *Kind of artistic craving causes interference*. This K initial, printed in bold, headed up the acrostic: KNOWLEDGE IS POWER—HAPPILY IGNORANT.

The final piece came up a treat. Picture a trifold of vaulted sash windows with wooden panels instead of glass. Printed on the central panel was the grid, with Across clues occupying the left wing, and Down clues the right. The configuration implied the altar, while a shaft of light on an empty foreground suggested the holy object to be absent. So too did the title: *retable for fountain*.

As for the fate of our collaboration, the piece stood for some weeks in a Melbourne gallery gaining polite feedback, though the object failed to reach the Guggenheim. Mind you, Andrew got that far, to the Bilbao museum at least. Since 2005 he has been working there as an art handler. He lives not far away, with his wife and their six-year-old son. And I'm prepared to bet that a garage in Biscay on the Cantabrian Sea is the only garage in the world to contain a cryptic reredos.

1999

美国历史最悠久的军事学院, 以严格 的规则和纪律闻名于世

Have you solved the clue yet? I'm not surprised. Unless you speak Mandarin, or know the nuance of each Chinese pen stroke, you'll struggle to identify *The oldest military school in the United States, world-famous for its strict rules and discipline.* That's the translation. Now you have a fighting chance to grab the answer. I'll give you a bonus clue: the answer has four words. Or, being a Chinese crossword, think four ideograms.

English-language setters get off lightly: we have a vowel or consonant to serve as intersection. But puzzle-makers for the *Southern Weekend*, based in Guangdong province, must think in pictures, so to speak. What two answers might marry in concept?

+ The euro is introduced.
+ Napster debuts.
+ *Big Brother* Mark 1 begins in The Netherlands.

New words: dot-com, staycation, bling

The term for crossword itself, the novelty introduced by the paper in 1999, is 填字游戏, which translates back as Chinese fill-in-the-blanks game. Of course, the concept is depicted with a kindred compound in English—a pairing of description (cross) and composition (word). But that's where the parallels cease. In English, if I want to cross a word with CROSSWORD, I have a riot of choices, thanks to the alphabet. My Guangdong counterpart, however, can only cross his crossword—or 填字游戏—with such candidates as 戏剧 which means theatre, where the Chinese character common to both is 'xi'—to play, or tease. This is the matching ideogram enlisted in the compound 游戏 (which means game, or 'youxi'), the very cluster to conclude the crossword's elaborate label. In other words, a Chinese setter depends on the interplay of notions and semantics, rather than the simplicity of letters: a proposition both poetic and refreshing, not to mention challenging.

Crosswords themselves are burgeoning in China, boosted by an online craze in which players can choose their own topics from an archive. With more black squares, the grids resemble completed Scrabble games in which words of only four tiles or fewer have been played. This pattern is more forgiving, making way for concept chains rather than the tight American jams. An added curio to the Western eye is how some 填字游戏 use Arabic numbers for the Across clues and Chinese numbers for the Downs.

So what is that American school famed for its discipline? West Point Military Academy (西点军校) is your answer, sharing the symbol for west (西) with the Across entry, Xishuangbanna (西双版纳), a popular tourist destination in China's Yunnan province. And yes, as you'd expect, Yunnan province lies in the far southwest, borrowing on the academy's mention of direction. Look at you: one small chapter, and you're already getting the hang of it.

2000

Must pay (3,2)

Check out this box:

A	M	E	R	I	C	A
M	A	R	A	C	A	S
B	U	R	G	E	S	S
I	M	I	T	A	T	E
T	A	N	A	G	E	R
S	U	G	G	E	S	T

+ The Olympics are held in Sydney.
+ The Tate Modern and the London Eye open.
+ Y2K is debunked.
+ A tree falls on the last Pyrenean ibex in the wild.

New words: global warming, click-through, intifada

Every line holds a word, across and down. (In case you're unsure, a *tanager* is a songbird, while the *Mau Mau* is a radical group arising from Kenya.) The grid was posted on an online crossword forum in 1996. The sender was a relative unknown named Frank Longo.

One person to see the box was Matt Gaffney. As he recalls in an email, 'I felt a chill run down my spine.' Thanks to Longo's Oblong, his professional future suddenly seemed in jeopardy. Gaffney was only 24 at the time, a rising star in the puzzle ranks, but the box was a sock across the jaw, because the interlock had been made by a computer.

Software was a game-changer in the 1990s. Every industry was overhauled by the arrival of smart machines, crosswording included. Frank Longo was an early adopter. Behind the scenes the New Jersey resident had been busy compiling a database, filling memory banks with potential crossword fill. He chose words from near and far, old and new. The foundation of his collection was straight dictionary stock, which was then overlaid with pop songs and astronauts, street slang and a bunch of African rebels.

His banks brimming, Longo tested the system with a few beta-grids. What you see is what emerged, jangling the hell out of Gaffney. Suddenly, the business of entwining letters seemed moribund. Matt says, 'The minute I saw this very clean 7 by 6, from someone I'd never heard of, I knew the days of the human-written themeless were numbered.'

Nowadays, any bit-brained computer can conquer the interlock phase—it can even supply pre-loaded clues from a captured archive of press records for most orthodox entries. Cryptic-setters have less to fear—for now, at least. The devilry of wordplay currently lies beyond a program's reach. But this frail complacency can't be shared by most Americans, who deal mainly in the quick brand of clues. The software boom had democratised the themeless puzzle, making it a feat any child with the right program can achieve.

Gaffney by this stage already had several major crossword clients in addition to running his own puzzle syndicate with fellow Brat Packer Matt Jones. But this box made him rethink his plans. If computers were destined to outrace *Homo sapiens* in the General Fill Handicap, then why compete in the first place? A better plan was to focus on those areas where machines fell short. Gaffney identified two. The first was theme selection—collecting weird subsets to serve as the key entries, oddball stuff like famous stutterers or bands with a z: quirky mini-lists no database would ever know. The second area Matt pretty much invented. Visit his website at xwordcontest.com and you will find ample evidence of the human brain at its screwiest.

Gaffney called them metapuzzles. Imagine a riddle wrapped inside a riddle. The new genre challenged solvers to crack the grid first and foremost, and then to discover a deeper message, a hidden word, a missing theme member, as part of the endgame. Building a puzzle within a puzzle like this is beyond the silicon head of a computer. Since 2000, a few years after seeing Longo's Oblong, Gaffney has dreamt up a slew of lulu metas to bewilder his solvers. In over 275 intricate puzzles he has spelt out questions as the principal entries like *What word in this grid can lose one letter to gain a syllable?* (FINANCE—which can become FIANCE), shaped clues to have two answers, like *Enveloped entirely* (TRAPPED or WRAPPED). He's even smuggled four sets of famous twins inside the major entries, which the solver had to pinpoint in the completed grid. (JACOBIN THESAURI, for example, held JACOB and ESAU, while PLEIADES FLUKES nurses the *Star Wars'* siblings, LEIA and LUKE.)

As part of the Gaffney fun, solvers must submit their completed diagram (in addition to the meta-answer) for the chance of prizes and kudos. The minute they find the solution-inside-a-solution, they email their triumph to lodge their name on a leader board. So goes the domain's routine, except for once: Gaffney's maddest coup of the whole series, entitled 'Please, No Calls'.

The meta in question had these key entries:

'k ttyl' e.g. = TEXT MESSAGE (short for OK, Talk To You Later)
Driver's license info for the person reading these words = YOUR SURNAME

Among the other answers were eight smaller words, which, in the interests of privacy (keep reading and you'll find out why), I shall present in random order: TRIO, WON, OWETO, TUE, OHHH, NEIN, TOO, FREE.

Can you latch onto the logic? Could you crack the meta? Gaffney now laughs at the creation. 'That puzzle was early on, when my solving audience was in the low hundreds—I would never try that stunt now!' Against all commonsense, the meta master had implanted his own phone number into the crossword (look again at those eight smaller words), asking shrewd solvers to text their surnames (look again at the first two entries) to his private mobile phone once they twigged. All up, 92 smart cookies bombarded Matt's phone, a unique lunacy in puzzle history. His wife, Kristin, suspected her man had lost his marbles, but such is the debt that crossword innovators *Must pay* (OWE TO) in the quest to outsmart computers.

2001

One of the film crowd with standard—
that's very unusual (13)

Quick start instructions:

1 Start up the program and hit F11 until the format is set to Crossword Compiler.
2 Hit the L key to enter Load Crossword mode.
3 Hit Y to accept the current format.
4 Use the arrow keys to select your example crossword—quick, basic cryptic or cryptic.
5 By default the Across clues are presented first.
6 To hear a clue, hit the C key.

+ The Twin Towers are attacked in New York.
+ Enron files for bankruptcy.
+ Sir Donald Bradman dies.
+ Wikipedia goes online.

New words: 9-11, facial profiling, weaponise

That last step is your biggest clue of all. The instructions you've just read are in fact meant to be heard when read aloud by a SAPI 5.1 American woman. (SAPI stands for Speech Application Programming Interface, and 5.1 is the technology's vintage.) The voice evokes a boozed robot: the words seem crammed, their emphases all over the shop. However, to a person with reduced vision, or none at all, Ms SAPI is a siren embedded in a breakthrough program called Blind Gamers Crossword Puzzle.

At one point, while trialling his cribbage game for those with vision impairment, Ian Humphreys used his own voice for the speech interface, but this proved too time-consuming. Enter Ms SAPI, a piece of ready-made software. But, if users don't warm to 'her' synthetic tones, the crossword program allows you to Windows-shop for another voice, again using arrows and audible commands. Such is the beauty of Ian's baby, in which every whim is covered. After so many years of exile and frustration, the blind solver has been let loose in the puzzle palace. Upload the program and shazam: almost any shift key on a Braille keyboard becomes a corridor to places those in the seeing community take for granted.

Take a 'look' at one of the Blind Gamer cryptics, for example. As soon as the cursor reaches the clue, Ms SAPI reads it out: *Arctic Lapp endlessly turns out to be good with hands (9)*. The grid already contains the initial, P, and the third letter, A. Cautious solvers are welcome to hit F, which stands for Fit and opens a virtual dictionary. The drunken robot prepares to announce all 143 possibilities, though the solver can scroll down or shortcut the list by supplying a likely opening cluster. The robot then identifies each item on request, from *peaceable* to *ptarmigan*. The solver highlights and enters their prime suspect, and the word is transferred to the solution grid, as typifies the PRACTICAL nature of Spoonbill Software.

The V key opens the Validate function—a running verdict delivered on any answer. The standard Delete undoes an error, while

Shift-R for Reveal is the function of shame. Anagrams are at the solver's fingertips too, assuming they know their clue types and what letters need mixing. Shift-F will Find specific words. Alternatively, if solvers wish to Quit (Q), they simply Save (S) their labours for another session. But if their Progress (P) is advanced, then why not tackle those last few clues? This will lead to the nervous moment when K comes into play, the program's key for Check.

Spoonbill is a not-for-profit operation. Ian, a retired computer programmer with the Department of Lands and Surveys in Perth, is British, migrating to Australia in 1968. As for Spoonbill, the name honours a beloved resident of the city's zoo. Nicknamed Spoony, the bird would perch on a railing near the main path, watching the strange bipeds walking past. If he closes his eyes, Ian can still see the glee etched on his children's faces when they stroked the bird, receiving ticklish pecks for their trouble.

Metaphorically, the retiree is trying to duplicate the pleasure that he saw in those faces. His software aims to produce smiles through a few simple strokes of a key, whether the players are indulging in poker or risk, hangman or stratego. The runaway success among the genres, though, in terms of downloads and feedback, has been the crossword. Not only was there strong demand in waiting, with the blind population locked out of the pastime, but the same tool allows users to interface with any other puzzle site that offers crosswords in the common Across Lite formats. As you read this paragraph, Ian's software is being downloaded around the world, with elated emails coming back in droves. Colin Glover, from Britain, wrote, 'I love crosswords so much and have been frustrated for many years not being able to do them. [Your program] has opened up a new world.' While Ruchi Patil from India said, 'I just tried it and found it to be incredible.' To solve a clue in the start-up's easy cryptic, the same sampler to give this chapter its title, the patient hobby of a retired programmer has become EXTRAORDINARY.

2002

صديق (5)

Lily Serna was born in Jerusalem to an Arabic mum and a Palestinian father with some Slovenian blood. (*Serna* is actually Slovenian for a small deer.) She moved to Australia when only young, where she grew into a pink elephant (the nickname for her school uniform) and later attained a masters of mathematics studying the dynamics of ocean currents on the Great Barrier Reef.

Lily's also a friend of mine. For two years we were opposing halves of a formula called *Letters and Numbers*, as aired on television from 2010. If you never caught the SBS show, then you may know the British version, *Countdown*, in which contestants have to jumble letters to make the longest word, and crunch numbers to reach a random total. Old-fashioned games in many ways, a refreshing antidote to a lot of brain-lite programs, and very addictive if the

---

+ Queen Elizabeth's Golden Jubilee is celebrated.
+ The Bali bombings kill 202 people.
+ *Kath and Kim* premiers on the ABC.

New words: google, blog, WMD

winner at home gets to escape washing-up duties. Lily was the numbers ninja, and I was the dictionary man.

Our host was Richard Morecroft, a comforter in terms of anagram and experience. Over two years we became close mates. Richard's key job description on the show was viewer's ambassador, doing his best to illuminate the cog-work of his two nerdy companions, though more often his gig was closer to boxing referee, trying to stop Letters taking cheap shots at Numbers, and vice versa. Because, despite being pals off the set, Lily and I loved to taunt each other under the Klieg lights. Our rivalry was part of the show's fun. Whereas Lily thought esoteric words like *esoteric* were a waste of time, I couldn't see the beauty (or point) of nine sevens making 56. Or 63. I forget.

School groups made regular trips to the studio. Our routine was to ask the kids to raise their hands, getting them to declare their bias when it came to letters and numbers. Which did they prefer? What was the greater strength? For some reason, Lily sewed up the adolescent male vote, while I converted my share of primary children, mainly due to (a) my constant puzzles and (b) the lolly prizes that went with them.

Each afternoon was a pantomime matinee. Lily booed Letters, and I hissed Numbers, the gist of our showbiz the ability to feign *yab-ghad* in a way. *Yab-ghad* means hate in Arabic, a word Lily taught me while loitering in make-up. Love is *hub* or *alfa*, which aren't easy words to forget. At least, that's how you pronounce the translations, since Arabic script is a filigree of twists and kinks that seems too beautiful to be language.

A year or so after the show was shelved—or rested, as the network execs prefer to say—I had cause to examine the Arabic swirls again. With bated breath, it must be said. When *Cluetopia* was first proposed, I'd set my sights on locating far-flung puzzles, the best among the rarest, having no inkling that Arabic would come into play. Such an ornate alphabet seemed at odds with the strictures of Across and Down. But I was wrong, as an Egyptian website schooled me. There, I unearthed 200 such puzzles, their lacework solutions as hypnotic as the clues festooning the screen.

The only catch was my lack of translator. Wait a minute—what about Numbers? I texted her, begging for a bizarre favour. As it turned out, in terms of nuance and idiom Toula Serna was my better shot. Lily was more than happy to recruit her mum for the chore, which is typical of mathematicians. All surds, no substance, those people.

Toula was brilliant. I'd chosen a puzzle posted on Christmas Day, 2002, as the date best illustrating the cultural leap. Look high and low: you won't find a Western crossword published on 25 December in any year, but in Egypt the population moves to a different beat—and a seductive, pictorial dictionary.

The grid obeyed the orthodox 15 by 15 of your everyday Anglo box, but thereafter the overlaps dwindled. Symmetry went out the window, while all Across entries ran right to left, in keeping with Arabic literature, except those words that ran in reverse to meet the challenge of intermeshing. The first clue alluded to a proverb, and the answer was ضرب البطل (accidental hero). As Toula explained, the term is a popular taunt of the Middle East which translates something like, 'Your brother has been forced and is no hero.' The nearest equivalent we have in English might be the misplaced glory we afford to the one millionth customer, or the cheers reserved for the player who scores a simple goal after all the hard lead-up work of other teammates. Perhaps the phrase is largely untranslatable, but then again I once thought the same of converting crosswords into Arabic.

Wafah was another answer in the diagram—namely, death. And *ya'saf,* meaning to be sorry. Tucked in to the same dense space was a film starring Omar Sharif, a Cairo football club, a Babylonian king and Molière satire. But the solution to spring from the blue, given the pseudo-hatred I nurse for Toula's numerically adept daughter, was ليمز (*khill*)—the answer to صديق (*sadiq*). And before you get the wrong end of the stick, *khill* (said with a guttural k, advises Toula, 'like the ch in loch') means friend.

2003

Greek god of war (4)

The Baltimore sheriff upends his pencil, using the eraser to undo his work. Across the table sits Omar Little, a career criminal in a bomber jacket. 'Ain't working out for y'all, huh?'

The sticking point is MARS, the name the sheriff had entered in the grid. *Greek god of war*, says the clue. But the letters don't gel. He shares his frustration with Omar, who takes a beat before suggesting ARES. The lawman does a double-take. He studies Omar's face, as if the deity is some kind of curveball. 'Greeks called him *Ares*,' adds Omar. 'Same dude, different name, is all.'

This extra detail persuades the officer. ARES must be right; the letters fit. And if that's not hard evidence, there's Omar's situation to consider. Despite a rap sheet extending to several pages, Omar is moments away from serving as a state witness. The trial is for

---

+ Saddam Hussein is captured in a Tikrit spider hole.
+ The Human Genome Project is completed.
+ Makybe Diva wins the first of her three Melbourne Cups.

New words: metrosexual, zhoosh, SARS, freegan

a murder charge against punk gangster Bird Hilton. This explains Omar's laundered leisurewear and the white silk tie he nooses around his throat before entering the dock, wishing to play the part of an upstanding citizen. However, Omar Little is a soldier, born to war—the drug kind—in Baltimore, the no-man's land of Maryland, where life and death come cheaper than dime bags.

The crossword encounter, a prelude to Omar's grace under fire, is how *The Wire* begins season 2, episode 6. Even the bomber jacket stresses the martial theme: the team emblazoned on Omar's back is the Hawaiian Warriors. That's why the sheriff knows the god is reliable. War is Omar's bread and butter. The man is a full-time commando in the city's trenches, the knife scar bisecting his face an occupational hazard.

The pencil gets busy. In goes ARES. Though OMAR—the name—seems another possibility.

2004

Drat and Double Drat! It's what we do (2,10)

For most teachers, the three Rs stand for *reading*, *'riting* and *'rithmetic*. But for Eric Westbrook, a teacher from Coventry, his three Rs are Rachel, Rosemary and Robert. Not that Eric teaches any more. Since leaving the classroom in 1996, due to failing eyesight, he has spent more time with his 'children'. The inverted commas are his. Eric and his wife, Ruth have five children in total, ranging in ages from 19 to 35, though over the years the three Rs among them have merited a little more attention than the rest.

Reasons vary. Rachel, the eldest, required brain surgery at the age of six, a marathon operation to remove a tumour. Even now, 30 years later, this vivacious woman is frozen on one side, with 50 per cent vision and cognitive impairments.

+ Facebook is launched.
+ The Indian Ocean tsunami devastates South East Asia.
+ Mary Donaldson becomes Mary, Crown Princess of Denmark.

New words: phish, blamestorm, stress puppy

Rosemary is 25. Born with chromosome abnormalities, she has no sense of time, a haphazard hold on numbers and the reading age of a young child, despite her sophisticated vocab. Her progress relies on regular supervision.

Meanwhile, Robert, the teen, has his own special-ed demands, thanks to a burning curiosity. 'Robert is bright—super bright. Ever since he was born, he's been asking questions.' Boyhood for Robert meant an endless quiz for Eric and Ruth. Why is grass green? How much does the sky weigh? Where does light go? Any parent knows the litany by heart. One of Robert's questions, however, led to a discovery for both father and son. The topic was salt, or sodium chloride, as scientists know it. Robert was fascinated by the individual crystals. How are they built? he wanted to know.

Eric dug out photos from electromagnetic microscopes, the kinds of images you'd expect a teacher to keep around the house. The two spent the next hour poring over nature's hidden geometry. Robert was engrossed. The moment was a turning point, swinging his course towards chemistry and molecular physics, which he now studies at university. For the father, the tangent inspired a new organism in many regards.

From his own late teens, Eric had always enjoyed tinkering with puzzles, yet seeing that delicate prism of salt made him view the hobby in a different dimension—in three dimensions, to be exact. The key lay in the crystal being multi-layered. 'You could make a crossword on one layer. And then, next level down, you could make another crossword, and then the layer after, making crosswords until you stop.'

Imagine a combination lock, the other metaphor Eric uses to explain his breakthrough. The gizmo comprises a set of rotating dials. Each dial has its own pattern, its own data, just as a crossword bears its own unique matrix. But once you arrange all the dials correctly, the patterns align, the separate imprints mesh, and the lock clicks open.

For Eric the salt provoked that light-bulb flash. Somehow, amid the care Eric lent his family in general, and the three Rs in particular, he found the time to experiment, recognising the salt crystal as the perfect model for a three-dimensional crossword. The structure allowed for the orthodox length and breadth of each level, but then introduced depth as well. Answers could rise and fall, column-like, through the mass, even obliquely in more ambitious designs.

'I sent some examples to the various crossword editors around the country,' Eric tells me. 'Most of them said they had not seen anything like it.' The inventor laughs. 'It took me a while to appreciate that comment's ambiguity.' Three-dimensional crosswords did exist before the salt incident, but Eric and his growing team of volunteers are taking the offshoot to a new level.

Google the genre and the search engine will send you straight to Coventry, where Eric and his cuboid blueprints are based. Meanwhile, the volunteers include the cream of British crossworders, career setters eager to get aboard the project, as Eric is using the new puzzle format to raise money and awareness for children with severe disability. Compilers to join the cause include Araucaria, Arachne, Qaos, Enigmatist, Lavatch, Dumpynose and a dozen more. Tournaments have been staged and calendars distributed. Just one look at the not-for-profit enterprise and you'll realise that 3D CROSSWORDS (*Drat and Double Drat!*) is precisely what they do.

2005

What're you doing tonight? (6)

'Jasper's bored in the coffee shop . . .'
This is how 28-Down begins, the story attached to the clue. The young man sits on a stool by the window as light drizzle falls on Adelaide. The newspaper at his elbow holds no interest, so he fires up his phone and plays a game that entails a slow-motion avalanche of bricks. 'If he times it just right he can drop a block into place at the same time as a new customer sits down on a chair.' The game is Tetris, of course, though that's never stated outright. Jasper becomes so fixated by his score, catching and manoeuvring the falling blocks, that he continues the game on leaving the cafe. Rain persists as he walks north to Victoria Square, in the centre of Adelaide, eyes glued to his screen. He stands at the window of an

---

+ Hurricane Katrina lashes southern USA.
+ The Cronulla riots erupt.
+ The dwarf planet Eris is discovered.
+ *Me at the Zoo*, the first YouTube clip, is uploaded.

New words: podcast, Chinglish, truthiness

ATM tapping buttons with one hand and arranging coloured bricks with the other. He's vaguely aware of three people behind him. He takes his cash and heads south to the edge of the crossword.

Sorry, did I just say crossword? I meant South Terrace, down King William Street. Along the way, still trapped in the game, he's aware of a man squatting on the footpath, looking for a coin, or maybe a contact lens. Near the pubs on Halifax, two young lovers are trying to start their car. Another man slumps in a doorway, wrapped in a blanket. And still the lurid bricks tumble from the sky, as Jasper puts them in their place.

Holly Gramazio is the writer behind Jasper and his city stroll. She's also the creator of the squatting man, the stranded couple, the blanket man, the drizzle. Each character is hostage to her extraordinary crossword, which mirrors the street map of central Adelaide, with stories as clues and the lives of the people intersecting at the junctions, just as answers cross paths in a grid. 'Adelaide is such a great shape for a crossword,' says Holly, on the phone from London.

'The core of the place—the city square—is surrounded on all sides by a thin band of parkland. The whole plan has right angles everywhere, with five public squares: one in the middle and one in each quadrant. It's just a crosswordy kind of place, geographically speaking.'

Holly graduated from Adelaide University in 2006, though this crossword project had been floating in her mind for twelve months or so before that. The multi-narrative puzzle, in fact, was part of her PhD in creative writing, along with a thesis exploring online fiction. While most other students in a similar stream plunged into cyberspace to craft their work, Holly preferred *terra firma*, weaving strands of fiction in a work she called *Sixteen Across*.

Readers-cum-solvers can view and solve it online at 16across.com, meeting Fiona the drain girl or Arnold the bassoonist, depending on which square they click. The beauty of Holly's grid is that the museum fundraiser at 3-Across, for example, is in the top-right frame of the matrix, the very point you'll find the museum on the city map. The answer is clued by the story's title: *So where do we find ourselves today?* (BARBECUE).

Adhering to the logic of crossword and space, the A of BARBECUE opens the way for ACCENT, thanks to a Frenchman named Lewsby who walks through the sausage smoke and past the characters encountered in 3-Across. Everything enmeshes and resonates on the narrative level as much as the alphabetic. 'I love fiction with silly structural gimmicks, stories that fold and intersect in strange ways,' admits Holly. At home in London she helps to arrange treasure hunts and site-specific games for Hide&Seek, keeping her postgrad skills at street level.

Sixteen Across was a complicated set of stories to assemble, but the limitations of the form had a hidden benefit. 'Constraints might make things seem harder to write, but they actually make things easier, at least for me, because you have a smaller set of choices to make about the kind of thing you can write.'

Crosswords, I find, can be equally liberating. Against common-sense, a tight space can loosen the imagination. Setters and solvers are forced to get more creative when the tools of expression—or deduction—are reduced. Often, the unfavoured words in my grids, those answers included because nothing else would fit, can inspire the stronger clues. I can't pinpoint why. Maybe a deeper stream of thinking comes into play—an obligation to toy with the unfamiliar. With no easy escape, you invent out of necessity, spurred on by deadline.

Taking us back to Jasper, the Tetris addict in 28-Down, just south of Victoria Square. As new tiles cascade down, he must rearrange, second guess, stack and unpack. As tablets and toys compete for our attention, there's a lost pleasure in the art of focus, the paradoxical freedom we feel when confined. Over and over, trapped in the matrix, the boy leaves the coffee shop, a venue faithful to the map, and walks past trees and pubs and phone boxes also fixed in the cityscape, the real and the duplicated. As he plays on his phone, a call comes through. Dylan wants to know what he's doing tonight. Does he want to come to the movies? He has cheap tickets.

But Jasper bails. He has things to do, TETRIS, in fact, all the while curating the blocks.

2006

_____ *greens (4)*

OPEN / FOAL
CLEAR / GRASP
SOAP / KISS

It almost looks like beat poetry. In fact, the words stem from an experiment held in San Francisco in 2006. The guinea pigs, so to speak, were Kent and Kevin Young, twins born from a single zygote in 1964. The genetic fluke was the basis of the experiment and its fancy name: *Another Monozygotic Experiment in Telepathic Conveyance.*

Kent and Kevin are painters and performance artists based in Los Angeles. Together they have staged over 30 exhibitions between New York, Belgium and their home state of Texas. Togetherness,

---

+ Serbia and Montenegro split.
+ Brant Webb and Todd Russell are freed from a Beaconsfield mine.
+ Wii is released.
+ Pluto is downgraded to a dwarf planet.

New words: affluenza, muffin top, cyberstalking

in fact, is a playful theme in much of what they do, highlighted by the crossword experiment the brothers conducted in the Steven Wolf Fine Arts Gallery.

Picture an open-plan office with two desks divided by a simple partition. Enter two men in identical suits and shoes. Around their necks are matching ties of black-and-white checks. They bow to the viewing public and take their seats. Kent sits at one desk, Kevin at the other. Above each space hangs a matching screen-print showing a blank crossword puzzle. The pattern is all the twins knew before the day started. As for the clues, the gallery has been keeping them under wraps, only now presenting them to be read—but just by Kent. This is the test: an artistic trial of telepathy, in which Kent has the clues and Kevin has zilch, except for the insights he can glean from his twin's alpha waves through the air.

As for the hit rate, the beatnik poem betrays a little of the shortfall. OPEN and FOAL hardly marry up. SOAP and KISS share something of a bodily connection, but that's clutching at straws. A stronger sense of thought transfer emerges in the puzzle's second phase. The twins scribble notes for the audience to kibitz. One clue says *Eli's school*, a reference to Eli Whitney, inventor of the cotton gin, who attended YALE university. Or that's what Kent has jotted on his notes, adding the four-letter campus to the grid. His brother, next door, oblivious to the clue and blind to his other half, enters YELL. They're certainly in the same ballpark, you'd have to agree. If this was a proper science experiment, a lab might rate that near convergence as an 8.3 out of 10, where 10 is verbatim.

But this monozygotic skit is less about science than art, and painting, and play. And subversion, turning the haven of a crossword, something we associate with designated clues and solutions, into a telepathic canvas. Or let's say a canvas of wannabe telepaths. While Kent and Kevin never hit the same nail on the head, they do creep even closer with the missing-word clue of _____ *green (4)*. In his notes, Kent writes LEAFY. One letter too long, of course; this is more a thought-starter. Perhaps LEAF is the answer. Meanwhile, across the divide, Kevin chews his fingernail and enters the word LEFT. The crowd oohs. This is close: not just in the phonic echo of LEAFY and LEFT but in the political leaning of the Greens, giving the stab a semantic overlap too.

After 45 minutes, the two grids hang incomplete and largely incompatible. No great shame—the twins have completed the game they set out to play. As one critic observes in the art media, the twins' grids 'are a psychogeographic guide to wandering away from the clues and getting lost in the field.' And even if that wasn't the experiment's purpose, hell, there's always the finale. Kent and Kevin put down their pens and finish with a line dance—in perfect sync.

2007

Johnny Mnemonic *director Robert (5)*

The story has Keanu Reeves playing a memory-courier. His brain can be uploaded with data too sensitive to email, like a virtual package lodged in his cortex. But there's a cost for every message Johnny Mnemonic carries, as he loses a few watts of childhood flashback in return. We all know the feeling in some way. The more we cram into our heads, the more some flotsam will drift away. For Frank Longo, a freelance crossword-maker based in New York, that cramming occurred in 2007.

Frank is the interlock king, a man we've met before thanks to his exceptional MAU-MAU diagram back in 2001, the Longo oblong. Veteran solvers will know the Longo handiwork owing to the scarcity of black squares in his diagrams. In 2005 he managed to make a crossword for *The New York Times* with just 52 entries,

---

+ Apple introduces the iPhone.
+ JK Rowling completes her *Harry Potter* series.
+ The first Earth Hour is held (in Sydney).

New words: carbon footprint, floordrobe, food mile

whereas your average puzzle of equal size is liable to carry between 70 and 78 entries.

Still hungry for records, Frank's next claim to fame was to make the world's longest crossword. The fold-out feat of 2439 answers packed inside a grid spanning 21 feet (6.4 metres) was Longo to the max. Imagine a chequered ribbon 9 squares high by 966 squares long. Solvers needed a hallway to unfurl the marvel. Sterling Publishing packaged the puzzle like a paper chain of panels, allowing solvers to fill in answers one segment at a time. The key entry was a quote from John F Kennedy, which stretched along the ribbon's centre.

But Mr Longo wasn't finished there—not by a long chalk. He wondered, since he could construct a 21 footer, then why not make a 22? A 23? After all, how long is a piece of crossword history? The biggest hurdle was repetition. It's one thing to make a verbal spool the length of an Olympian leap, but quite another to ensure no word recurs among the 2439 answers. Or more, if Longo was to go longer.

And he did, in 2007 releasing the '25-Foot-Long Crossword Puzzle', the greatest cram of his career, jamming 2813 answers into a single grid without a double-up. To quote the fold-out's flyleaf, 'That's more answers than you'd encounter in an entire month of daily and Sunday newspaper crosswords.'

Cleverly, the clues progress from easy to ornery the further you move along the length, all the way from 1-Across to 2592-Across. To maximise his performance space, Longo bundled the length and breadth of Hamlet's famous soliloquy inside the grid, from 'to be or not to be . . .' until the conclusion 35 playscript lines later: '. . . be all my sins remembered.' That's a grand sum of 276 words, as spoken verbatim by the moody prince, every last syllable captured in the criss-cross, though Frank must have been tempted to tap Shakespeare's more fitting work: *Measure For Measure*. The puzzle was a great SUCCESS (320-Across), stretching well over 7 METRES (2421-Across) and selling 50 000 copies in America and Canada.

Longo the name is now synonymous with outsized feats, etched in crossword history and the solver's memory. Which reminds me—*Johnny Mnemonic*. If you ever did know the film's director, I'd hazard to guess you've since forgotten him. Frank didn't, however, and his movie trivia appeared in 2251-Across. The name also appeared, however, on the crossword's slipcase. Has that clue helped? The director of *Johnny Mnemonic* was Robert LONGO. No relation, but Frank's modest way of autographing his elongated miracle.

2008

Small window (9)

Behind every great crossword is a remarkable story. Or ten storeys, in the case of Sergiy Petlyuk. The rectangle ranged from the foyer to the penthouse, his puzzle adorning a residential tower in Lvov, in western Ukraine. In terms of rows and columns, the grid was 19 squares across by 34 down. Small potatoes on the printed page but a total wow if you paint them on a building roughly 32 metres high. Sergiy's brainchild was the tallest crossword in the world.

Developers in Lvov, which is called Lviv by locals, wanted to make a bold statement with their new apartment block, so they put the job out to tender to see what the creative sector could do. A recent graduate from the local art college, Sergiy caught the bus to the building to get a better feel for it. Standing at the base,

---

+ The subprime crisis erupts on Wall Street.
+ Fidel Castro steps down as Cuban president.
+ The Tamil Tigers mediate with the Sri Lankan government.

New words: bromance, lolcat, shovel-ready

looking at the wall of blank concrete squares, he had an epiphany. The developers' statement was painted in black-and-white gloss.

Crosswords are popular in the Ukraine, and locals soon afforded the novelty landmark status, saying things like 'I'll meet you at the crossword building,' or 'I live two blocks south of the crossword.' The puzzle was there for all to see as well as to solve, since a vital part of the artwork was a booklet duplicating the grid and supplying the clues.

Word soon spread. The giant puzzle lured both tourists and Lvov urbanites into the city's dormitory suburb long before anyone had a chance to occupy the block. A popular custom among the pilgrims was solving the crossword in the booklet and then going at night to Sergiy's tower, on which a special paint invisible by day luminesced in the streetlights, displaying the solution.

The clues were crafted by a professional setter, on commission from the local Lviv paper. As part of the brief, Sergiy was adamant that the key entries should toast the giants of Ukrainian art and culture, which is why ARCHIPENKO, the avant-garde cubist of Kiev, was there, and NARBUT, the graphic artist behind the nation's coat of arms. The entry offering the best peek into Sergiy's vision, however, was a rare English word.

Correct. The clues and answers were bilingual, thanks to the booklet. While the puzzle on the wall carried only Ukrainian answers, a second compiler named Sergiy Makovskiy styled an English counterpart, in which alternative clues and answers were offered to please (or tease) tourists. Both puzzles were built around the pantheon of Ukraine greats. Yet at 7-Across in the English version, *Small window* was a FENESTRAL, something only an architect might pounce on, nine storeys in the air.

2009

Dinin ayrilmsi devlet (7)

Mustafa Kemal Atatürk cuts a dashing figure in the crossword's centre. The father of modern Turkey is gazing dreamily upward, out beyond the frame. He wears a tailored suit with a white poppy in the buttonhole. His tie is silk, his jaw lantern.

Atatürk was the republic's first president. Even today, 75 years after his death, pigeons snooze on his bronze anatomy across the land. His image adorns the nation's lira. In 1923, when he ejected the caliph, a moustachioed version of his face decorated *Time* magazine. The revolutionary was hailed by the West as a liberator. Indeed, *Atatürk*, the title, translates as father of the Turks. On repelling the Allies and banishing the theocrats, the man announced a nation

---

+ Barack Obama is sworn in as US president.
+ Michael Jackson dies.
+ The swine flu pandemic sweeps the world.
+ *Avatar* takes the world to Pandora.

New words: sexting, buzzkill, fauxhawk

reborn. Turkey aspired to be an extension of modern Europe, a democracy of secular values and state-funded education.

Hence the day on which Atatürk gained office, 29 October, is hailed as Republic Day. As you'd expect, every town and village kicks up its heels. Red flags fly. The fiesta is so grandiose that the day itself lasts 35 hours, with rockets exploding from one o'clock the night before. Naturally, the liberator's face bobs up on posters and banners in every square and byway—and in 2009 inside the crossword grid of *Cumhuriyet* (Republic), a national daily.

The puzzle was entitled 'Neyi Kutluyoruz?' (What Are We Celebrating?). The question felt so obvious it bordered on rhetorical. Even a stray backpacker, losing her way en route to Gallipoli, could guess the hoopla had some link with the handsome dude in the picture. On top of that, a million Turks knew this special puzzle was coming. *Cumhuriyet* had paid a prince's ransom to air two teasers about the crossword on television a few days short of the national holiday. Is this the first time a national telly spot publicised a crossword? Possibly. It's the only one I encountered on this global walkabout. The baritone voiceover said, 'Down—what are we celebrating? The solution is in *Cumhuriyet* on 29 October.'

The second ad was identical to the first, barring a single word. Instead of 'Down', the second ad said 'Across'. This may seem trivial, but the two prepositions carry special significance in Turkish. The word Down (or *Aşağı*) not only applies in the standard elevator sense, but also translates as 'from top to bottom'. As my Istanbul insider, Gülce Özkütük, insists, the word 'Down' here could well be interpreted as extending from the higher to the lower classes. In a similar vein, Across (or *Karşısında*) not only evokes a shuttle crossing a loom, or a ferry cutting across the Bosporus, but also captures the sense of left to right in a political sense, the full spectrum of Turkish ideology. The implications were deliberate.

After so much suspense, the grid itself was pretty standard, obeying the Swedish model, with clues and arrows inside an asymmetric pattern. Where it differed from the average fare was in a smattering of 25 circles inside some of the squares, each circle numbered to help solvers arrange a message along the base. CUMHURIYET BAYRAMI (Republic Day)—the obvious answer—has 17 letters, too short to be the final phrase. Perhaps the holiday puzzle offered more than it first promised? This was putting it mildly.

When Atatürk chased the Allies from Anatolia, preserving the rickety Ottoman Empire in 1922, he did so with cunning and force. Eighty-seven years later, it took a single crossword to almost undo his good work. For this was more a bomb than a puzzle, a stick of gelignite tossed at the feet of the ruling party. In order to grasp the territory at stake, we need to quickly map the political landscape.

After Atatürk wrested power from the caliphate in 1923, the lone party on the ballot sheet, for some 25 years, was the CHP (Republican People's Party). Its central planks sat left of centre. Social democrats in most regards, the members were known as Kemalists, honouring their founder.

Since World War II, however, the Turkish drift towards conservatism has strengthened, with successive national governments displaying a distinct lean to the right. The ultimate blow to the Kemalist garrison was the election of the AKP (Party of Justice and Development) in 2002, which exhibited a strong Islamic bias. That the AKP entertains a state agency of Religious Affairs is viewed as heresy by the Kemalists, who believe that god (any god) and state have no place being in the same sentence.

Earthquakes form just one bane of Turkish life. Another is the constant political anxiety formed along these historical lines. Upheaval can seem a breath away. Sentiments intensify every October when the red banners appear and tend to overspill when a national crossword goes beyond marking the occasion.

Neyi kutluyoruz? was the puzzle's question. As the paper's name suggests, *Cumhuriyet* was a Kemalist rag, and it often succumbed to propaganda for fear of an Islamic-friendly regime unravelling all of Atatürk's stout deeds. The spectre of widespread mosques gnawed at the editors. Burqas for every woman. Compulsory Korans in the schools instead of compulsory Atatürk. The rising panic reached fever pitch in the Republic Day puzzle, which seemed to be a call to arms as much as to biros. A few of the entries will give you an idea:

> *Colour of our flag* = RED
> *Shape in our flag* = CRESCENT

A fourth clue mentioned *Sect houses closed by the republic*. The answer was TEKKE—places of religious education that were outlawed by Atatürk. While our last sampled clued is the translation of this chapter's title, *Separating religion from the state* (SECULARISM).

The puzzle's final message was delivered by the circled letters. Despite the promise of the heading, it did not reveal the cause of the celebration. Instead it was a cry for direct Kemalist action, translating as PROTECT THE VALUES OF YOUR REPUBLIC.

In true Atatürk fashion, the patriotic pose was struck, and the incumbent enemy outlined. Yet this time round, the message arrayed in a crossword, there was a dulling of the rebel leader's usual impact. Almost a century ago, when Atatürk made his call to the people, they rose, broke their shackles, they followed his commands. That was in 1923; this was 2009. The landscape had shifted. Modern Turkey was no longer a gung-ho pinkish hotbed, an epithet that might have applied two decades prior. Besides, *Cumhuriyet* had done so much to denigrate the average Turk for his growing conservatism that the average Turk didn't give a flying fig for more of the same propaganda. The Molotov cocktail the crossword longed to be turned out to be a damp squib. Or, if it did explode, *Cumhuriyet* sustained the damages—financial and otherwise. Mustafa Kemal Atatürk remained in his box, the father of Turkey rooted to the spot, staring stage-left. All around him, beyond the puzzle's limits, modern Turkey continued to evolve.

2010

It's upsetting to teach sheep to sing 'Shoot the Boer' (4,6)

Till now our search for clues has mostly been racing from puzzle to puzzle, with the occasional IKEA ad thrown in. But what if there's no puzzle involved? Imagine a clue adrift of any grid, a fragment, with no puzzle beyond the clue itself. That's how things work in South Africa, where a crossword junkie called Jonathan Ancer writes a column in the *Cape Times*.

Ancer is a journalist by training, a satirist by nature. His weekly columns explore politics and fatherhood, arts and sport, his text awash with African language. Words like *tjatjarag* (excitable) and *yebo* (yes) pepper the copy. As a rule, the tone is comical. He plays

---

+ A massive oil spill occurs in the Gulf of Mexico.
+ Eyjafjallajökull erupts in Iceland, disrupting air travel world wide.
+ Mary McKillop is canonised.
+ Justin Bieber is idolised.

New words: googleganger, pocket dial, vuvuzela

with a topic, often taking an irreverent angle, concocting one clue among the 600 words.

A constant focus for a large part of Ancer's work for several years has been Julius Malema. In media circles this firebrand is known as a gift that keeps on giving. Malema once ran the African National Congress Youth League. His pugnacity was hard to ignore, if not his lack of intellect, though in April 2012 his hostile peacocking saw him ditched from the league altogether. Demerits in office included a knee-jerk impulse to cuss at reporters and a radical belief in erasing all private mining interests; and then there was the song he sang before a rally at the University of Western Cape. The number was entitled 'Dubul' iBhunu' ('Shoot the Boer', or 'Farmer'). To all intents and purposes the leader was encouraging the massacre of whites. The stunt was condemned by the vast majority of South Africans. Eventually, the chant led to charges of hate speech and incitement to unrest.

Predictably then, Malema draws his share of media flak. Cartoonists depict him as a squalling infant, a hot-air blimp or a magician with every card in his deck the race card. Editorials have slammed the demagogue's bent for violence and Stalinism. That much you'd expect. But a cryptic clue every second week mocking his latest failings? Well, that's outside the box in more ways than one.

Ancer's column is relentless. If the scribe spots a flaw in the latest Malema message, he jumps on it. Kicks it. Clues it. Hence the obvious target of March 2010, when Malema led the crowd in that bloodthirsty chant. Under the leader's spell the campus lapsed into anarchy.

Ancer was poised to yell back his own answer: *It's upsetting to teach sheep to sing 'Shoot the Boer'*. Whether Malema had the skills to decode the ribbing, I can't tell you. That's no real problem, however, as the column typically ends on the solution, a punchline to compensate for the absence of crossword. In this case the formula was an anagram, asking solvers to upset *teach sheep*, an elegant dig at the potential for mob behaviour that day. Mix the letters and there's your verdict: HATE SPEECH.

2011

Woman stares wildly at calamity (8)

Proofreaders turned the paper inside out. Lawyers, too, and section heads. Every page, every article, searching for mischief, as this was the last edition, and Rebekah Brooks, the editor-in-chief, was expecting trouble. For ample reason. Brooks had been accused of playing a hand in the phone-hacking scandal that ultimately shut the paper down. For years a culture of espionage had been fostered among a corps of journalists, bugging voicemails and bribing police in order to gain an edge over rivals. But the jig was up. The *News of the World* was dead in the water, a tabloid icon toppled after 168 years. At one stage, this Sunday redtop was the biggest selling paper on the planet, racking up almost eight and a half million readers in 1950, but those heydays were gone. The last issue was hitting

---

+ The Arab Spring occurs across North Africa and the Middle East.
+ Aung San Suu Kyi wins a seat in the Burmese parliament.
+ Occupy Wall Street protests occur in New York.
+ *Two and Half Men* fires one man, Charlie Sheen.

New words: burqini, totes, fracking, amazeballs

the streets on 10 July 2011—and Brooks was on the lookout for in-house shenanigans.

Cosmologists insist the world will end with a bang. The poet TS Eliot was more inclined to think a whimper. Seems they both have it wrong. For going by the crossword on page 47 of that last edition, the *World* ended with a hardy-har-har-har.

There were two crosswords, in fact, beside the bingo game in the Mindbenders section: the cryptic and the quick. Both sets of clues yielded the same answers in the one grid, a 13 by 13 that every proofer overlooked, every lawyer, every senior editor. Mind you, once the word spread, nobody on the street missed a thing.

Warning bells should have sounded, yet the sweepers overlooked the likes of *Stink* (STENCH) and *Cease* (DESIST). They ignored the red rags of *Lamented* (DEPLORED) and *Flan* (TART). They merrily flicked past *Criminal enterprise* (RACKET), and somehow they failed to notice *Brook* (STREAM). And that was just in the quick. The real ridicule was lurking in the cryptic clues.

Even if the copy-checkers were not cryptic-solvers, they should have baulked at the narky surface of several clues. Take *String of recordings (4)*. Look inside RECORDINGS, and there's your hidden string: CORD. Surely enough rope to hang the nameless culprit behind the crossword? But no.

The comical was there too. Say you're a *World* journalist. You've just been turfed out onto the street. What do you do? I'd suggest you'd drift towards the decision declared by 8-Across: *We're off to get a jug* (EWER). Later, nursing a retrenchment hangover, you could resolve to *Master new course* (STREAM) or find *New desire to live* (RESIDE). Why? All because your *Domestic wages* (RETAINER) and STATUS (*Figures university internally is standing*) are significantly DIMMER (*Switch to being more stupid*).

The sucker punch was hiding in the final Across clue. The surface reading prompted the image of a bereft woman, perhaps a power-broker on borrowed time who contemplates her toppling empire. The clue declared: *Woman stares wildly at calamity*. To reach the answer, scramble *stares* and place the new combo behind DI (*woman*), and there's a DISASTER waiting to happen.

Which it did the week after the last crossword ran. British PM David Cameron launched an inquiry into Hackgate after the police had finished their digging, and news went from bad to worse for Brooks and her employers, News International. Two years later, as this book goes to press, the fallout continues, with vast compensation payouts, perjury charges, document seizures and company attrition.

So, tabloid editors, take a leaf from *News of the World*. Why pay a freelance astrologer when your in-house crossword-setter can see the future far more vividly?

2012

Nombre del líder supremo que rige nuestro destino? Barbado (5,6)

Hugo Chávez was the face and voice of Venezuela. The ex-army heavy was elected to power in 1999, serving four terms in office, negating one coup along the way, and annoying the bejesus out of America with *ad hoc* Latin socialism. His death, in 2013, was probably met with a collective phew from Washington, but there was a lot to admire about the hotspur. A dirt-poor child from the sticks, Hugo rose through the ranks to command 29 million citizens and three million Twitter followers.

Publicity shots often showed the president in full regalia, a tricolour sash across his barrel chest, a red beret of combat lodged on

---

+ The Higgs boson particle is discovered.
+ The Transit of Venus occurs for the last time until 2117.
+ Psy goes Gangnam Style.
+ Felix Baumgartner space-dives 39 kilometres above Earth.

New words: crowdsourcing, YOLO, hashtag, fiscal cliff

his skull. Among his heroes he listed the liberators Simón Bolívar, Che Guevara and Fidel Castro.

A name unlikely to be on the list was Neptalí Segovia. Talk of Segovia made the airwaves in May 2012, as part of a news show called *Cayendo y Corriendo* (Falling and Running), a pro-Chávez vehicle hosted by a punchy motormouth called Pérez Pirela. One night he declared there was treason afoot. '*Mira!*' he said, holding up a newspaper. The page was folded to the crossword section. '*Mira*,' he repeated, '*esta un mensaje*' (Look, it's a message). He felt sure of it. He brandished the puzzle's solution to his studio audience. Eight answers had been highlighted, including RAFAGAS (gunfire) and ASESINEN (murder). A fluke, perhaps, but not when ADAN, the brother of Hugo Chávez, is found in the same grid.

Pirela ramped up the histrionics, referring to the secret codes used by Charles de Gaulle during World War II that passed on valuable details to Resistance fighters in the guise of news bulletins. (Surely he meant the D-Day coincidence across the Channel, that other great scapegoat puzzle?) Pirela pulled out his phone and tried to call a mathematician to have him calculate the odds of such an outrage being accidental, but the mathematician wasn't at home. The show's host didn't miss a beat. (You can see the whole hysteria yourself, as it was uploaded onto YouTube by Iguana TV.) The main message was clear, he felt, and Neptalí Segovia was the traitor at the conspiracy's heart. Sorry, was the bloke who made the crossword. Within hours the Caracas English teacher had gone from part-time setter to public enemy number 1.

The next morning, intelligence agents raided the offices of *Las Últimas Noticias* and seized all relevant documents. They spent time grilling the editor about Segovia's political ties. How long had he been with the paper? Who were his associates? Did he hum any tunes while working at his desk?

Before things went too far, assuming they hadn't already, Segovia took himself to the central police station in Caracas. 'I have nothing to hide,' he told reporters on the steps. 'The work I have been doing for the last seventeen years has only a cultural and educational intention, and is transparent.' In the company of police he went through other queried entries in the 'traitorous' crossword. CAMINO meant road and nothing more, as opposed to being a sniper's location. BASE meant base and didn't imply a resistance cell. PROBABILIDAD was just that, a probability. As for RABAT, it wasn't a festival on 19 July, as Pirela had kept insisting on television, but the capital of Morocco.

The next day, in all probability, the news of this murderous crossword reached Rabat, and every other capital city under the sun. The grid was reproduced in *The New York Times*, *The Age* and *The Guardian*. Segovia had become the cynosure of world media, despite the absence of any ASESINEN, the lack of any RAFAGAS and the Chávez brothers' walking unscathed down the CAMINO.

Indeed, if Pirela had really wanted to rumble a call to rebellion, he needed only to wait 48 hours, when a paper called *Tal Cual* (As is) reached the streets. Unlike the mainstream press, this was a tabloid with strident anti-Chávez views. A blind man could see as much in the editorial, which declared that 'a Venezuelan crossword has no Down clues as our homeland apparently lacks any verticality. Instead, a submissive and horizontal population would rather leave the many blank spaces for the world to fill in, for fear of deprivation.'

The parody came complete with a mock-up crossword on the front page. Its creator was so kind as to provide the answers, too. Three clues jumped out, each capable of getting Pirela's goat, if not infuriating *el presidente*. Translated, they were:

What officials do when they misuse public funds = CORRUPTION
Perhaps the most abused law? = CONSTITUTION
Name of supreme leader who governs our destiny? Bearded = FIDEL CASTRO

2013

Sign of growth (6)

Starting this clue tour back in 1913, I had a pebble in my shoe. Of course, as a diligent guide, I remained stoic. Unflustered. We pushed ahead. We visited Glasgow and Guangdong, sitcoms and novels, taking in the scenery. But while we travelled this pebble kept bugging me, this one annoying question: how will the whole folly end?

Back in 2012, I emailed every library in the atlas, every media storehouse in the book, asking for stories of a crossword nature. The exercise confirmed my hunch. No matter what language, what patch on the globe, the crossword is known. Even if my inquiry yielded a polite shrug, the *palavras cruzadas* of Rio and the *sanaristikko* of Helsinki were still out there wooing their share of solvers.

+ Pope Benedict XVI resigns.

+ Queen Beatrix of The Netherlands abdicates.

+ Arthur Wynne's baby turns 100. (The royal telegram must be lost in the mail.)

New words: watch this space...

But that pebble remained. For all the stories my research uncovered, the yarns the libraries dug up, the snippets I chanced upon, the question still nagged. My timeline from Arthur Wynne's eureka to a century later had this constant void as a climax. I don't care what sci-fi writers say—it's pretty hard to write about the future before the future arrives.

I carried on. I feigned courage. If worst came to worst, I figured, I could take inspiration from Wynne himself. After all, desperation mothered the word-cross, so why not put my faith in a deadline's adrenalin? The blankness that embodied the 2013 chapter would find its fullness out of necessity. In the end, I told myself, the end would emerge. I didn't know how right I could be.

The finale arrived in *The Guardian* on 22 January 2013, a few months before the manuscript was due. The setter was John Graham, a man we met half a century ago, back when he chose the alias of Araucaria. In 2013 the reverend was 91, having arrived in the world just eight years after the crossword itself. Not that you'd guess as much: despite his age, his mind was still a toybox of zestful and zany ideas, though his body was frail. Frailty, in fact, was his puzzle's motif. The sobering news lay in 18-Down: *Sign of growth (6)*.

For an added hint, think zodiac. Or mortality. Or, better still, ignore Margaret Petherbridge Farrer's Sunday breakfast test, the one outlawing death and disease.

1 Across, a magazine catering for British crossword addicts, had the bonus of a title when this puzzle first ran, in December 2012. There, the crossword was labelled 'An Unwelcome Visitor', which solvers deduced to be CANCER (18-Down). John Graham was beyond CHEMOTHERAPY (27-Across), and was using a crossword to relay his predicament.

Hugh Stephenson, *The Guardian*'s crossword editor, was compelled to rerun the puzzle to a wider audience. This was major news. Araucaria was a *Guardian* darling; he had made his name at the paper, a name as household as any cryptic-setter can own. Solvers could be forgiven for presuming the chap immortal, as Graham had been dazzling for over 50 years, prolific and diabolic at every turn. Yet here was a puzzle that declared an end of sorts, a coded farewell.

Instructions accompanied the grid in what is known as a stand-first. This tiny paragraph helped solvers to string the key answers together, which summarised the reverend's health plight. Extensive ENDOSCOPY had isolated the CANCER in the OESOPHAGUS. The crossword-maker was 'being treated with 13 15' (PALLIATIVE CARE).

I remember the day I solved this puzzle. Lying in the local park, grabbing what shade I could find, I felt the chill infiltrate my blood the deeper I entered the labyrinth. Every second answer angled back to the reality: STENT, NARCOTIC, NURSE. Even a neutral entry like SUNSET (*Fat round Poles at end of day*) took on a macabre pallor. But then the puzzle's wonder began to shine. What at first seemed sinister—relying on a puzzle to announce one is dying—was really something more ingenious, sacred and inclusive. As Araucaria himself told Sam Jones, a *Guardian* reporter, 'It seemed the natural thing to do somehow. It just seemed right.'

To my knowledge, the feat is a world-first. Wedding proposals, we know, have been encoded in grids before now, along with many other wonders, but I cannot recall another imminent death notice in one, however long a maestro might have flourished. You may think this seems a sombre way to end our helter-skelter chase, a downbeat note to darken what's been a rollicking melody. But this end also feels right. The crossword gods have delivered our climax on cue. As this is not the death of the crossword or the end of the chase, necessarily. 'An Unwelcome Visitor' is more milestone than gravestone.

The year 2013 found a lifelong compiler doing what he knew best. His mortal theme was as elegant as ever, and as the master passed on his mantle to the next compiler, his clues made peace with the world and left his solvers well. For even in his frailty, Araucaria conceived to add MERRIMENT to his matrix, where *matrix* is Greek for womb. So in the end is the beginning, and in the beginning, the end.

A word of thanks

O ne by one, mango fill basket.

That Caribbean proverb was my mantra in writing *Cluetopia*, the inner voice of calm to reduce the panic, the insomnia, the disbelief I'd ever promised my publisher 100 crossword stories along the century of their existence.

My basket, so to speak, was a giant sheet of cardboard. I'd drafted 100 boxes into a tidy grid, the semblance of a virgin crossword somehow going to steady my pulse. Square One was obvious, the word-cross of Arthur Wynne. Then came a few more must-have milestones—the D-Day flukes of 1944, the Beerbohm hoax of 1940, the CLINTON/BOB DOLE gotcha of 1996. After that the gaps began to gnaw. Night and day.

But I held my nerve. (Deadlines are handy that way.) I googled and tweeted. I haunted op shops and newspaper archives. Flea markets and garage sales. I raided dental clinics for old magazines. Made pathetic pleas on radio stations, in language columns. I followed leads and vague recollections. And over summer I hammered the Send button on Outlook Express, emailing the world for help.

In a patchwork way, the world responded, turning this book into a possibility. When it comes to saying thanks, I'm stumped to know where to start. Maybe if I break the force into platoons, you'll appreciate the campaign's scale. Let's start with the librarians, for whom every writer carries a secret torch.

I want to thank the angels of continental Europe: Kathrin Schmiedel (Germany), Valéria Szeli (Hungary), Eleonora Tsvetkova (Russia), Lenka Válková (Czech Republic), Martijn van Wensveen (The Netherlands) and Bernard Krespine (France). I'd also like to apologise to the staff at the National Library of Croatia for outlining my quest in Serbian, and vice versa for their counterparts in Belgrade.

Across the ditch I'm indebted to Lona Jones at the *Llyfrgell Genedlaethol Cymru* (The National Library of Wales) for telling me that *croesair*, the Welsh word for crossword, first appeared in 1833 as a term meaning paradox. You can't make that sort of stuff up.

Closer to home, the staff at Victoria's State Library and Sydney's Mitchell Library were quick to enter the quest's spirit. To every archivist I pestered, from Afghanistan to Zimbabwe, I'd like to say thanks. Despite your catalogue's shortage of mangoes, you took the time and trouble to look.

Canadians Lori Pothier and Sara Parkes were brilliant in unlocking the story of Kingston Penitentiary. Likewise Steve Younis was a stalwart guide in the Superman vault, while Bill Hillman was brilliant in the Edgar Rice burrow. Which brings me to the translators, the great elucidators of language.

I'd like to make special mention of Dr Margarita Pavlova, not only for her splendid name, but for finding the headspace in her frantic academic schedule to illuminate Nabokov and Russian game shows. Others in my corner were Angelika Stoll (who unlocked German), Andrew Godwin (Chinese), Marie Trinchant (French), Rangi Faith (Māori), Nicole Else (Esperanto) and Frederik Ekman (Barsoomian).

Lingo by lingo I was also aided in Arabic (Toula Serna and Rima Atme), Italian (Lorena and Moreno Mazzocco, Nadia's mum and

Barabra Amalberti), Turkish (Gülce Ozkütük and Libby Effeney) and Dutch (Wieb Bosma, Bruno Herfst and Henk Verkuyl).

As for the American tongue, I was guided to untold gold by T Campbell and David Steinberg. (If you don't know David, he's a teen aiming to digitise the entire backlist of *New York Times* crosswords with a battalion of fellow believers. Check out their progress at the Pre-Shortzian Puzzle Project online.)

Still in the States, Judith Long is a mainstay of *The Nation*, and the editor to enliven the Frank Lewis tale of 1975. Speaking of heroines, how can I look past the spunky Elspeth Knox, who shared her coffee and memories on several occasions?

Companion questers, if that's a word, include such amateur sleuths as Peter Biddlecombe and Big Dave in the UK, Australia's Dr Kelvin Edwards (crossword tutor of the first degree) and Professor Alistair Thompson (whose campus library card I must have maxed out).

Next in line are the setters, most of whom are mentioned in these pages, yet plenty warrant particular mention. Among the champions are Tom Johnson (alias Doc, Gozo, Anorak and Didymus), Roger Squires (the ex-magician who conjured favours out of thin air), Patrick Street (Australian Crossword Club president), Coimbatore Gopal Rishikesh (better known as Rishi, or Chatuvarsi of *The Hindu*), Hans Christian Nygård (my Swedish ambassador), Matt Gaffney, Frank Longo, Eddie James (Brummie and Cyclops) and the whole Lovatt clan (Christine, James and Dominic).

South Africans Jack Dunwoody and Jonathan Ancer were first-rate safari guides, while Holly Gramazio lit up the streets of Adelaide. For their breakthrough philanthropy, and individual genius, I salute Ian Humphreys and Eric Westbrook.

Maker of the ten-storey crossword Sergiy Petlyuk, was a hard man to catch, but always worth the chase. Clone that for the monozygotic twins, Kent and Kevin Young. Thanks as well to Perth's Andrew Tinning for unleashing his IKEA idea. As for the parodists—Andrew Gangoiti, Doug Files and Tim Pulju: the world is richer for your rule-breaking. To the librettist Stephen Sondheim and your champion supporter David Ovenden: bravo!

I'm also indebted to umpteen editors—Will Shortz, Eugene Maleska and Colin Inman to name but three—to allow readers to see what wonders have been wrought during their watches. In the same vein, I'd like to underline my gratitude for all literary estates, novelists, poets, scriptwriters and other creators, for granting permission to reproduce material here. You'll find specific acknowledgements in the preliminary pages.

Equal generosity was shown by the scad of newspapers and magazines cited, and sighted, in *Cluetopia*, from the mainstream to the make-believe. I can't believe our chequered century romped from the *New York World* to *The Guardian* via *The Daily Planet*. Seems only fitting a folly like this book took a turn for the comic.

Lastly, when it came to taming the travelogue into a seamless escapade, the editing talents of Ann Lennox and Penny Mansley, and the proofreading skills of Davina Russell, were supreme, as was the in-house counsel of Tracy O'Shaughnessy. Thanks to Sue Hines, my publisher, for daring to think this project could fly. And three rousing cheers to anyone I've neglected in the thankless exercise of trying to remember the 101 people to thank.

As the flyleaf tells you, this book is dedicated to my father, a man we lost *en route*. But if I can be greedy, I'd also like to add a young East German boy called Lars from 1981, as well as every solver across the planet. Without your ardour, the sun would sink on the joyous art of setting.

David Astle
www.davidastle.com

Permissions

The following permissions, by chapter, have been sought:

1924   Material from *The Cross Word Puzzle Book*, by Margaret Petherbridge, Simon & Schuster Adult Publishing Group, © 1924

1933   The Barsoomian crossword by Frederik Ekmans, as it appeared in the *ERBzine*, is reproduced with kind permission of the compiler.

1940   The partial reproduction of the Max Beerbohm letter as it appeared in *The Times* of London, 1940

1943   Material from the IKEA advertisement is reproduced with the courtesy of Andrew Tinning, Marketforce.

1974   Permission for reproducing the extract from the poem, *Unfinished Crossword*, is granted by the poet, Faith Rangi.

1980   The extract from Dr John Kolia's story, 'A Crossword Puzzle' from *Without Mannerisms: And other stories*, Institute of Papua New Guinea Studies, 1980

1986   The extract from *Spelling When Yoo Dont No How Crosswords*, Peter George Hannan, Falcon Publishing, n.d.

1988   The reproduction of material from *Crosstalk*, Eugene Maleska, Simon & Schuster, 1993

1991   Material from the *Speculative Grammarian* crossword is reproduced by kind permission of the setter, Doug Files.

1996   Material from the *New York Times* crossword is reproduced by kind permission of the newspaper's puzzle editor, Will Shortz.

2000   Permission for reproducing the 'Longo Oblong' grid is granted by the compiler, Frank Longo.

2000   Material from the Matt Gaffney's crossword site is reproduced by kind permission of the compiler.

2001   Material from the Spooner Blind Gamer site is reproduced by kind permission of the programmer, Ian Humphreys.

2005   Material from *Another Monozygotic Experiment in Telepathic Conveyance* is reproduced by kind permission of the artists, Kevin and Kent Young.

2006   Material from the 16-Across project is reproduced by kind permission of the creator, Holly Gramazio.